DEATH OF A CAPO

As Eddie Lino turned his head, Caracappa pulled out his gun, extended his arm, and aimed directly at the back of his skull. And pulled the trigger. Boom. Boom. Boom. Traffic racing home on the Belt Parkway more than smothered the sound. Caracappa kept firing into Lino's body. Boom. Boom. Nine times.

Lino bled out all over the new leather seats. His foot slipped off the brake and the car rolled forward, dead man driving, until it crashed into a fence.

Caracappa put the gun back in his pocket and the two New York City police detectives walked casually back to their car. Just another night in the life of the two dirtiest cops in NYPD history.

"[The authors] keep the narrative moving with a good balance of police work, politics, and Mafia drama, channeling with authority . . . the voices of the street as well as the police force . . . True crime fans should be happy to get past the hype and into the nitty-gritty of this infamous case."
Publishers Weekly

FRIENDS OF THE FAMILY

THE INSIDE STORY OF THE MAFIA COPS CASE

TOMMY DADES and MICHAEL VECCHIONE

with DAVID FISHER

HARPER

An Imprint of HarperCollins*Publishers*

This book was originally published in May 2009 by William Morrow, an Imprint of HarperCollins Publishers.

HARPER

An Imprint of HarperCollins*Publishers*
10 East 53rd Street
New York, New York 10022-5299

First Harper paperback printing: April 2010
First William Morrow hardcover printing: May 2009

The William Morrow hardcover edition contains the following Library of Congress Cataloging in Publication Data:

Dades, Tommy.
   Friends of the family: the inside story of the Mafia cops case /
Tommy Dades and Michael Vecchione, with David Fisher. – 1st ed.
      p. cm.
1. New York (N.Y.). Police Dept.—Corrupt practices. 2. Police corruption—
New York (State)—New York. 3. Murder for hire—New York (State)—
New York. 4. Mafia—New York (State)—New York. 5. Dades, Tommy.
6. Vecchione, Mike. 7. Caracappa, Stephen. 8. Eppolito, Lou, 1948-
I. Vecchione, Mike. II. Fisher, David. III. Title.
HV8148.N5D28   2009
364.152'309227471—dc22

                                                    2009005623

FRIENDS OF
THE FAMILY

To my beloved mother, Della, you will forever be in my heart. Thank you for everything. To my daughter, Nicole, and my son, Frankie, I love you both. You are my life, God bless both of you. And to my sweet Lorraine, thank you for your trust and your love. God created an angel when he made you.

TOMMY DADES

To Mom and Grandma Rachel, although you're not here, I know you're with me all the time. To Pam, my wonderful sister, I know your hand will always be on my shoulder. I miss you and I will always love you. To my Dad, who throughout his life has taught me by example to always do the right thing, and to my sons, Brian and Andrew, for being the best sons a father could ask for.

MICHAEL VECCHIONE

FRIENDS OF
THE FAMILY

PROLOGUE

This is the way the Eddie Lino hit came down: Lino was a capo in the Gambino crime family, John Gotti's main guy. Lino was a made man; his greatest claim to infamy was that he had gunned down the Godfather, "Big Paulie" Castellano, in front of Spark's Steakhouse in 1985. On the night of November 6, 1990, a little after seven P.M., Eddie Lino left the Cabrini Social Club on Avenue U in Bensonhurst. Supposedly he was on his way to a Gambino induction ceremony. Somebody was going to get made that night. He was driving his new Mercedes on the service road of the Belt Parkway. He probably never noticed the dark sedan following him.

Louis Eppolito was driving. Eppolito was a big guy, in both size and personality; he liked to tell people he was the most decorated detective in the history of the NYPD. Sitting next to him was his former partner, Steve Caracappa, the skinny guy. At that time Caracappa was assigned to the Organized Crime Homicide Unit inside the NYPD's prestigious Major Case Squad, so he had access to all the verified information, gossip, and speculation about every wiseguy in the city.

Who knows if they had a plan or were just waiting for the right spot. But as Lino approached the Ocean Parkway exit, Caracappa slapped the red flasher on the dashboard and turned it on.

Lino had to notice it right away. Chances are he figured it was just another one of those pain-in-the-ass bullshit harassment stops. Some cops just busting his balls. But it was the cops, so he knew he had to stop. He pulled over to the side of the service road. Apparently he put the car in neutral and kept his foot on the brake. Whatever this was, it wasn't going to take long. Probably Lino was looking in the rearview mirror as both doors of the unmarked cop car opened and two guys got out and walked toward his car. Lino rolled down the window.

Maybe they had met before. Wiseguys and detectives often get to know each other. It's part of their business. Ships crashing in the night. As Caracappa walked the cop walk with Eppolito toward Lino's car he probably kept his hand in his coat pocket, so Lino never saw the gun. Eppolito said in his big cop voice, "Hey, Frankie, how are you?"

Lino knew he was right; this was just a ball buster. They had stopped the wrong guy. These cops were looking for his cousin, Frankie "Curly" Lino, a Bonanno soldier. So maybe he relaxed a little bit. Maybe he even laughed at them a little, the jerks. "You got the wrong guy," he said. "Frankie's my cousin."

Eppolito pointed toward something on the passenger-side floor. "What's that on the floor?"

It was nothing. Some garbage. Lino leaned across the seat to pick it up.

As Lino turned his head Caracappa pulled out his gun, extended his arm, and aimed directly at the back of his skull. And pulled the trigger. Boom. Boom. Boom. Traffic racing home on the Belt more than smothered the sound. Caracappa kept firing into Lino's body. Boom. Boom. Nine times.

Lino bled out all over the new leather seats. His foot slipped off the brake and the car rolled forward, dead man driving, until it crashed into a fence.

Caracappa put the gun back in his pocket and the two New York City police detectives walked casually back to the car. Just another night in the life of the two dirtiest cops in NYPD history.

Christmas Day 1986 was a beautiful day for twenty-six-year-old Nicky Guido. As usual, his whole family was together at his parents' house in Brooklyn, on Seventeenth Street in the Windsor Terrace neighborhood. Nicky's mother, Pauline, had given him a gold Christ head and then made her special manicotti. Things were going great for Nicky: He was working at the telephone company but he'd put in his papers for a city job with the fire department. But more than anything, he was thrilled about his new wheels, the bright red Nissan Maxima that was parked right outside the house. After dinner he brought his uncle Anthony outside to show off the car. It was overcast but warm for Christmas.

Nicky slid into the driver's seat, and Anthony got into the passenger seat. Everything about Nicky was legitimate; he was a good kid working hard and earning a living, so there was absolutely no reason for Nicky Guido to pay any attention to the Cadillac that was drifting slowly down the block. When that big car pulled up right next to him and stopped just a few feet away, maybe he turned curiously to see what was going on, maybe he saw the three men in that car, and maybe he even saw the guns before they opened up at him from point-blank range. Nicky dived across the front seat, trying to protect his uncle—but he never had a chance. These shooters were from another world, a world that Nicky had no connection to.

The family heard the shots from inside the house. They came running outside. His mother, Pauline, looked into the bullet-riddled car. "I saw his heart was bleeding," she said. "I went to touch his hand, but he must have died, because his fingers were cold . . ."

To the police none of this fit. This was clearly a mob hit, but Nicky was an innocent kid. Totally innocent. They looked hard, but they couldn't find any connection. None. Why would the mob decide to go after this kid? The thing made no sense. So the case sat there, unsolved, for more than a decade.

Even after the whole thing was done and the Mafia cops had been put in a cell to rot forever, there was still one question that never got answered: At the beginning, were these guys killers who became cops or were they cops who became killers? One thing for sure, though: They were the two worst men ever to wear the badge of the New York City Police Department.

CHAPTER 1

Tommy Dades didn't bother knocking. He'd earned walk-in privileges a long time ago. He and Mike Vecchione had become close friends while solving a series of freezing cold cases. The two men formed a great team: Dades the detective, Vecchione the assistant DA in Brooklyn District Attorney Joe Hynes's office. Tommy investigated and Mike prosecuted, real-life law and order. Mike looked up from the pile of papers stacked neatly on his desk. As always, he was dressed impeccably in a tie and jacket. "Hey, Tommy, what's going on?"

Tommy settled down in the comfortable wooden chair on the visitor side of Vecchione's neat desk. As always, his black leather jacket was hanging open and he was wearing a pair of absolutely spotless white sneakers. In his streets-of-Brooklyn accent he said, "I think I got another Dades Special."

"Dades Special" was the catchphrase the two of them had invented to describe some unsolvable cold case that Dades had dug up from somewhere and decided to solve. Sometimes it came the other way, from Vecchione's desk, and those were "Mike Specials." Whatever this one was, Vecchione knew it was going to be good. One thing Mike knew for sure: Whenever Detective Tommy Dades got involved, life was always going to be interesting.

Maybe this story actually began the day they shot the union rep in the ass and accidentally killed him. Or maybe it began the day "Gaspipe" Casso tried to blow up John Gotti and got the wrong guy, a guy who made the mistake of dressing too well. Or it could have started when Mickey Boy Paradiso tried to kill Gaspipe, who escaped by running into the basement of a Chinese restaurant. Who knows, the whole thing might have started when Burt Kaplan, the One-Eyed Jew, went to jail in 1980 for conspiring to sell a million dollars a week in quaaludes. But for Tommy Dades it started, just like all the important stories of his life, with the mother.

Wherever it started, whenever it started, there is no question where it ended; it ended with the worst scandal in the history of the New York City Police Department. It ended with killer cops. Two highly decorated retired detectives charged with providing information to the Mafia that resulted in eight dead bodies—including a couple on which the cops were the triggermen. It ended with Detectives Louis Eppolito and Stephen Caracappa convicted of being on the Mafia payroll—$5,000 a month, with bonuses for extra work like a murder, for betraying more than forty thousand fellow New York City police officers. It ended with two lowlifes, two skells, disgracing the badge.

That's a very big thing, the *worst* scandal in NYPD history. That history covers more than a century, and it includes half a million cops. Maybe more. The last time anything close happened was 1914, when Lieutenant Charles Becker—an associate of the street gangs who were running the city in those days—was charged and eventually executed for the murder of a gambling-club owner, Beansie Rosenthal, who was threatening to testify against him.

Police Lieutenant Becker ran his district tougher than a king, and he killed at least that one guy. But compared to these two cops that was nothing. That was a minor scrape. The extent of the damage that Eppolito and Caracappa did to the department may never be completely totaled. They gave up informants to the mob, who then murdered them. They informed the mob about wiretaps and investigations, they warned men who were about to be arrested to go on the lam, they forced innocent people to confess to crimes they hadn't committed by threatening to kill their families, they provided whatever information the mob needed, they kidnapped people and turned them over to the wiseguys to be tortured and killed, and finally they put on their badges, pulled their guns, and murdered at point-blank range. There's no possible way of figuring how many investigations they destroyed, how many people died because of them. They were the absolute worst. No contest.

And like Charlie Becker, for a long time it looked like Eppolito and Caracappa would get away with murder. Both Eppolito and Caracappa had retired and were living in Las Vegas when a woman named Betty Hydell called Tommy Dades in 2003. Eppolito and Caracappa had bought large houses across the street from each other in a pristine subdivision named Spanish Palms. Things seemed nice and comfortable for

them. "The Stick," as the slender and taciturn Caracappa was occasionally called, was working for a security firm. He was known around Spanish Palms for
rescuing stray animals and going to bed so early that
his wife was always complaining about it. But his
partner, from all reports the guy who gave the orders,
Louis Eppolito, was still trying to catch the spotlight.

Even when he was a cop everything about Eppolito
had been big and loud; his bodybuilder's physique, his
booming voice, his flashy clothes and expensive jewelry. He raised exotic snakes as pets and wore a
serpent-head ring. Tommy Dades remembers meeting
him twice, at Christmas parties two years in a row.
The first year, Eppolito was wearing a black shirt with
a white tie and was loaded down with jewelry. Dades
remembers, "He looked like he was going to a Hal-
loween party dressed as a gangster. He had nine
bracelets, sixteen rings; he definitely wanted to be noticed. He was the kind of guy people either loved him
or hated him. There was no in-between. I didn't know
him to judge him, but going by first impressions, I
didn't like him."

Mike Vecchione knew him a lot better. "I had
known about Louis Eppolito most of my life. I'd
grown up in Brooklyn's Prospect Heights with the
white sheep of the Eppolito family.

"Everybody in the neighborhood knew all about
the Eppolitos. There were four brothers; three of them
ended up associated with the Gambino crime family,
while the fourth brother was totally straight. In fact, to
completely disassociate himself from his brothers, Joe
Ippolito even spelled his name differently, starting it
with an 'I' rather than an 'E.' My family was friends
with the Ippolitos. We always referred to Joe and Ray

and Paul as 'the good Ippolitos.' We all knew that 'the bad Eppolitos' were the mobsters, even if at that age I wasn't sure what a mobster was. Joe's wife, Ray, worked closely with my mother and my aunt helping the nuns from the local church, St. Teresa of Avila. We were always at each other's houses. I grew up playing with Louis Eppolito's cousin Paul.

"I knew that Louis Eppolito had become a cop. Believe me, that was not a career choice anybody expected the son of one of the 'bad Eppolitos' to make. I'd never met him, but I guess I figured it was possible that crime didn't run in his genes. Maybe Louis had rejected his family background."

Eppolito had grown up in the Mafia. His father, Ralph, was a soldier in the Gambino family known as Fat the Gangster. An uncle, Jimmy the Clam, was a capo. Another uncle was also with the Gambinos. Louis supposedly had turned his back on his family to become a cop. Supposedly.

In Vegas Eppolito bought a $360,000, four-thousand-square-foot two-story house with a five-foot-high fountain on the lawn, two white pillars at the front, and the first swimming pool in the neighborhood. After retiring, he'd written a book about his career, ironically titled *Mafia Cop*. Maybe that title was an inside joke he shared with Caracappa. To earn a living he got bit parts in fourteen movies—his once-muscular build long gone, he had played a wiseguy appropriately named Fat Andy in *Goodfellas*, a drug dealer in *Company Business*, and an assassin in *Da Game of Life*—and had written the screenplay for a Charles Durning film called *Turn of Faith*, which had been financed by former boxer Ray "Boom Boom" Mancini and actually received decent B-movie reviews, particularly for the "authenticity of the dialogue." By 2003 he was pretty well known in Vegas. He was hustling to raise money to produce his screenplays and telling friends that *Mafia Cop* was about to become a TV series. Photographs he'd taken with celebrities hung all over his office walls and he proudly entertained cast members of *The Sopranos* at the house. Louis Eppolito was still trying desperately to run with the fast crowd. The one thing neither he nor Caracappa seemed worried about was the past catching up to them.

While Eppolito and Caracappa were out in Vegas, Detective First Grade Tommy Dades was running out the string on his extraordinary twenty-year career. He was assigned to the Intelligence Division in Brooklyn, basically trying to stay out of the way of his new boss. "I'd had great bosses for most of my career. But after 9/11 the whole business changed. We ended up with a deputy commissioner who came out of the CIA and his only concern was terrorism. Nothing else mattered. Terrorism, that was it. We'd done great things. We'd solved twenty-five murders; we'd put at least a hundred wiseguys in prison. We'd established a better working relationship with the FBI and DEA than anybody in the history of the department. But the only thing this new boss wanted to know about my squad was when were we all retiring. He couldn't care about anything else. He didn't want to know from organized crime. When they finally closed our unit most of our files, years of work, just got thrown out in the street. It was a shame. I stood in the street going through the garbage and I actually found a tape that ended up being used in a federal trial."

Tommy Dades was spending his last months on the job he loved deeply cleaning up old business when

Betty Hydell called just to say hello—and within a few sentences the very old business became his future.

Betty Hydell was one of the mothers. Throughout his career Tommy had often taken the time to forge special relationships with the mothers. Mothers of victims, mothers of suspects, even mothers of killers. Long after his work on the crimes that had brought them together ended he kept in touch with them. If they needed help with something, navigating the system, figuring out where to get the best price on car repairs, even running the occasional errand, they called and he responded. Tommy was one of those people who had made friends everywhere. He had his own network, the Tommy Network. He helped people and they helped him. Whatever needed to be done, Tommy had a friend he could call to get it done. Sometimes his relationships encompassed the other family members, the father, brother, or sister, but the mother was always the heart of it. A lot of them loved him for it. They had his home number and they called him often, knowing he really cared. Knowing that their husband, their son, was more than a forgotten file somewhere. Each Christmas Tommy and Ro, his wife, received cards, flowers, and gifts from the families of cases he'd worked. With Tommy, it wasn't hard to figure out where the caring came from.

Tommy had never met his father. His whole life he had believed he was an only child, raised by his mother. The two of them became extremely close; he remembers, "When I couldn't find her, I'd get panicky. She was an amazing woman, and beautiful, really beautiful. She worked for her whole life at Maimonides Hospital in Brooklyn, ending up as an administrator in the mental health department. The same hospital where I was born. She earned a decent living, so we weren't starving, and she was satisfied as long as she had enough money to buy nice clothes and play the numbers. We lived in Brooklyn, in the same code forever.

"I was a tough kid, an aggressive kid. I was basically on my own from the time I was eight or nine years old. Starting when I was thirteen she'd run to Atlantic City for weekends with her loser boyfriends, leaving me alone. I easily could've gone the other way. I was offered a lot of opportunities to do the wrong thing, but most of the time I walked away. Most of the time. But the truth is that I stole a few cars, I stole copper from construction sites. Things of opportunity. I never planned anything illegal. There were times when it was tempting; I had no money. I used to stand with my friends on the corner of Eighth Avenue and Forty-seventh Street in Brooklyn. The people I was with were selling anything anybody wanted, pot, coke, whatever. They were my friends. One of my best friends growing up is a made guy today in Queens. We see each other—not as much as we used to—but we never talk about what we're doing. I could have easily been in that mix; I don't know why I didn't do it. I think I just didn't want to make life any tougher for my mother.

"We had this amazing connection, me and my mother. The morning she died I was working. She'd been sick but lately had been feeling a little better. For some reason about seven o'clock in the morning my throat started to close up, I started hyperventilating. I was having a complete anxiety attack. I told my partner Jimmy Harkins that I must've eaten something bad, because I'd never felt that bad before. I said,

'Maybe I should go to the hospital and get a shot before I end up dying in the car with you.' Instead I signed out early and figured I'd stop at the hospital near my house. But I started feeling a little better and decided I'd take a nap and see how I felt. I was half-asleep when my aunt called to tell me she couldn't get in contact with my mother.

"I started calling my mother's house but nobody answered. I was trying to ignore this whole thing, pretend if I didn't pay attention to it everything would be okay. I called my close friend and partner Mike Galletta and asked him to go by my mother's house. I couldn't do it myself, I just couldn't. Instead I went to the doctor's office. This was a doctor I didn't know so the nurse gave me some forms to fill out. One of the questions was 'Are your parents alive?' I put down for my father 'Unknown,' and for my mother I put down 'Yes.' But as I was checking the box I knew the answer was going to be no.

"All the dead bodies I'd seen in my life, all the murder victims, I couldn't go to the house. When EMS got there they said she'd been dead about five hours. Which was almost exactly the time I started hyperventilating. That's a fact, that's exactly the way it happened."

Growing up Tommy learned what the streets could do to a kid—and to that kid's mother. So even when he found himself dealing with a real lowlife, he tried to make reality a little easier for the mother. "When you speak to the mother," he said, "it's not about the kid. You're doing it for her."

Through the years the Dades had become especially close to Betty Hydell. Betty Hydell's two sons, Jimmy and Frankie, went bad early. Real bad. Jimmy Hydell was a stone-cold killer. He had even arranged the murder of his longtime girlfriend, an innocent young woman named Annette DiBiase, after he beat her up and she started talking out loud about him. A friend of his shot her in the head five times and buried her in the woods. It probably was a favor. But by the time Tommy met Betty, Jimmy was long gone. All that was known about his disappearance was that one day he'd walked out of his house on Bangor Street on Staten Island to go to a meeting in Brooklyn and no one ever found his body. Nobody cared too much about another dead wiseguy either, nobody except the mother.

So Tommy Dades never knew Jimmy Hydell. But he got to know the brother, Frankie Hydell, real well. In fact, he felt responsible for Frankie's murder. This was one of those cop things that ate him up. Frankie wasn't as tough as his older brother; Jimmy had earned a mob reputation, while Frankie probably was more of a wannabe. Frankie's real expertise was in bank burglaries, with a minor in drugs and extortion. But in March 1988, Frankie Hydell was convicted of manslaughter. The key piece of evidence against him was a confession he made to a junkie who was wired, a confession that turned out to be more bragging than reality. His real crime was stealing the car that his brother used in the hit. Frankie served eight years, and when he got out he went right back to work.

Not too long after being paroled Frankie was in a social club on Thirteenth Avenue in Brooklyn when a mason tenders union official named Frankie Parasol was murdered. He wasn't supposed to be killed. This was supposed to be a simple beating, ordered by a heavy hitter as a warning, but it went bad. Parasol was shot in the ass; it should have been an embarrassing flesh wound, but the bullet opened an artery and he bled to death. Frankie Hydell actually tried to save him; after everybody else ran away he called 911. His voice can be heard on the tape pleading for an ambulance. While nobody could have known it at the time, this was one of those moments where a butterfly flapping its wings in the Southern Hemisphere leads to a hurricane in the Northern Hemisphere: It started a long chain of events that ended two decades later in a Brooklyn courtroom.

Tommy Dades's partner Mike Galletta caught the murder case. Within days Tommy and Mike learned from a confidential informant that Frankie Hydell and several other men were involved. A confidential informant, or CI, will provide information but will never testify in court, while a cooperating witness, a CW, will take the stand. Dades and Galletta had forged an unusual and productive relationship with an FBI agent named Matt Tormey. The three men often worked as a team, ignoring completely the legendary NYPD-FBI rivalry. Galletta and Tormey believed that if Frankie got jammed up, rather than go back to jail he would flip, meaning he would agree to become a confidential informant. And Frankie could be very helpful; not only did he know where bodies were buried, he knew who had buried a lot of them. They decided to take a shot at turning him.

Galletta knew that Frankie Hydell was shaking down stores on Thirteenth Avenue in Brooklyn. He was in the business of money for nothing. Mike and FBI Special Agent Bill Hickel installed video cameras and a tape recorder in one of those places, a twenty-four-hour convenience store. Steven Spielberg couldn't have directed a better scene. Hydell was arrested and locked up. Another two years in the joint for parole violation was the best outcome he was looking at. The worst thing was doing major time. Hydell's parole officer laid it out, then threw him a lifeline. The FBI wanted to talk to him, he explained. If Frankie was looking for a deal they could help him.

Tommy had turned a lot of guys. He was pretty much an expert at it. He was a good talker; he had a feel for telling people what they needed to hear. But even for an expert it sometimes is very tough to convince a street guy to change his future. A couple of years earlier, for example, Tommy and Matt Tormey had spent three days, eight hours a day, trying to flip a guy named Joey Gross. They bought him breakfast, lunch; they let him make phone calls and laid out his options. They explained to him over and over how it would benefit him to work with them and warned him what would happen if he didn't. For two days Gross didn't say too much, but at the end of the third day he agreed to think about it. For a long time that was as far as he would go: thinking about it. It took months, but eventually he ended up testifying for the government in several cases. Instead of spending a decade in prison he did a year and a half and went into the Witness Protection Program.

Frankie Hydell was easy. He was feeling real bad about his participation in Parasol's murder. Matt flipped him in a single meeting. It went exactly as it had been planned. Tormey registered Frankie Hydell as an FBI confidential informant, although the NYPD had complete access to him. From that first meeting, Frankie was adamant he would never testify in the Parasol murder; instead, he supplied information about bank robberies, car thefts, big marijuana deals, and an array of other crimes.

Initially Frankie Hydell told Tormey he didn't want anything to do with Detective Tommy Dades. He distrusted cops in general, claiming that two cops had been involved in his brother's disappearance—but he had a special hatred for Tommy Dades because, Hydell told Tormey, "This guy, he's always looking to break everybody's chops."

Little by little Tormey convinced Hydell that Tommy Dades was an okay guy. "I've been working with him a long time," he said. "I'm telling you he can be trusted a hundred percent. He's a good guy."

Tommy met Frankie Hydell for the first time in an FBI safehouse, a sparsely furnished apartment in a high-rise on Manhattan's Upper East Side. Hydell had a gruff voice and he spoke street: "You know that everybody hates your fucking guts. Both you and your motherfucking partner. You guys're destroying the whole neighborhood, locking everybody up, breaking chops for no reason."

Instead of arguing with him or defending himself, Tommy treated Frankie with respect. He focused the conversation on subjects where they might find some level of agreement. By the end of that first meeting, maybe they weren't best friends, but there was the foundation of a good rapport. That made a lot of sense. They both came from the streets; they knew a lot of the same people, talked the same talk. And Frankie Hydell pretty much sealed their relationship during that first meeting when he told Tommy that a psycho kid named John Pappa was looking to kill Tommy. "He even sat on your house for two days. He saw your wife and kids go in your house. He was waiting for you to come home and then he was going to kill you in front of them."

This story winds around a lot of corners before it gets to Louis Eppolito and Steve Caracappa, but it all leads directly to the murderous detectives. John Pappa was loosely affiliated with the Colombos. He definitely was a heavy hitter, credited with ten murders before celebrating his twenty-first birthday. As Frankie explained it to Dades, when Pappa found out that Tommy was looking at him for a couple of those hits he figured he could end the investigation by killing him. Nobody ever claimed he had brains. Somehow Pappa managed to get Tommy's address. And according to Hydell, Pappa then spent several days sitting in his red car in front of Tommy's house on Staten Island, waiting for Tommy to come home. Waiting to kill him.

A few weeks later a second CI confirmed Hydell's information.

Dades's wife, Roseann, took the news that some lowlife had been waiting patiently in front of her house to kill her husband pretty matter-of-factly. This wasn't the first death threat Tommy had received. A year earlier there'd been a series of letters warning him that he and Galletta were going to be machine-gunned to death. But this threat was as real as the red car parked in front of the house. No one doubted Pappa was serious. And no one knew if he had been working alone. Tommy told Ro what to look for, how to be careful, how to get help fast. The department stationed a squad car in front of the house twenty-four hours a day, seven days a week, for the next six months.

Ironically, about a month before getting this information, Tommy had arrested Pappa. The investigation that Pappa had tried to stop had resulted in his indictment for multiple murders. "We got word that Pappa was going to be a member of the bridal party at a friend's wedding on Staten Island," Tommy recalls. "There was only one thing the groom didn't know: Pappa had been one of the guys who'd killed his brother. So we were going to arrest Pappa when he showed up at church for the wedding rehearsal.

"I was sitting in the car across the street when he showed up. We waited until he started climbing the steps to the church and then I jumped out of the car and started screaming. 'Police, John! Hold it right there.' I had my gun in my hand. I was maybe ten feet away from him when he pulled a nine-millimeter out of his waistband; at that distance that gun looked about as big as a basketball.

"I screamed at him, 'Dump the gun, John! Dump it now!'

"Instead he took off running. Just as he opened the door to the church he turned around and aimed right at me.

"In those situations you don't think, you react. 'Don't do it!' I screamed at him. I aimed my gun at him and started to squeeze the trigger—and just as I did the church door opened and I saw a whole bunch of people inside the church. I didn't fire.

"Pappa ran inside. I grabbed the door before it closed and raced inside right after him. I wasn't more than ten steps behind him, but I didn't see him throw away his nine-millimeter. Instead I heard it hit the floor over to my right. I never saw the gun, but I heard it. In situations like that every one of your instincts is pumping. You see things, you hear things, you feel things that otherwise it's impossible. But I heard that gun hit the floor and slide.

"The whole wedding party was screaming, trying

to scramble out of the way. They didn't have any idea what was going on. There were people diving into the pews. About halfway down the aisle I took a flying leap at Pappa and tackled him. As we hit the floor I slammed my knee into the side of his head to keep him down, then I pointed my gun at him and I started screaming loud as I could, 'Don't anybody fucking move! Don't move! I'll kill anyone that moves!' I didn't know who any of these people were. All I knew is that they weren't friends of mine. 'Everybody get down,' I yelled. I ended up putting the priest on the floor.

"John Pappa wasn't done. He started getting wild on me. I grabbed him around the throat with one hand and warned him, 'Try me and I'll break your fucking neck.' As the backup raced into the church I was shouting to them, 'Get the gun! Get the gun! It's under the pews over there on the right.' Pappa's nine-millimeter had fourteen bullets in the clip—and one in the chamber."

After learning from Frankie Hydell that Pappa had intended to kill him, Tommy figured he'd better set that one right forever. As a result during Pappa's trial the judge had Tommy thrown out of the courtroom. Pappa's defense attorney had caught him mouthing silently, "I know what you did and if you beat the case I'm gonna kill you." Eventually Pappa was convicted of five murders and received two life sentences plus sixty-five years. He was twenty-one years old and he was never going home again.

So at their very first meeting Frankie Hydell may have saved Tommy Dades's life. That made a pretty strong foundation on which to build a relationship. As the months passed Frankie turned out to be a very productive informant. He was involved with a mob crew that was in the marijuana business, bringing in four-hundred-pound crates from Mexico through Arizona. They would put sheets of the laundry freshener Bounce in each crate to blunt the scent so the drug dogs couldn't detect it. Frankie told them about each shipment. The information Frankie provided resulted in the arrest and conviction of five major players.

The whole key to working successfully with a confidential informant is maintaining secrecy. Paid informants literally sign contracts under fictitious names; their real names are known only to their law enforcement contact. Tommy and Frankie had a good thing going and both of them knew it. While they only met face-to-face three times, they spoke several times a week. Then one night the situation changed. Frankie was told by the head of his mob crew to go up to the Bronx, supposedly to meet with people who were shipping stolen cars out of the country. It turned out that the real reason for the meeting was to confront him. One of the other members of the gang had gotten word from somewhere that Frankie was cooperating with the Feds. They assumed he was talking about the union guy's killing, which put them all in jeopardy. Frankie managed to laugh his way out of the situation, but as soon as possible he met with Tommy and Matt. "They think I'm working with you guys," he said.

This information, it turned out, had come from someone in the Brooklyn DA's office. In order to flip Frankie Hydell, to make the convenience store shakedown disappear if he agreed to cooperate, Tommy and Matt needed the DA's cooperation. Notes were scribbled on sheets of paper; folders had been flying all over the office. Anybody could have known about it.

Later, Joe Ponzi, chief of the DA's investigative force, had conducted an extensive internal operation to try to identify the leak. He'd dumped phones, set up a sting; he tried everything possible. Joe Ponzi was a friend of both Tommy Dades and Mike Vecchione. This leak was an itch he was desperate to scratch, but he was never able to discover its source.

In fact, where it came from didn't matter; the damage was done. Hydell was compromised. Tommy and Matt decided to shut down the operation, telling him, "You got no choice. You're gonna have to go full boat now. Witness protection, the whole thing."

If Hydell realized he was in a real bad jam, he didn't show it. "Ah, don't worry about it," Frankie told them, "I blew 'em off. The whole thing's bullshit. Everything's cool."

Tommy did worry about it. Several years earlier the mob had found out about another CI he was working with and they had killed him. Just as in this case, there'd been a leak in the system that had never been found. So Dades knew the consequences if Hydell was wrong. He tried again to talk him in, but Frankie continued to refuse, insisting he had the whole problem covered.

It turned out he was wrong. It wasn't his fault, but he was wrong. More mistakes got made. The big one occurred after Frankie informed his handlers that the crew was planning a bank robbery in New Jersey. The cops decided to grab the crew during the robbery, confiscate the evidence, and then release them without any explanation. That bust would serve to corroborate Hydell's information, as well as make the rest of the gang very confused and very nervous.

The U.S. Attorney's office will allow registered CIs

to participate in certain crimes if it is deemed absolutely necessary to continue an operation. But in this situation there was a chance that an innocent person could get hurt, which would be a public relations disaster, so Hydell was ordered to stay away. Tormey told him, "You know you can't go, right?"

He knew. "Don't worry 'bout it, I got it covered."

Five guys planned the heist; four guys went. Probably because it was taking place in Jersey, Matt Tormey's FBI supervisor would not let the NYPD cover it. Instead the assignment was given to a bureau surveillance unit, which was simply going to film it as evidence. The night of the robbery the unit staked out the bank for more than five hours, then decided the job must have been postponed or canceled. But instead of just packing their cameras and walking away, they notified the Jersey state police. They sent a teletype that included all the information about the robbery, adding the fact that this information had come from an informant. When the crew finally showed up to pull the job, the state police grabbed them. Nobody got hurt.

The problem was that an inexperienced officer gave a copy of that teletype to the defense attorney representing the crew. It wasn't done intentionally; it was just a simple, and deadly, mistake. The teletype didn't identify Frankie by name. It read, "An FBI confidential informant indicated . . ." But five guys planned the job, and four guys went. Combined with the previous information from the DA's office, it was obvious that Frankie was working with the Feds.

Tommy, Matt, and Mike sat down with Frankie in the safehouse and laid it out for him. "We begged him," Tommy remembers. "We did everything we could to

convince him to get out of there. 'This is really bad,'
Matt told him. But we couldn't force him off the street.
We couldn't force him to become a witness. There was
nothing we could do. Frankie had a mouth; he figured
he could talk his way out of it."

He couldn't. One night in April 1998 Frankie went
to a strip joint on Staten Island, a place named Scar-
lett's, with his best friend, John Mattera. When they
walked out of the place four men were sitting in a car
waiting for him. The shooter put three bullets into him
from just about point-blank range. Frankie Hydell was
probably dead before he hit the ground. Tommy
learned later that this was an up-the-ladder sanction.
People from the social club on Thirteenth Avenue had
gone to the bosses in the family and told them they
had a piece of paper from the DA's office that proved
Frankie was a rat. Then they exaggerated, claiming
they'd caught him with an FBI check, proof that he
was working for the government. That was impossible; the bureau doesn't pay informants by check. But
based on that evidence permission had been granted
to kill Hydell.

As Tommy recalls, "We were devastated. You get
to know these guys, care about them. It wasn't just
that we lost an informant; this was a person we liked
and cared about. And the family had already been
through so much with the brother, who had disappeared into the air. This was just too much." Professionally, if you can't protect your informants you're
out of the business. And personally, each of them
liked Hydell. He had a sort of roguish charm. And
once he'd made the decision to cooperate, he'd shown
as much dedication to providing information as he had
in the past to running scams. If he had continued,

been a little luckier, he might have even had a shot at a legitimate future. Stranger things have happened.

The morning after the shooting Tommy, Matt, Mike Galletta, a deputy inspector, and a lieutenant drove out to meet the Staten Island detectives who'd caught the case. They met with the lieutenant who ran the squad. It was a sensitive situation; they had to be extremely careful what information was divulged to the investigating officers. So without giving the detectives working the case all the details, they explained that they were pretty certain they knew who'd killed Frankie Hydell. Maybe not the name of the wiseguy who pulled the trigger, but the people who made it happen. The names would come.

The lieutenant was polite. He told them thank you very much and then completely ignored them. Apparently a cab driver claimed he had seen the murder and identified the shooter as a local crackhead. This driver was a street guy who had done some light work for Hydell. Tommy knew this was total bullshit, this was a mob hit, but the lieutenant wasn't interested. Arresting the crackhead enabled Staten Island to clear the murder. The suspect spent fifteen months in jail.

Dades believes that Matt Tormey was so upset about Hydell's murder that he decided to put in his retirement papers. But for Tommy the situation soon got a lot worse. A mob hanger-on facing five years in prison—based on information provided by Frankie— reached out to Dades and Tormey. This guy was a member of the union working on a building under construction in Manhattan while out on appeal. Tommy and Matt met him in an unfinished apartment in the building. He had some important information for them, he explained, but there was a price. His mother had breast cancer and he didn't want to go to prison, but he couldn't go public. He couldn't testify. When Tommy asked for a taste of what he had, the guy looked right at him. "You're the one who gave out the information that compromised Frankie," he said.

"What are you talking about?" Tommy was rocked; this was a cop's worst nightmare, but he'd learned a long time ago to conceal his emotions. "That's bullshit," he said evenly. "How do you figure that?"

The guy smiled and said, "You told somebody on your side of the fence about him cooperating. That person told somebody on our side of the fence."

That was all the information this guy would give up without a deal. Maybe it was true, maybe not. Informants all have their own agenda. This guy wanted to beat prison. Tommy laid it out for him: "If you're offering to take the stand we'll get you out of prison, but you just telling us, that isn't going to do us any good."

The guy couldn't take the deal. There was an irrefutable logic to his position: If he testified he would be killed; dead forever was a lot longer than five years in prison.

Tommy didn't believe that his talking had resulted in Frankie's death—except when he did. He just didn't know the truth. It was possible. But it was hard to accept that he could have been that careless. He never spoke about his informants around people he didn't know, and it was impossible to believe that someone he knew and trusted could give up the information. He spent a lot of time trying to figure out who the informer might be. It was incredibly frustrating. The possibility that someone working in the NYPD or the DA's office, or someone affiliated with one of those offices, would give up an informant, knowing that he was going to die, made him furious. But without more information about the source he was wasting his time, just pissing in the wind.

Unable to find the source of the leak, he turned to finding Frankie Hydell's killers. And that's when he met Betty Hydell. "Matt had a pretty good relationship with the family," Tommy recalls. "When he retired he left them my phone number. I called them first. In the family there was just Betty and her husband and their two daughters. The two sons were dead. The father had been a bus driver for twenty-nine years, a totally legitimate guy. Betty had worked for twenty years; she was totally straight. I called her to break the ice. Basically, I just told her that I intended to solve this homicide and maybe she could help me. She knew Matt and me were close, but she didn't trust any New York City cops.

"Building a relationship with her took time. Eventually she invited me out to the house on Staten Island. First thing I told her was that I was sorry about Frankie and I was going to do the best I could to find his killers. 'Thank you,' she said, but she said it without a lot of conviction.

"Betty Hydell was in her late fifties. She was a real pleasant person, and because of all the things she'd been through she was street-smart. She was very leery of me. Right away she told me that it was going to take time to earn her trust because she'd been screwed over by both the FBI and the NYPD. She didn't tell me why at that point and I didn't ask. Basically, she was challenging me to prove that I really was interested in solving her son's murder."

Matt had retired and moved to Florida. When Tommy began working the case, the last thing he figured was that it was going to take him to two filthy dirty cops. His real objective was to give the mother some peace.

When you're connected to the streets, as he was, a lot of cases start at the end: From the first day you know who committed the crime, then you have to work backward to reach the beginning and prove it. One of the first things he did was subpoena the cell phone records of the people he thought might be involved, from a few hours before Frankie was killed till a few hours after the shooting. It turned out that right after the murder the phones were blasting at each other. A couple of unexpected numbers also turned up. As Tommy had guessed, these were the same guys whose names had popped up in the killing of the union official. They were afraid Frankie was going to rat them out—that was never going to happen, but they didn't know that—so he had to go.

Tommy shared each piece of information he developed with Betty. The one thing he found out that he didn't tell her was that her sister's husband, Frankie's uncle through marriage, who was a Gambino capo, *may* have known about the contract and let it happen. Betty and her sister didn't have much to do with each other, but Tommy kept that piece of information private. He just didn't see a reason to hurt Betty any more.

Frankie Hydell had been registered to the FBI, so officially this was the bureau's investigation. In the past that wouldn't have mattered; Tommy and Matt would have worked together. But Tormey had retired and the special agent who replaced him wasn't a member of the Dades fan club. So Tommy was completely shut out of the loop. Eventually Hydell's best friend, John Mattera, pleaded guilty to participating in the hit and a second man was tried and convicted. The three other men believed to have been involved, including the actual shooter, were also charged with the crime.

One of the last things Mike Galletta did before retiring was solve the murder of the union official, Frankie Parasol, and lock up the guys who did it.

While Tommy was no longer involved in the actual investigation, his work on the case had enabled him to establish a good relationship with Betty and her daughter Lizzie. He really liked both of them. As he explains, "These are really nice people. She just got stuck with two boys that unfortunately went the wrong way. But Frankie wasn't anything like his brother; mostly he talked a good story, and eventually he paid for that. But none of that was her fault. All she got was the heartache."

Over time, Tommy got very close with the family. He would speak with Betty about once each week, more if he had heard something about the case he could share with her. He would call Betty on Mother's Day and the other family holidays, and she called him on his birthday. And sometimes when she called she talked about both of her sons, Frankie and Jimmy. "Both of them are dead," she complained to Tommy, "and I doubt anybody is going to do anything about it."

Tommy never gave the mothers false hope. After the losses they had suffered, that would have been too cruel. But when he gave his word, he always followed through with it. Always. He'd told Betty Hydell that he was going to chase this case until he found some answers. He didn't promise her that he would solve it; he just knew he was going to.

CHAPTER 2

Good cops live for the rest of their life with the cases they never solved. Long after they put their badge in a frame or in a drawer they still wonder about it. Tommy Dades kept this one close to the edge, just waiting for a familiar word to pop, looking for someone to roll over and bring it back to life. He owed that to Betty Hydell. And through the years he heard a lot of cop talk about Jimmy Hydell's disappearance. Most of it centered around claims made by Lucchese boss Anthony "Gaspipe" Casso.

In 1993 Casso had been captured by a twelve-member SWAT team after spending thirty-two months running from a racketeering indictment. Even in a world ruled by violence Casso was considered unusually bloodthirsty. He had killed his way to the top of the Lucchese family. Supposedly he would order people killed if he simply dreamt they were cooperating with the cops. He once said that he wanted to kill the twenty-five members of the family believed to be cooperating and he didn't only because he couldn't figure out how to get rid of twenty-five bodies. He even broke the rules by which the Mafia had been strictly run for decades by ordering a hit on the completely innocent sister of mob turncoat Peter "Fat Pete" Chiodo, after his attempt to kill Chiodo failed. The woman was shot after dropping off her children at school but survived. Inside the mob and in the newspapers he was known as Gaspipe, supposedly because his father had been an enforcer on the Brooklyn docks known for using lead pipes to bust heads. But cops and prosecutors sometimes referred to him as Lucifer, because they considered him to be a complete psychopath.

When he was finally caught, in addition to the racketeering charges, he was indicted for fifteen murders. In fact, the actual number of murders in which he had been involved was at least thirty-six. They were going to slam the cell door behind him and melt down the key. He was fifty-three years old and he was never going to drive a car, wear a suit, walk along a beach, eat in a nice restaurant, or touch a woman again. He knew it, his attorney knew it, and the government knew it.

So Gaspipe flipped. He agreed to cooperate with the federal government. In addition to admitting to all the racketeering charges, he pled guilty to fifteen murders and a variety of lesser crimes. He also agreed to tell the government everything he had learned about organized crime; that included the details of every crime in which he had been involved as well as everything he had heard about throughout his entire career, from fact to rumor. The incentive is that the cooperator gets immunity for any crime to which he confesses—and his testimony can't be used against him. And finally, Gaspipe agreed to testify against other mobsters. The deal was that when all of that was done, when the government determined that he had honestly fulfilled his cooperation agreement, federal prosecutors would give him what was called a 5K letter. This relates to the Federal Rules of Criminal Procedure, which say, basically, that if a defendant gives substantial cooperation to the federal government his cooperation will be made known to the judge by the U.S. Attorney. Based on the recommendation of the federal prosecutor the judge has the power—but not the obligation—to substantially reduce the sentence of the cooperator.

Sammy "the Bull" Gravano, for example, admitted to participating in nineteen murders, but after providing information or testifying in trials that resulted in about forty convictions or guilty pleas he was sentenced to five years in prison. Five years for nineteen murders. Eventually he was released and admitted to the Witness Protection Program. The government gave him a new life—with financial support. It was the best deal a mass murderer had ever gotten. Gaspipe got the message. After all, he was only pleading to fifteen killings—although he claimed that he had been involved in thirty-six murders. Complete cooperation was his only shot at freedom.

The day he signed his cooperation agreement he called his wife at the women's lingerie shop she owned in Brooklyn and told her, "Sell the store. Take the money and the kids and go to Florida. I'll never see you again."

In response she supposedly said, "Drop dead."

On March 2, 1994, at the federal correctional institution La Tuna on the Texas–New Mexico border, Anthony Casso began revealing the innermost secrets of organized crime to FBI agents. During the next three years he met frequently with various agents and told an extraordinary tale of life and death in the Mafia. Particularly death. He admitted to being involved in thirty-six murders, and based on his reputation even that count seemed low. His 302, the official file in which his testimony was greatly condensed, was more than five hundred pages long. The crimes he described in detail ranged from major crimes like his attempt to kill John Gotti to more mundane efforts like putting rat poison in a judge's dinner at a restaurant in Little Italy. He named all the names and explained how the mob ran the garment industry, the construction trades, the garbage collection business. He explained how the enormous profits from an extraordinary variety of crimes were divvied up. He identified the retired detective involved in the theft of the "French Connection" heroin and how the money from the Lufthansa robbery was split. He explained how cops and prison guards were bribed and how the mob owned the Little Italy street festivals. It was a chillingly matter-of-fact, day-to-day account of a life lived without rules or morality.

One of the crimes he described was the kidnapping and murder of Jimmy Hydell, who was killed for his participation in a failed attempt to murder Casso. Gaspipe confessed that he had shot Hydell himself. As he later told Ed Bradley of *60 Minutes,* "Maybe I shot him ten times, twelve times. Really, I don't know the exact amount. It coulda been fifteen."

But when he began telling the FBI the whole story of Jimmy Hydell's murder, he stunned the agents when he mentioned casually that two New York City detectives had played a key role in the killing. At the time of the killing, he continued, he didn't even know their names. He knew them only as "the cops." And it wasn't until after the Hydell thing that they began working for him on a regular basis.

It was an incredible revelation. According to Casso, he literally had the cops on his monthly payroll. And unlike other rogue cops in the past, these two men weren't simply providing information, they were doing the dirtiest kind of work for the Lucchese family. They were hired killers.

In his 302 Casso claimed he had started working with the the cops in 1986, after he survived an attempt on his life and he started trying to find out who had set him up. He reached out to everybody he could trust, demanding answers. Anthony Casso was one of those people who got answers sometimes before he even asked the questions. Among the people he asked was a mob associate named Burt Kaplan, who told him that he had cops inside the Sixty-third Precinct, where the assassination attempt had taken place. Kaplan eventually handed Casso a manila envelope containing all the crime scene photos and reports—and the names of the men who had tried to kill him: Jimmy Hydell, Bob Bering, and Nicky Guido.

Right on top was a photograph of Hydell. Jimmy Hydell wasn't a made guy, but he was around. At first Casso didn't believe Hydell was involved. "That's crazy," he said. "I just got him a job with the unions." Casso and Hydell apparently went back a few years. At one point Casso had been in a luncheonette when Hydell and some friends were tearing up a nearby Chinese restaurant. When the owner of that restaurant appealed to Casso for help, Gaspipe had confronted Jimmy Hydell and his friends. Hydell had his dog with him, a big dog who kept leaping toward Casso.

After warning Hydell three times to get that dog away from him, Casso screwed a silencer onto the barrel of his gun and killed the dog. "Put him in the fucking trunk," he ordered Hydell.

Casso had never heard of the other guys. They were hangers-on, wannabes, small-time shooters with big-time ambitions. They came from who knew where and then they went back. Nobody knew how to find them. But more than anything, Casso wanted to know who had paid the bills for the attempt on his life. That was the one name he really needed; until he knew who had put out the contract on him, his life was in danger, and he knew that Jimmy Hydell could tell him. So he put the word on the street that he wanted Jimmy Hydell—alive. It was the two cops who delivered Jimmy Hydell to him, ironically in a car trunk.

That was the beginning of a beautiful relationship. Mob guys spent their lives worrying about rats, people who got jammed up and started talking to the law. But cops on the inside providing information to the mob? Getting them whatever information they needed? This was a very special gift. This just didn't happen too often. Kaplan owned them and he knew what he had, so he wasn't about to give up their identity, even to a friend like Casso. They were Kaplan's life insurance policy. Any business they did for Casso had to go through him. That's just the way it was and that was okay with Gaspipe.

Casso ended up doing a lot of business with the two cops. His "crystal ball," he called them, and in his 302 he claimed they had been involved in eight murders, including two in which they actually pulled the trigger. They were on his payroll for more than a year before he learned their identities.

Kaplan gave them up. One night he was telling Gaspipe that his cops had a hard-on for a guy named Red Calder, who somehow had been involved in the killing of one of "Lou's relatives." The relative turned out to be Jimmy "the Clam" Eppolito, a member of the Gambino family. Jimmy had been whacked because his son had gotten involved in a charity con that involved President Jimmy Carter's wife, Rosalynn, and Ted Kennedy. That had brought down too much heat. He had to go. So Casso finally learned the cop's name: Lou Eppolito.

It was more than a year later, Casso told the Feds in his deposition, that he finally learned the name of Eppolito's partner. Kaplan showed him a copy of the autobiography Eppolito had written, *Mafia Cop*. Look at this, he said, showing him a photograph of Eppolito with Steve Caracappa. The caption over the photograph identified them as "The two Godfathers of the NYPD." Casso immediately recognized the two cops as the men who had delivered Hydell to him. Kaplan told him that Caracappa was really pissed at Eppolito for putting his picture in the book.

The FBI agents were stunned by Casso's story. There were bad guys in just about every police department; everybody knew that. That was reality. Some guys took advantage of the shield. No question. But cops on the Mafia payroll? If he was telling the truth, this was a story that was going to rock New York City: killer cops.

The problem was that nobody actually knew if anything Gaspipe Casso said was true. Casso was a crazed killer; it was reasonable to assume he might also be a liar.

The primary condition of the agreement Casso had

made with the government required him to divulge the complete details of every illegal activity in which he had been involved or of which he had knowledge—and then he had to stop doing it. He had to go straight. If he didn't, if he withheld information or continued to be involved in criminal activity, the government could throw out his cooperation agreement and prosecute him for every crime he'd ever committed, from murder to jaywalking.

It turned out that from the very beginning Casso had been a lot less than completely honest. For example, he neglected to mention to the FBI that he had been involved in plots to kill federal judge Eugene Nickerson and federal prosecutor Charlie Rose. And while in prison he bribed guards to provide him with everything from cash to sushi, then attacked 350-pound mobster Sal Miciotta for informing prison officials that he was smuggling in contraband. Gaspipe had even planned an elaborate prison break—he was going to escape on horseback! But the information he continued to provide to the government was so valuable that the Feds probably would have overlooked these problems—if he hadn't made the mistake of accusing Sammy Gravano of lying.

Sammy the Bull had been the government's key witness against John Gotti. It was Gravano's damning testimony that put Gotti in solitary confinement until the day he died. The government had a big investment in Sammy's testimony; the absolute last thing they wanted to know was that he had lied on the stand. That might have been enough to allow Gotti to appeal his conviction.

But after Sammy had testified against mob boss Chin Gigante, Casso wrote a letter to prosecutors claiming that Gravano had lied under oath. Casso also accused Gravano of ordering the stabbing of the politically active reverend Al Sharpton and claimed that Sammy had been involved in drug trafficking.

The accusations against Gravano were easily disproved, but as a result of Casso's letter the government claimed he had breached his plea agreement. Rather than providing him with a 5K letter requesting leniency, they allowed the judge to sentence him to thirteen concurrent life sentences plus 440 years in prison.

The government had stated that Casso was a liar. So none of the claims he made in his 302—including those against Eppolito and Caracappa—could be pursued without jeopardizing the Gotti conviction. Casso's two cops walked away without a legal problem, but not without the accusations against them becoming publicly known. Three weeks after Casso had begun cooperating the *New York Post* ran a major article headlined I HIRED COPS TO WHACK GOTTI FOE: MOB CANARY GIVES NAMES TO PROBERS. The article reported, "During secret, out-of-state debriefing sessions Casso shocked his federal handlers last week by disclosing how he had enlisted two city cops to carry out a contract killing . . ."

The names of the two detectives spread rapidly through the city's law enforcement community. Tommy Dades heard about it from several different people in the NYPD. Many of the cops who had worked with or knew Lou Eppolito or Steve Caracappa refused to believe Casso's story. They knew the two cops as tough, effective, and brave officers, while Casso was a true nut job. But a lot of others weren't so sure. There had always been something edgy about Eppolito, something that just didn't feel right. By the time this story appeared both men had retired, so the department took no action. Without corroboration from a legitimate source there was no case, just the word of this skell, and the department wasn't working overtime to find someone to back up Casso's claims. There was little benefit to the NYPD to keep a scandal like this in the headlines. Mostly they hoped the story—just like Casso—would be locked away and forgotten forever.

The thing was, Tommy Dades believed Casso. Maybe Gaspipe wasn't the most honest guy in the world, maybe he wouldn't make a credible witness, but the stories he told squared with what Dades had learned working organized crime cases for almost two decades. It was the kind of stuff you just couldn't make up. Not only the stories implicating the cops, but all of it, all the other plots and crimes and betrayals he recounted. It all had the ring of truth. Like a lot of cops, Tommy had read Eppolito's autobiography, *Mafia Cop,* when it was published in 1992. That was years before Casso starting talking. The premise of the book was that Eppolito had grown up in a Mafia family: His father and his two uncles were with the Gambinos. His grandfather had been a close friend of Lucky Luciano. But supposedly he had gone straight—even though at his wedding the band played the theme from *The Godfather.*

Tommy thought the book was total bullshit. What kind of cop writes a book in which he admits, "Every time we went on a call where a husband smacked his wife, I went back that night and smacked it to her too . . . battered wives were the most vulnerable." He didn't believe any of Eppolito's going-straight stuff, particularly when Eppolito bragged in the book, "At least the mob guys treated me with respect. Not because I was a cop, but because I was a man of honor."

A "man of honor"? That was the phrase used by the mob to describe a made guy, a member of an organized crime family. No cop Tommy had ever known claimed proudly to be a "man of honor." Back then Tommy didn't know what Eppolito really was doing but he figured he was doing something. Casso's testimony confirmed that.

There was nothing Tommy could do about it though, except file all the details in his mind. There was a lot of information stored up there, bits and pieces of five hundred cases, names and relationships and crimes, a lot of dots waiting to be connected. But this wasn't his case, so it wasn't his business. It was more office gossip than work.

And that's the way it stayed for more than three years, until Frankie Hydell told him about the day his brother disappeared. "I was sitting with Frankie in a safehouse, an apartment, going over some information, when I saw he had this tattoo on the back of his neck, just above the top of his tank top. It said, 'Gaspipe's a Rat.' 'What's that all about?' I asked him.

" 'The guy's a no-good scumbag,' he told me.

"I knew right away what that was all about. Obviously Frankie believed Casso's claim that he had killed Jimmy. So we got to talking about that, nothing specific, just bullshitting. Finally I ask him, 'So what's your take on all that shit about the two cops being there? Think that's true?' I wasn't looking for anything, so I was pretty surprised what he told me.

"He kind of laughed at that and shook his head. 'You shitting me? I know they were fucking involved.'

"That's when I started paying close attention. 'Yeah? Like how?'

" 'I'll tell you how.' I could see the anger building in him as he told me about it. 'The day they killed Jimmy they grabbed me first.'

" 'What are you talking about?'

"He nodded yes. 'Yeah. They grabbed me first. I'm telling you, it was those two guys. I was driving my brother's car so they musta thought I was him. I come home and they was waiting by the house. They had an unmarked car, a police car. They show me their shields and try to stick me in their car. Fuck you, I told them, I ain't going nowheres with you till I know what the fuck this is all about. I was giving them a hard time and then one of them goes to the other one, "This isn't him." So they let me go.'

"He told me the whole story. About a half hour later, he said, he was driving away from the house when he saw the two cops again, this time heading toward the Verrazano Bridge, going to Brooklyn. Right at that moment he didn't think that had any meaning. In this world there are things that happen every day that no one can explain. Sometimes good things, sometimes not so good things. But there's nothing you can do about it, that's just the way things are, so you just shrug your shoulders, next. Frankie said it was only much later that night, when Jimmy didn't come home, that he figured out what had happened.

"I asked him, 'How do you know it was the same cops Casso was talking about?'

" ' 'Cause they looked just like he said, a fat one and a skinny one. Like Laurel and Hardy, you know what I mean?' When he saw their photographs in the newspapers he knew for sure it was them; he said that's how he found out their names."

Frankie hadn't told anyone about this. Tommy didn't bother asking why—he knew the answer: Cops had kidnapped his brother and were somehow involved in his murder. As far as Frankie knew, maybe they had even killed him. When the NYPD was told that cops were involved they didn't even bother to investigate. So the last thing Frankie was going to do was go to the cops. It was obvious to him that he couldn't trust cops to investigate cops. "I know they killed my brother," he told Tommy, "and nobody's doing nothing about it."

Tommy knew he was right—the case was dead. "There was nothing I could do about it either. Frankie was a confidential informant, not a witness. If I told this story to a lieutenant, he's gonna want to know the source of that information. That would mean exposing Frankie, which could put Frankie's life in danger. There wasn't any upside; Frankie was never going to testify against those two cops, and even if one day the world turned upside down and he agreed to take the stand in a courtroom, prosecutors would still need someone to corroborate his testimony. Nobody was going to take the word of a street guy like Frankie against a detective like Eppolito."

An active cop collects a lot of information during his career. Tommy knew a lot about a lot, much more than he had time to investigate. Most detectives maintain relationships with half a dozen informants; Tommy had about fifty people on the streets telling him what was going on. People trusted him to use the information they provided without burning the source. Even Sammy the Bull would call him regularly after he got out of prison just to talk. Now he knew another secret: He knew what had happened the day Jimmy Hydell disappeared. Not every detail, but enough to get him real interested. But it wasn't enough to do anything about it. What he needed to open an investigation was a reputable witness willing to testify against the cops. Without that he had nothing. And then when Frankie was murdered he had less than nothing. Dead men don't testify.

So the information had about as much value as knowing that Tashkent is the capital of Uzbekistan—until the day you're on *Jeopardy!* and the category is "Capitals of Former Members of the Soviet Union." Tommy never forgot about the case though. You never know when the category is going to come up. That was the debt he felt he owed to Frankie.

One afternoon in September 2003, six years after Frankie's murder, Tommy was sitting at his desk at the Intel Division at the Brooklyn Army Terminal when Betty Hydell called. She was calling to ask Tommy the usual question, was anybody doing anything about the alleged leak in the Brooklyn DA's office. But after a while their conversation moved to the subject that cemented their relationship, the murders of her two sons. "Let me ask you this, Betty," Tommy began. "You know I don't want to aggravate you, but there's gotta be something more you can tell me. Just try and think."

After a long pause, Betty replied, "Believe you me, Tommy, there's a whole lot I could add, but what good would it do me? I told it all to the FBI five years ago and they never even called me back."

That was news to Tommy. The FBI had some additional information? "Well, why didn't you ever talk to me? You know I would've listened."

"I know you're working on a lot of other things; I read about them. And if the FBI didn't do anything about it, why would I think you could?"

Because for me this is personal, Tommy thought, although he didn't say it. Instead he suggested, "Why don't you go ahead and tell me the story?"

On the day Jimmy disappeared, she said, he'd been picked up at the house by a friend of his, Bob Bering. He'd left his car behind because Frankie needed it to go to work. A little while later Frankie left, but he came back inside a few minutes later and told Betty that when he'd gotten into Jimmy's car two cops had come out of nowhere flashing their badges. "They tried to grab me," he told her. "They thought I was Jimmy." When they realized they had the wrong Hydell brother they'd let him go. Then they got back into a dark, unmarked police car and drove away.

Having chased a lifetime of bad tips, Tommy rarely got excited. But this time he couldn't help himself. This was the same story Frankie had told him before he'd been popped—but this time it was coming from a clean source. "What are you telling me, Betty? Are you saying you saw these guys?"

It was even better than that. "I wanted to know what was going on, so me and Lizzie, we went out and got in my car. We went around the corner and there they were, still there waiting. I pulled up right next to them. There were two men sitting in the front. I rolled down my window and asked, 'What's your problem with my son?'

"The fat one pulled out a police badge and held it up." Betty had seen far too many police shields in her life to be intimidated. "'So what's that supposed to mean? I asked you why you're bothering my son. He hasn't done anything.' "

"It's none of your business," the fat one told her. "Police business."

Her son was her business, Betty told them. "You just leave him alone." Then she drove away.

Tommy thought about all this. The wheels were turning. "Let me ask you this, Betty. Would you recognize those guys?"

Another surprise. "Oh, I know them," Betty said. "I saw them on *Sally*. I told that to the FBI too." One afternoon she had been watching a repeat of *The Sally Jesse Raphael Show* and who should Sally have on but retired detective Louis Eppolito, who was there promoting his book, *Mafia Cop*. "Oh my God," she'd said aloud. She recognized him instantly. Louis Eppolito was the fat guy who mistakenly had tried to pick up Frankie Hydell the day Jimmy was murdered. She immediately went out and bought his book and looked at the photographs. It was him. There was absolutely no doubt in her mind. It was him, the cop. You don't forget the face of the man who killed your son. "Lizzie'll tell you the same thing. She was right there with me."

Betty had immediately called the FBI. They took a statement from her. But no one from the bureau had ever called back about it.

"Can I talk to Lizzie about this?"

" 'Course you can."

"Let me ask you this, Betty. If I ever got to that point, would you talk to a prosecutor about what you just told me?"

She replied that she would do whatever he suggested,

then asked, "You think something could happen about this? After all this time?"

Tommy was honest with her. "I can't promise you anything. All I can tell you is what you're telling me gives me a foundation to work on. Give me a few days. I'll either tell you they shut me out or I got the green light to do it."

The last case of Detective Tommy Dades's career had just begun.

CHAPTER 3

Mike Vecchione was frying judges that day in late September 2003 when Tommy Dades bounced jauntily into his office. Vecchione was the head of the Rackets Division in Brooklyn DA Joe Hynes's office, an empire of investigation and prosecution that encompassed everything from organized crime to civil rights violations. Six months earlier Vecchione had arrested New York State Supreme Court Justice Gerald Garson for accepting a bribe. In the hope that he'd receive a reduced sentence, Garson had flipped almost immediately and given up Clarence Norman, head of the Brooklyn Democratic Party. Norman had been caught committing a variety of crimes involving political corruption. Vecchione was going to prosecute the case.

In Brooklyn, the Clarence Norman case was the big bang of local politics, the past and the future coming together with explosive force. The Brooklyn DA is an elected official; Hynes is a Democrat and Norman ran the local Democratic organization. A lot of promising careers have ended when crime met politics, so this investigation was getting Vecchione's complete attention. This was going to make Second Coming headlines, and as everyone in law enforcement knows, big headlines often mean big headaches. There was a lot of pressure on him to get it right.

"The timing couldn't have been worse," Vecchione remembers. "I was in the middle of preparing several of the most important prosecutions of my entire career. The other bureaus I supervised were overloaded with work. We had a hiring freeze in place so I was spending a couple of hours every day just juggling lawyers to make sure everything got covered. And then Tommy walks in and tells me he's got this great case. I almost laughed. There was no way I had the time for it, whatever it was, no way. But with Tommy . . . I didn't know what he had, but I knew my life was about to get a lot more complicated."

Dades and Vecchione had met in 1992, just after Mike had been named Chief of the Homicide Bureau. Tommy was still assigned to the Sixty-eighth Precinct Detective Squad. The first case Tommy brought to him, the Casatelli case, wasn't even a homicide. That was typical Tommy. It was a brutal assault that put three college kids in the hospital. And it wasn't precisely a cold case; at best it was lukewarm. It wasn't even an important case; maybe it would make page 16. Below the fold. It was the kind of case most detectives would have long since forgotten. But as usual, when Tommy got involved, the mother was in the middle of it.

Casatelli started one night in 1992. Five college kids were celebrating a birthday in a Brooklyn bar. When they came out of the bar they got into some kind of dispute with three neighborhood tough guys.

It was the basic egos-and-alcohol argument. The college kids then got into their car and drove away. Most nights it would have ended there, but not that night. That night lives changed.

The locals followed in their own car. When the college kids stopped to buy cigarettes the street guys attacked them with baseball bats and knives. Three of the five of them were left lying in their own blood on the sidewalk; each of them had been beaten and stabbed at least ten times.

After spending more than a year in the hospital two of the victims eventually recovered, but the third one remained in a semicomatose state. So technically it still wasn't a homicide. Not as long as the machines kept him alive.

Tommy caught the case. The two kids who had escaped injury had given the police a solid description of their attackers. Within a couple of days Tommy got one name from the streets, a punk he'd arrested twice before named Tommy Kane. Dades got photos of Kane, his brother, and some of the guys they hung out with and glued those pictures to a sheet of paper, creating a rudimentary lineup. The witnesses picked out Kane, his brother Paulie, and a third tough guy named T. J. Hynes. Dades quickly arrested Paulie Kane, who pleaded guilty. But Tommy Kane and Hynes ran. They disappeared.

The newspapers never bothered with the case. A lot of detectives would have let it go. A file in a drawer. But Tommy got to know the mother of one of the victims, Mrs. Casatelli. They spoke regularly. *How you doing, Tommy? I'm fine, is everything okay? Why can't they find the people who did this to my son?* Tommy promised her he wouldn't forget her son. And he didn't.

Tommy was plugged into Brooklyn. If Kane and Hynes were hiding in a Brooklyn sewer, Tommy would have known about it. Believing they'd left the state, he knew eventually he was going to need legal assistance to bring them back. That's when he went up to see Mike Vecchione.

Vecchione's office was on the fourth floor of Brooklyn's old Municipal Building. It was a dingy corner office, the kind of office that could have come out of a black and white B picture. The windows were covered with so many years of dirt and grime you had to put on the fluorescent lights to find them.

In the days before terrorism changed the world the DA's office was run pretty casually. The more productive detectives could pretty much pick the DA they wanted to work with. Tommy Dades knew just about everyone in the office and he knew the Casatelli case was going to be a problem. There were a lot of conservative lawyers in that office, men who needed to see the smoking gun before they would get involved in a case. Tommy barely had smoke, and those people weren't going to roll the dice on his evidence.

Tommy needed someone in the DA's office to issue a subpoena to force a potential witness who had left New York State to return to testify. Initially he took his evidence to a prosecutor he'd worked with several times before. As Dades remembers, "I told him what I had and he laughed in my face. He told me to forget it, he'd never be able to get an indictment with what I had. He told me to come back when I had enough evidence to go to the grand jury. I decided to go over his head."

That's when he approached Mike Vecchione for the first time. The two men liked each other immediately.

Both of them spoke Brooklyn and neither one of them had any illusions about the law. Both of them knew how it worked in real life. Tommy was straight with Mike. He told him what he had, what he needed, and how he intended to get it. He admitted it wasn't much of a case yet. It wasn't even a homicide. But he promised Vecchione that he would do whatever was necessary.

What impressed Vecchione most at that first meeting was Dades's passion for justice. He made this ordinary case seem unique and important. Vecchione had worked with literally thousands of police officers, but he'd never met anyone who spoke as deeply from his heart as Dades. Tommy told him about the mother and how much this case meant to her, saying, "It's all she's got, the hope that we're gonna nail these guys." He told Mike he had promised her that he would give this case his maximum effort and that he intended to do exactly that. It was a masterful selling job. And when he was done Vecchione agreed to work with him.

It was two years before they finally got a break. Somehow Vecchione had managed to convince a grand jury to indict both fugitives based on Tommy's admittedly flimsy evidence. An arrest warrant had been issued. Two years later that warrant paid off. Tommy Kane was picked up in Florida for driving under the influence. When the arresting officer ran his driver's license the warrant popped. He was extradited to New York and sentenced to nine and a half to twenty-two years. Two down. The Kane brothers were in prison, but Hynes was still a fugitive.

Tommy's relationship with Mike continued to grow stronger. During this time they worked together to solve several other seemingly impossible cases. In one of them, they worked with FBI agents Gary Pontecorvo and Jimmy DeStefano to successfully put a name on a skull that had been fished out of a small river several years earlier and used it to put the killer in jail for murder. But as their friendship grew, even as they wrapped up old cases, the Casatelli case just hung there, a dark cloud that wouldn't float away.

More than three years passed. Tommy Dades was still speaking regularly to the mother. Finally, one afternoon he sat down at his desk and he just decided, *I'm gonna find that scumbag today.*

He began rereading his notes, searching for the key that would open up the case. He knew it was there; it was always there. He just had to be smart enough to find it. He began by searching for a connection to the system—an application for license plates, a tax return, maybe credit problems. Anything that would leave an identity trail. But if Hynes was in the system, he couldn't find him.

Then he remembered a rumor that he'd heard a while back. Supposedly Hynes's mother had left Brooklyn with him. That was curious. Checking his notes, he discovered that she was a nurse. It was just a detail, one of those bits that easily could have been overlooked. But Tommy figured that wherever she was she had to be working. Bills had to get paid. He knew she couldn't get a nursing job under an assumed name. Whoever hired her would have checked her license. "I figured what the hell, let me take a shot. If she's stupid enough to be working as a nurse under her real name, I'm going to get him."

Whatever she was doing, he figured she needed a car to do it. He did a massive computer search, looking for a car registered in the mother's name. And there it was. A woman with that name had leased a car in Florida and after a couple of years had stopped making payments. The car had been repossessed. Tommy called the precinct in Florida covering the area in which the car had been repoed. He spoke with a detective and asked, "You got any hospitals around where you are?" There were two of them. "Do you have any connections to them?" The detective knew people in administration. "Do me a favor, would you? Call your people at those hospitals and see if they got a woman with this name working there."

The Florida detective called back fifteen minutes later. A woman with that name was working in one of the hospitals. Unfortunately, that hospital was in a different precinct. It was out of his jurisdiction.

Two hours after Tommy had sat down determined to solve this case he was speaking with a detective in the correct precinct. This detective contacted the head of security at the hospital and got the mother's home address. Tommy faxed the arrest warrant to Florida. Less than an hour later, three hours total, the detective called Tommy. "He was sitting on the front stoop when we got there," he said. "He didn't give us any trouble." Hynes pled guilty to the assault and was sentenced to five to fifteen.

Turned out Hynes was very lucky. Ironically, after Hynes had been sentenced one of the college kids died of his injuries. The case had finally become a homicide. Tommy spoke with the victim's family, asking them what they wanted the DA to do. Vecchione was willing to go back to court with the more serious charge. But the family had had enough. They didn't want to dredge up those memories.

When Dades and Vecchione began working the Casatelli case their relationship had been strictly professional. Cops and lawyers often get along about as well as cats and Chinese chefs. A lot of detectives consider the DA's office their enemy. They've spent too much time working with prosecutors who didn't believe them, or found a thousand ways to make their job more difficult, or just wouldn't get with the program. Some prosecutors aren't exactly passionate about cops either. But Tommy got along very well with most of the people in Joe Hynes's office. In fact, he got along with them so well that other detectives used to kid Tommy about these friendships, warning him that if he ever got in trouble in Brooklyn the DA would have to appoint a special prosecutor because everybody in the office was his friend. He was up-front with his objectives and always delivered what he promised.

Occasionally Dades and Vecchione would have dinner. Occasionally eventually became frequently. There were barbecues at their mutual friend Joe Ponzi's place on Staten Island. Mike was divorced but Tommy got to know his two sons, whatever new woman he was dating, and his father. Mike got to know Tommy's wife, Ro, and their kids and Tommy's mother. Mike and Tommy got together about once a week, but they'd speak on the phone at least once a day. If they were working a case they might speak three or four times a day. Their conversations covered all the ground between the gossip about the latest mob hit and Mike's son's football game. When Tommy started boxing in NYPD shows and fund-raisers, Mike and Joe Ponzi were usually sitting ringside.

And they worked together as often as possible. So on that day in September 2003 when Tommy walked in his door with a big, knowing, maybe even a little sheepish smile on his face and flopped down in that wooden chair, Mike knew he was about to go on another interesting legal journey that was guaranteed to be unusual. "Whattya got?" he asked him.

"You know those two detectives, Eppolito and Caracappa? I think we can finally get them," he said matter-of-factly. "I can corroborate Gaspipe. You interested?"

Mike leaned back and clasped his hands behind his neck. "It isn't too often a guy just drops into your office and changes your life in a couple of sentences," he recalls. "But as soon as I heard him mention Eppolito and Caracappa I knew I was in. I didn't know where Tommy was taking me, but I was going with him.

"Just like everybody else in law enforcement, I had heard all the stories about those two guys. I knew all about Louie my whole life so nothing about him surprised me. Tommy and I had even discussed the case a few times over dinner. I didn't know any of the details. I hadn't read Casso's 302s. I knew Eppolito and Caracappa were supposedly dirty, but I didn't know how deep the mud went. I also remembered that the case had fallen apart when the U.S. Attorney tore up Casso's cooperation agreement. The fact that they hadn't pursued the allegations meant they didn't have enough evidence to support Casso and they probably didn't believe him. So when Tommy asked me if I was interested I told him, 'Are you kidding me? Of course I'm interested. What've you got?' "

By the time Tommy finished relating his conversation with Betty Hydell, Mike was pumping out ideas. "This is great," he said several times, "this is great."

Tommy explained to Mike that he had already made some moves. The first person he'd called after speaking with Betty Hydell was Joe Ponzi. Ponzi was Chief of the District Attorney's Investigations Unit, and Tommy worked with him all the time. Investigations is a squad of 115 people with powers equal to NYPD officers' that works directly for the DA's office. They do mundane things like serving subpoenas and finding witnesses, but they also conduct high-profile and dangerous investigations. They do insurance fraud, tax violations, they work undercover, they even do organized crime cases. Whatever needs to be done to help make a case, that's what they do.

Joe Ponzi had spent two decades in the Brooklyn DA's office, gaining a reputation as one of the best interviewers and polygraph operators in the business. He had the gift for making bad guys want to talk to him. He'd been responsible for an impressive number of confessions. People used to say Ponzi was so smooth he could talk an oyster into giving up its pearl. After meeting more than a decade earlier, Dades and Ponzi had almost immediately become close friends. As Tommy summed up their friendship, "The day we met I would have given him my kidney."

Ponzi also had a personal investment in the case. The flamboyant Eppolito had met the immaculately dressed Caracappa in 1979 when both detectives were assigned to the Brooklyn Robbery Squad, which was then commanded by Ponzi's father. Sergeant Larry Ponzi had been their boss for about two years. In fact, in his introduction to *Mafia Cop*, Eppolito acknowledged, "Sergeant Larry Ponzi . . . who taught me how to be a detective, I send my respect."

Joe Ponzi knew Eppolito very well. "I would see both of them, Eppolito and Caracappa, in social settings. When the precinct had a 1013, a fund-raising party for cops having financial problems or medical problems, or a promotion party, I'd see them there. Louie more than Steve. I didn't know Steve that well; he was always a mysterious character as far as I was concerned.

"But Louis . . . I can remember Louis coming into the Homicide Bureau on the fourth floor of the Municipal Building with his tie draped loosely around his neck and wearing a flashy chain and a snake ring and holding court. He'd tell joke after joke about the broads he'd banged and the crazy things he did. He was out of control.

"My dad was fairly close with both of them. One time Louis volunteered to fight in an exhibition boxing match. My father was his cornerman that night. Louis talked a good fight, but if he couldn't knock out his opponent in the first thirty seconds he was finished. The guy he was fighting that night didn't like him at all. He toyed with him. He just took him apart. In the dressing room they had to give Eppolito oxygen. But he still told people he won.

"I knew everything about the case before Tommy called me. I saved every newspaper that was ever written about Casso's allegations. I talked to my father about it: 'What do you think? You think it's possible?'

"My father didn't know. 'You know what, I don't know them like that. I just can't fathom them in that context. Casso's crazy as a fucking loon. The government wouldn't have dropped the case if they had anything.'

"When Tommy called and told me what he had and asked me to get involved, I hesitated. Before I committed myself to this I needed to get my father's approval. That was critical for me. I needed him to be comfortable with the idea that I would be investigating cops. My father is my best friend, my mentor, and in my life it's always been taboo to hunt cops. I've steered clear of it for twenty-nine years; this was going to be the first time. But this . . . this was so far over the line. I told him, 'If they didn't do it, that'll play out, but if they did these things there's no way they should be able to just walk away from it. I don't know that anybody'll be able to put together something a prosecutor will deem court-worthy, but it's something I want to do.'

"My father told me it was something I had to do. He was a great cop and if this was true, he wanted these guys to pay. He gave me his blessing."

Ponzi had already had a small taste of the case. After the mob found out that Frankie Hydell was cooperating and killed him, Ponzi had run an internal investigation trying unsuccessfully to find the leak. So when Tommy told him about his conversation with Betty Hydell he immediately understood its relevance. It was a flimsy foundation on which to build a murder case against the two detectives, but it was a start. He owed it to his father, to himself, to every cop who had ever put on the uniform, to see where it went. "I'm in," he said.

Ponzi quietly gave Tommy a tiny office with a desk, a phone, and a computer on the eighteenth floor. They were investigating cops, so nobody else knew about it. He and Tommy had the only keys. Even the cleaning staff wasn't permitted to open the door.

Vecchione and Ponzi sat down to figure out how they'd work the investigation. Both men supervise relatively large departments. Vecchione runs the prosecutorial side of the Rackets unit; Ponzi is in charge of the investigative side of the entire DA's office. This was a really unusual situation: As a chief Ponzi rarely had time to get personally involved in investigations. Vecchione was already in the midst of several major cases. "What do you think?" Ponzi asked.

"You kidding me?" Vecchione replied. "Of course we're going to do this. I'm gonna do it myself. I'm going to try this case and put those two motherfuckers behind bars. What are you gonna do?"

Ponzi nodded firmly. "Let's do this one."

Dades's team was now three strong. The strategy was pretty straightforward: Dades and Ponzi would handle the actual investigation; Vecchione would clear the legal path for them.

Mike Vecchione's concern from the very beginning was how to keep this investigation on the state level rather than making a federal case out of it. That was going to be a little tricky, because they would need to get carloads of old files from the Feds, and eventually they would need to speak with Gaspipe Casso, who was still in federal custody. But with a little luck and a lot of hard work he felt it could be done.

It wasn't just ego that made Vecchione want to keep the case in Hynes's office. It was obvious from that first day that this was going to be a difficult investigation with only a limited chance of success, but he was convinced that legally it would be substantially easier for the state to get a conviction. Vecchione was going to use Betty Hydell's statement to try to make the Jimmy Hydell murder case against Eppolito and Caracappa. Any additional charges he could make stick would be a nice bonus, but a murder conviction would put them away for twenty-five years to the rest of their lives.

The federal government couldn't prosecute Jimmy Hydell's murder. There is no straight murder statute on the federal level. In extreme cases the federal government uses the civil rights laws to bring murderers to justice, based on the concept that they have deprived an individual of his or her civil rights by killing them, but in this situation that would be a tough charge to make stick. The only charge under which the Feds could prosecute the two cops was a RICO. RICO, the Racketeer Influenced and Corrupt Organizations Act, was passed in 1970 to give law enforcement a potent legal weapon to fight the Mafia. RICO allows the government to prosecute people for a pattern of criminal activity rather than specific crimes. They could be prosecuted for being a member of the Mafia. Specifically, to be found guilty under the RICO statute an individual has to commit a minimum of two "predicate acts," or crimes, in cooperation with at least some of the same people over a substantial period of time. One crime, no matter how heinous it might be; several criminal actions committed within a very short time span; or a series of criminal actions that can't be connected in some way don't qualify for prosecution under the RICO statute.

Vecchione didn't see how the Feds could charge Eppolito and Caracappa under RICO. The two or more underlying crimes that constitute a RICO violation have to be committed within ten years of the indictment. No matter what crimes the two cops committed for Casso, their relationship with him had ended more than a decade earlier. Casso had been arrested in January 1993. Eppolito had retired in 1990, Caracappa two years later. Dades had learned that the two cops were living out in Las Vegas, presumably no longer involved with the Lucchese crime family. Unless they were still committing crimes in the desert for the Luccheses, the statute of limitations had run out for a RICO. And if the Feds couldn't make a RICO case, they couldn't prosecute the cops.

But on the state level there is no statute of limitations on murder charges.

Vecchione knew that the Feds might be extremely unhappy if the Brooklyn DA was able to make a murder case against cops that the Eastern District had in its hands years earlier but failed to pursue. That's not exactly the type of publicity any U.S. Attorney wants. So they might make it difficult for the state to proceed, but they wouldn't dare risk blocking the investigation. Eventually they would hand over whatever materials they had.

Network television has recently popularized the concept of a "cold case," a case that hadn't been solved within a reasonable period of time and is no longer the subject of an active investigation. In other words, a case nobody is losing any sleep over. The media has made cold cases a hot concept. And law enforcement has plenty of them to solve. It is estimated that there are more than a hundred thousand unsolved murders in the United States. Cold cases. It's an old theme with great dramatic possibilities.

Cold cases live forever on paper, in neglected files crammed into overstuffed file cabinets. The first thing Tommy Dades and Joe Ponzi needed was all the old files. They contained every bit of evidence that had been gathered against the cops. This included Casso's 302s and all the supporting documents, the reports of any independent attempts to verify Casso's claims, transcriptions of interviews, the cops' personnel folders, maybe some newspaper clippings, and all the official reports and notes on the investigation of the murder of Jimmy Hydell. The Feds had a lot of the material. The Brooklyn DA's office had some of it in its archives; Tommy had his own files, consisting of his own notes and newspaper clippings collected throughout his career, and Ponzi had his clippings. But the Feds would have the most complete files; as far as anybody knew they hadn't been touched in a decade and they were probably stuffed into the back of a cabinet, maybe like a Sleeping Beauty, just waiting for the right prince to come along.

To begin, Ponzi, Dades, or Vecchione would have to make an official request for the files to the United States Attorney's Office, Eastern District, specifically to federal prosecutor Mark Feldman. For Vecchione that was a slight problem.

Mark Feldman was another kid from Brooklyn who went way back with all the big players in this case—including Eppolito. Years earlier he had run the Rackets Bureau in the Brooklyn DA's office. And just as Vecchione had gotten to know Detective Tommy Dades, Feldman had gotten friendly with Detective Louis Eppolito. "One of the reasons we all knew Louis so well," Feldman was quoted as saying in *Mafia Cop*, "was because his relatives kept turning up dead."

In his book, Eppolito describes Feldman as "a tough Jew if I ever met one." Their relationship, apparently, was cordial, respectful, and strictly professional. When Eppolito needed legal advice, just as Dades turned to Vecchione, Eppolito turned to Mark Feldman.

Dades agreed with Eppolito's assessment of Feldman, believing, he says, "Mark was probably the best prosecutor of organized crime cases in New York. Bar none. We got to know each other in the 1990s, while I was part of a unique organized-crime task force in the early 1990s. Everybody hears the stories about the battles between the Feds and the state, but this was an unbelievably productive team, consisting of FBI agents and DEA agents and NYPD detectives. It was run by a U.S. Attorney named Jim Walden and Chris Blank, who was cross-designated from the Brooklyn DA's office.

"We probably created the biggest marriage between the state and the Feds that they've had in years. It was one big happy family. We were taking down cases left and right with no arguments, no problems, because it was a complete team effort. We knew all the players in organized crime. We had lists of old homicides. We'd decide, let's solve this one—and we did. It was an amazing group and it worked because nobody was fighting for glory. Eventually we indicted forty Luccheses.

"Mark Feldman was a big part of that team."

While Dades and Feldman were friends, Mike Vecchione's relationship with Feldman was strained. At best. The two men had started their careers in the Brooklyn DA's office at roughly the same time. For several years both Vecchione and Feldman had worked in the Homicide Bureau. Vecchione remembers very well how supportive Mark Feldman had been on the toughest day of his legal career. "I was trying a paroled criminal for the cold-blooded murders of two police officers. I had reliable witnesses and I had substantial forensic evidence—but I also had a racially mixed jury at a time when Brooklyn was on the edge of exploding.

"The trial lasted five weeks and the jury reached its verdict on a Saturday morning. Not guilty. I couldn't believe it. Not guilty? I was stunned. This scumbag had killed two police officers and he was going to walk out of that courtroom. I was just overwhelmed with emotion; it was my responsibility to speak for those two cops and I'd failed. For whatever reasons, I'd failed. After the verdict was announced I went into this little office outside the courtroom, closed the door, and started crying. That was the lowest point in my professional career. It was Mark Feldman's day off, but he had cared enough to come to court to lend his support. The only person in the office who was there."

Mike had left the DA's office in 1980 to run the NYPD Advocate's Office, but Feldman stayed and eventually became head of the Rackets Bureau under DA Elizabeth Holtzman. When Joe Hynes was elected Brooklyn DA in 1989 he wanted to put his own people in leadership positions and Feldman left, maybe with a little bitterness, eventually landing in the U.S. Attorney's office. Vecchione and Feldman got along with each other until 2001, when Vecchione took over the Rackets Division. Vecchione was city, Feldman was federal. There is a great deal of competition in New York between the U.S. Attorney's office and the DA's office in each borough. It's a potent brew of ego, ambition, and power, fueled by publicity. Several prosecutors, most recently Rudy Giuliani, have used the publicity generated by high-profile prosecutions to build political careers. So when jurisdictions overlap, egos get stepped on.

Feldman's boss for almost two years was U.S. Attorney Alan Vinegrad. Vecchione had a history with him too. When Vinegrad had been an assistant in the

U.S. Eastern District office Vecchione had tried a difficult case with him. An ultra-Orthodox rabbi had kidnapped a young boy, whom he believed to be the Second Coming, from his mother. The Feds did not have jurisdiction because the rabbi had not taken the boy across state lines, but the rabbi could be charged under New York State law for secreting the boy in a place he could not be found. Working together, and sharing the publicity, Vecchione and Vinegrad had convicted the rabbi and his wife, and while doing that they had become friendly.

As far as Vecchione was concerned, the already complicated relationship between the Feds and the state had begun deteriorating when Mark Feldman joined the U.S. Attorney's office. More than ever before, the Feds were taking cases and informants from the state. Vecchione assumed Feldman was still mad at Hynes for forcing him out of the Brooklyn DA's office. Feldman believed that Vecchione had complained about that to Vinegrad, blaming him specifically for the deteriorating relationship.

So it was against that background that the state had to approach the Feds to get the old files on Eppolito and Caracappa. Tommy Dades made the first call to Feldman. "What's up, Tommy?" Feldman asked when he called. Like everybody else, Feldman knew Tommy was always on the edge of an adventure.

"Listen to me for a second, Mark. I got some information on the Jimmy Hydell murder," he said. "So if I was looking to jump in and reopen the Eppolito and Caracappa investigation, and I thought I could corroborate Casso, would you give me the paperwork you guys had when you were investigating? I want to take a shot at doing a state murder case.

"I got to ask you one thing though: If I come to you and ask you for everything you've got on it, you gotta give me your word you won't interrupt me, you won't force the FBI down my throat, and you'll let me work on it alone. Can you do that?"

Feldman told him, "I'll call you back in a half hour." True to his word he called back less than a half hour later and told Tommy, "Go see Bill Oldham and take whatever you need." Oldham was a veteran investigator in the U.S. Attorney's office, another guy who knew his way around. He had been working in that office when Casso had originally made his claims, so he was very familiar with the case.

Several nights later, Dades, Ponzi, and Mark Feldman had dinner at a local restaurant named Two Toms. It was more social than business; the three men were friends with a shared love of the law enforcement world and got together often. Somewhere between the veal and the pasta they began discussing this case. Dades had a lot of respect for Feldman and told him about his conversation with Betty Hydell. "There wasn't any other reason for Eppolito and Caracappa to be looking for Jimmy Hydell," he said. "There was no investigation going on, they weren't even supposed to be working together, there was nobody that even knew Jimmy Hydell was part of the crew that shot Casso, there was nothing else out on him. What happened was that they don't know what Jimmy looks like so they pick up Frankie by mistake, then they let him go. No harm, no foul. But while they're waiting for Jimmy to come home Betty catches up with them and has that conversation with them. A little while later Frankie sees them going over the Verrazano to Brooklyn. The last place anybody knows Jimmy was alive was in

Brooklyn less than an hour later." Tommy shrugged. "What else could they have been doing but picking up Jimmy, just like Casso says?"

Feldman was a prosecutor. He'd been involved with hundreds of cases. That seemed like a lot of speculation to him, a lot of blanks to fill in. No one except Casso had seen the two cops with Hydell. Maybe it made sense over a table at Two Toms, but Feldman knew that the only possibility the state had to make the case was to convince Casso to testify—and that Casso was not going to testify.

The only other guy who could make the case was the go-between, Burt Kaplan. But Feldman knew from his own experience that Kaplan fancied himself a stand-up guy. He was in jail pretty much for the rest of his life. In 1998 he'd been convicted of marijuana trafficking and sentenced to twenty-seven years in federal prison. He was sixty-five years old. After his conviction he'd been given an opportunity to corroborate Casso's testimony and maybe walk out of prison, but he'd turned down the government's offer. He made it clear that he wasn't "a rat." He wasn't a "stool pigeon." He was an old-time, hate-the-coppers stand-up guy. He wasn't talking to anybody.

"Don't even think about Kaplan," Feldman told them. The odds against them making the murder case weren't exactly astronomical, and it wasn't a bet anybody with good sense would make. Especially without Casso or Kaplan. "Betty Hydell isn't enough," he said. "You're going to need a lot more."

Tommy remained the optimist. "Yeah, I know. But we've made tougher cases." They all knew that Tommy and Mike had turned an unidentified skull fished out of a creek in 1999 into a murder conviction.

All the teeth except one molar had been knocked out, and it proved impossible to extraxt a usable DNA sample, so there was no way of identifying it. It sat on a shelf in the Medical Examiner's office until 2003, when a guy Tommy flipped gave up a murder he knew about, hoping to make a deal. The story was that a kid had been shot and beaten to death and his body was left out in the woods under a pile of old tires for several years. But when the killers found out somebody was planning to put up a mall in the area they went back for the now decomposed body. They broke the skull off the backbone and tossed it in a creek.

Tommy took that story to Mike. At first he didn't know about the skull. But when he began doing his research he discovered that a skull had been found not far from the site of the murder. Now they had a victim's name and a skull, but no way of proving the skull had belonged to the name. Checking the victim's rap sheet, Tommy learned he had been in prison. He said to Mike, "Let's take a shot and see if he had dental work done in the can." Incredibly, they found his dental records. A forensic dentist made the match to the skull. They were able to put the killer away.

Feldman knew all about Tommy's persistence, but he also knew that without Casso or Kaplan he could spend the rest of his life banging on doors and he wasn't going to convict the two cops. He offered whatever cooperation he could give them; he had absolutely nothing to lose. In fact, at one point he told Dades that his office was time-barred from bringing a RICO case against the cops. And he also suggested that they add Bill Oldham to their team. Not only did Oldham know the case, he pointed out, but he knew how to maneuver inside the federal system. As an investigator for the U.S. Attorney's office he had routine access to federal facilities that state investigators did not have. He could save everybody a lot of time.

It made sense. Bill Oldham became the fourth member of the team.

The question of jurisdiction continued to bother Vecchione. While he didn't say anything, he didn't trust the Feds to stay out of the case, particularly if it looked like Brooklyn might be able to get an indictment. Two cops indicted for committing murders for a Mafia capo? That was going to make big bold headlines. Big bold headlines make careers. Mark Feldman was an ambitious guy.

But both Dades and Ponzi assured him that Feldman's word was gold. Better than gold. Besides, they told Mike, Feldman knew and accepted the fact that the U.S. Attorney couldn't bring murder charges against the cops. "Why don't you go ahead and speak to Mark yourself?" Ponzi suggested to Vecchione. "You guys are the lawyers; get it all squared away."

"So I called Feldman," Vecchione remembers. "This was business, and we're both professionals. We started talking about the case and he told me, 'Look, I think we're time-barred. The acts look like they're too far in the past for us to be able to make a case. We don't have any indication that these guys have been involved in any kind of continuing criminal enterprise, so it's a single murder. We don't have a statute for that. So go ahead, knock yourself out.'

" 'That's great, Mark,' I told him.

" 'Just one thing though,' he added. It was almost as an afterthought. 'If it turns out that somehow we can make a RICO out of this, you guys can keep the Hydell murder, but we'll do the RICO.' That sounded reasonable to me. I knew that Feldman was protecting his claim, but he didn't sound optimistic.

"'All right,' I agreed. 'As long as we can do the murder.'"

That was the plan. The state would go first, prosecuting the Jimmy Hydell murder, and then, if the Feds could find a RICO charge in there somewhere, the state would then hand over all its evidence and the federal government would proceed. It was an easy deal for Feldman to make. As it might have been described on the streets, it was nothing for nothing.

When Mike hung up he figured maybe he was wrong, maybe Tommy and Ponzi were right, maybe the Feds weren't going to get involved. From nailing the two cops to jailing them, this was going to be all Brooklyn. But Vecchione still had this feeling, this little legal itch that just wouldn't go away, that it wasn't going to be as easy as it sounded.

Besides, Feldman had already proved his word was good. The day after his initial conversation with Tommy Dades, he handed over the investigative material the Feds had in storage. Less than an hour after Dades had parked his car in front of the U.S. Attorney's office at 1 Pierrepont Street he was trying to figure out how to fit five very large boxes in his trunk and backseat. He had no idea what he might find inside those boxes. Apparently the Feds had taken Casso very seriously, at least until he'd threatened the Gotti conviction with his accusations against Sammy Gravano. So it was likely there was a lot of valuable information in those boxes in the back of his car. Right then, right at the beginning, before Tommy carried those boxes up to the eighteenth floor and opened them up, he felt like a little kid on Christmas morning, waiting excitedly to see what surprises he would find.

A lot of cops aren't great readers. It's a job that promises action; it doesn't require going into the office, sitting behind a desk, and working through a pile of papers. So much of the time the type of kid who decides to become a cop is looking for action more than intellectual challenge. Even on the job there are numerous assignments that don't require a lot of reading.

Anybody looking at Tommy's background would have figured he wasn't much of a reader. He came from a broken home and spent as much time on the streets as in school. He was never a great student; he'd dropped out of school after his freshman year in high school to join the marines—although instead of taking the oath he'd ended up working in Vegas. But it turned out that Dades was an avid reader. That was just another one of those little surprises about Tommy Dades.

That came from his grandfather. His name was Eddie Schwartz—"Blackie" they called him on the loading docks of the *New York Daily News,* where he worked for most of the forty years he spent with the paper, because of his dark complexion. Blackie Schwartz was a self-educated guy from the Lower East Side who ended up foreman, and every night he'd bring home a fresh-smelling copy of the "night owl," the first edition, for his grandson. The *Daily News* wrote about the two things that most interested Tommy, crime and boxing. Tommy read anything to do with organized crime, anything. When the other kids were reading books about sports heroes or the children's classics, Tommy was reading the biography of Monk Eastman, a tough guy from the nineteenth-century Five Points gang that once owned the city. Rather than collecting baseball cards, Tommy kept stories about mob guys. Learning about organized crime was his hobby long before it became his profession.

But he didn't stop when it became his profession. He continued to read everything he could find about organized crime and remembered it, and in his mind he made the connections. Tommy was a great talker; he collected informants like Trump collected rent. Few men who haven't had a mass card burned in their hand and taken the oath of omertà knew more about organized crime than Tommy Dades.

But as much as Dades loved being on the streets, it was this ability to mine documents that made him a great detective. He'd read piles of documents to figure out how the pieces fit. He'd find the anomalies that other detectives had overlooked. He remembered the names and the connections and the crimes that went with them. He had the necessary patience to sit and read and the talent to understand every word of it.

To the five boxes of dusty material he'd carried into the war room he added his own collection of clippings. And then he opened the boxes and went to work learning about the incredible betrayal of Detectives Louis Eppolito and Stephen Caracappa. If there was a nugget in the piles of papers and tapes and transcriptions that would enable him to put those guys away, he was going to find it.

When Dades sat down at the very beginning of the investigation the investigators already knew quite a bit. They knew that officially Louis Eppolito and Stephen Caracappa had both retired from the NYPD with their full pensions, meaning that any outstanding problems they may have had were resolved: Their records were clean. They knew that Eppolito claimed in his book to have been the eleventh-most-decorated officer in department history. He also wrote about participating in several gunfights. Describing the first one, in which he was one of several officers who killed a bank robber, he claimed, "I learned something about myself during that gunfight. I not only had the capacity to kill, I had the capacity to forget about it, to not let it bother me."

That's strange, Dades thought. According to Eppolito's records cited in the federal indictment, while on the job he hadn't been involved in a single shooting.

They knew that Louis Eppolito had come from a mob family, that three members of the Eppolito family had been murdered in mob hits. They knew that he liked playing the role of a wiseguy; he dressed large, spoke loud, and carried a big ego. In *Mafia Cop,* Eppolito's coauthor wrote that Eppolito told him he had committed "a litany of felonies while wearing the badge, but they were all in the name of 'honor' and 'respect.' "

Caracappa, they knew, fit the role of the quiet sidekick. Caracappa played Ed Norton to Eppolito's Ralph Kramden—if those two TV characters had been cold-blooded killers rather than city workers.

They knew that Eppolito and Caracappa had attended the police academy at about the same time and first worked together under Larry Ponzi in the Brooklyn Robbery Squad. And that in 1984 Caracappa had become a member of the Major Case Squad, an assignment that gave him easy access to the department's most sensitive investigative information. And that three years later he assisted in the founding of the

Organized Crime Homicide Unit inside the Major Case Squad, giving him routine access to highly confidential intelligence about the FBI and the NYPD's plans to attack the Mafia—particularly the Lucchese family.

They knew that although Eppolito and Caracappa had separate assignments most of their careers, they remained close friends and were often seen together.

And they knew that, once before, Eppolito had been caught apparently working with the mob—and had gotten away with it. In March 1984, police had raided the Cherry Hill, New Jersey, home of Rosario Gambino, a capo in the Gambino crime family. Gambino had been indicted for selling heroin and had been on the run for almost a year. During the raid they recovered thirty-six law enforcement reports—and found Detective Louis Eppolito's fingerprints on several of them. It didn't seem like a coincidence. An investigation discovered that one afternoon Eppolito had shown up at the offices of the Intelligence Division supposedly to ask detectives questions about the case. He told them that he had recently seen Gambino at a Brooklyn restaurant and was curious about the status of the investigation.

The documents found in Gambino's home were copies—the originals were still on file at Intel. How they got from Intel to the house was the story of the fingerprints. Eppolito was brought up on departmental charges. But to the absolute astonishment of just about every cop who knew how the disciplinary system functioned, Eppolito had managed to beat the case. No matter which way you turned it, it didn't make sense.

Mike Vecchione in particular always believed that

something very unusual had taken place inside the trial commissioner's courtroom. The trial commissioner's office is where the police police themselves. Under New York State law a police officer is a civil servant and enjoys all the protections of the civil service code. So no matter what violation or even crime a cop might be charged with committing, from minor infractions like being absent from a post to extremely serious charges like murder, the city can't penalize or suspend them, or fire them or take away their pension, without giving them due process. In the police department due process means a full administrative proceeding in front of an independent hearing officer, a judge, with the right to confront witnesses and face your accuser. The hearing takes place in a courtroom setting and it is conducted just like a civil trial. The primary difference is that there is no jury; the judge makes all the decisions.

Most cops consider it a kangaroo court. They think it's stacked against them: No cop who goes in comes out innocent. That's what made the whole Eppolito case so strange.

In 1980, while Dades was out on the street, Mike Vecchione had left the Brooklyn DA's office and accepted Police Commissioner Bob McGuire's offer to become the NYPD's Chief Prosecutor. "I prosecuted hundreds of cases against cops as well as supervising a forty-person staff. We convicted cops for minor infractions like being out of uniform and for serious crimes like extortion. I remember I prosecuted two cops who had a nice little business going; they were stopping trucks for minor traffic violations like a broken taillight as they left the Hunts Point market and then negotiating a payment instead of a ticket. I tried a cop for shooting a kid to death; this was a complicated case in which the Manhattan DA didn't have enough evidence to bring criminal charges against him, but the NYPD could bring lesser charges of mishandling his weapon. We convicted him and he was fired, with the loss of his pension. It wasn't much, considering the gravity of the crime, but it was the best we could do."

It was in the advocate's office that Vecchione first encountered cops doing business with organized crime: He was preparing to try two detectives for tipping off the local wiseguys running Vegas nights for churches and synagogues that they were going to be raided, when they took a plea. Those cops lost their jobs but they were allowed to keep their pensions.

So Mike knew the system. That's why he couldn't understand what had happened in the Eppolito case. In his book, Eppolito claimed he was the victim of a police vendetta against him, that the department was going after him only because his family was mobbed up. His explanation for the fact that his fingerprints were found on documents in the possession of a Mafia drug dealer was about as clear as a kaleidoscope. Some of those prints were photostats of his prints, his lawyer explained. The crime lab reported that the two original prints they found were "similar" to Eppolito's, meaning the quality of the prints was not good enough to make a unique identification, but in all the ways they could be compared they matched Eppolito's.

"That was his defense to the primary evidence against him," Vecchione remembers. "And it never made any sense at all. The trial commissioner's name was Hugh Mo, who took over after I'd left the office and gone into private practice. Hugh Mo found Eppolito not guilty. I just didn't get it. Did they find

Eppolito's original fingerprint on a copy, or a copy of his fingerprint on an original, or on another copy? But the fact is even that doesn't matter. The fact that his prints were there is pretty strong evidence that Eppolito handled the documents. Mo said you can't base a finding of guilt on a copy of a fingerprint, or on a fingerprint on a copy of a document. I thought that was ludicrous. If a copy of a document comes out of a machine with my fingerprint on it, it means I touched the copy. I've been involved in at least a thousand cases and believe me, the presence of those prints in addition to all the other evidence—the fact that he happened to show up at Intel and happened to discuss the case with a detective—is either proof that Eppolito was guilty or it's the worst series of misunderstood events since Rosemary Woods 'accidentally' erased twenty-one minutes of the Nixon tapes.

"Let me be clear about it: There is absolutely no evidence that Mo or anyone else involved in this administrative proceeding did anything illegal. Apparently Mo even concluded that Eppolito had the documents in his possession. But he still dismissed the charges against him."

So they knew that Eppolito had had at least one confrontation with Internal Affairs and somehow managed to beat the charges against him.

They knew the U.S. Attorney had tried to flip both Anthony Casso and Burton Kaplan. Casso turned out to be a liar and Kaplan didn't want to know from nothing.

They knew that long after both detectives had retired they remained extremely close. They lived across the street from each other in Vegas and Eppolito on occasion introduced Caracappa as his cousin. They suspected the two retired detectives still had excellent contacts within the NYPD. Both men had made a lot of loyal friends on the job, many of them still active, many of whom would happily pick up the phone to tell them that somebody was looking at the old charges against them. But they were confident that neither man was aware that four men had reopened a twenty-year-old investigation.

They knew that Eppolito and Caracappa had been both smart and very lucky for more than twenty years. That's what they knew when they went to work.

But they believed the two detectives had gotten away with murder, and that's what they intended to prove.

CHAPTER 4

During his career Tommy Dades had seen the potpourri of events that life as a cop has to offer. There was the nutcase who killed two people and then decapitated their bodies. He sat one of the headless bodies in an easy chair and jammed a smiling head under each arm, then took several photographs. He did it, he explained after he'd been caught, as a present for the detectives.

In the Sixty-eighth squad Tommy worked with a female partner named Fran for five years, whom he'd met originally when they both were working narcotics. One afternoon they were told to go interview some guy about a complaint made by a neighbor. When they knocked on his door he shouted for them to come in. He was waiting for them in his living room—sitting on a portable potty going to the bathroom. Fran looked at Tommy, who shrugged his shoulders and said, "Interview him." So they did.

Tommy saw it all. Accident victims decapitated. Murder victims with their throats slit or nine thousand bullets in them. He'd seen the body of a man who died alone in his apartment in August and lay undiscovered for several weeks—long enough for his maggot-covered body to melt into the couch. He'd been present in an insurance office when a baby was born and been on the floor of the stock exchange watching men literally step over the body of a man who died of a heart attack.

Like every cop who has put in their time, he's been there. He's seen it. But as he sat there alone in Ponzi's little office reading Casso's 302s over and over even he was stunned by the range of Gaspipe's allegations against Louis Eppolito and Steve Caracappa.

Dades had heard the many stories about police corruption. He knew all about Frank Serpico and David Durk and the Knapp Commission, which had once cleaned up the police department. He knew about the Prince of the City and infamous inside theft of the French Connection heroin. He knew about the cops with reputations inside the locker room for using their weapon too easily, cops who got passed from station house to station house because everybody knew they were dangerous. He had heard the stories about the old days, when the cop walking the beat expected—and happily accepted—tips, meals, and holiday presents. He knew that some cops still looked the proverbial "other way" rather than enforce quality-of-life crimes. He knew that every precinct had at least one "house mouse," a cop who did nothing on the job but pass the years until he had earned a pension.

And he was familiar with the legendary "blue wall of silence," the cop code that forbade police officers from talking to anyone about the mistakes, misjudgments, and even crimes of fellow officers. He knew all the locker-room stories of bad cops and crooked cops and violent cops and even crazy cops—although, improbable as he knew it sounded, in his own career he had never actually seen another cop take even a small bribe, walk away from his duty, or perform some crazy, unnecessary act.

He knew all that, but there was nothing he knew about in the whole history of the NYPD that prepared him for the tales Casso told.

A 302 isn't a precise transcript; it's a summation written by an FBI agent after conducting an interview. The debriefing of Casso had taken place over a three-year period. These interviews were conducted by various agents investigating different crimes. And in these incredible pages Casso told the story of his relationship with the detectives from the day it began.

It turned out that the Hydell killing was only one of the murders in which they played an active part. As Gaspipe told the FBI, after a Gambino associate, a heroin-addicted drug dealer named Eddie Lino, was stopped and shot to death on the Belt Parkway in Brooklyn, Kaplan told him, "After the cops had shot Lino, some guy who was just crossing the street saw Steve . . ."

Steve? That's how Casso learned the first name of Eppolito's partner.

Casso claimed they were on his payroll for a long time. He told the FBI that "the cops" had been paid $50,000 for picking up Jimmy Hydell. After that he'd given Kaplan $10,000 every three months to pay them for the information they were providing. After a few years he even gave them a $5,000 raise, paying them $15,000 every three months, until he was arrested in January 1993.

Those payments covered all kinds of work. For example, when Casso and his underboss, Vic Amuso, decided a mobster named Anthony Dilapi could no longer be trusted, they put out a contract on him. The problem was Dilapi was running, supposedly hiding out somewhere in California. Casso asked Kaplan if Eppolito and Caracappa could find him. Caracappa got his address by contacting Dilapi's parole officer. A mob guy named Joe D'Arco carried out the contract. Once Casso began talking he didn't stop. It turned out that after killing Dilapi, D'Arco just tossed the gun out his car window—and "the cops" found out that, incredibly, the LAPD recovered it.

It took Casso more than five hundred pages to chronicle his growing reliance on his "crystal ball," his spies inside the police department. In addition to serving as an early warning system alerting the mob to wiretaps, providing the names of informers, and providing details about the progress of investigations the NYPD launched against the mob, the cops became Casso's personal Google, quickly responding to every request for information he made. Among the many secrets they revealed was that the FBI had planted a bug, a microphone, inside a railing directly in front of a social club in Little Italy run by Genovese capo Pete DeFeo.

Sitting there, reading this stuff, Dades couldn't even begin to calculate the amount of damage Eppolito and Caracappa had done to New York City, to American law enforcement's war on organized crime. These were cops—cops!—and every day they were giving up other cops. They were the worst kind of scumbags imaginable. Fighting this war the department had come to depend on informers inside the mob for intelligence.

Detective Steve Caracappa—detective? Tommy almost had to spit out the word—had access to almost all of that information. Numerous operations that initially seemed promising had ended in sudden failure, and until Casso opened his mouth no one knew why. For example, when the cops told Kaplan that a Colombo family member named Dominick Costa was cooperating, that piece of information was passed from Kaplan to Casso to Vic Orena, the acting boss of the Colombo family, who ordered Costa's relatives to get rid of him. End of Costa.

It was the cops who warned Kaplan that John "Otto" Heidel was a rat and was trying to get out from under his own problem by catching Casso on tape. Casso told Lucchese capo George "Georgie Neck" Zappola to take care of the situation. According to Casso's testimony, Zappola later told him what had happened. Vinny Zappola and Little Sally Fusco Jr. got the contract. They slashed a tire on Heidel's car and waited for him to show up. As Heidel started to change the tire Vinny Zappola approached him. Heidel took off, running for his life, with Zappola right behind him. Heidel was hit a couple of times and grabbed a motorcycle; for a few seconds there was a chance he might live. But Fusco was driving the getaway car and he had raced the wrong way up a one-way street to cut off Heidel. Finally, Zappola caught up to him and put the fatal bullet in his chest.

As soon as Heidel's body was identified NYPD detectives raced to his house to search it before the mob got there to clean out any evidence. No telling what might be found there—diaries, phone books, you never knew. Incredibly, either Eppolito or Caracappa—Kaplan didn't tell Casso which one, but it turned out to be Eppolito—managed to get inside as part of the team. Whichever one of them it was found microcassettes hidden in a secret compartment in the bathroom and slipped them into his boot. Later, when Casso played the tapes, he heard Vic Amuso's voice pointing out to Heidel that it was a cold night and asking, "You want anything?"

Amuso replied, "Yeah, soup." Apparently the tapes were destroyed.

To Tommy Dades, this all seemed like a bad movie. Casso had first told these stories more than a decade earlier—and absolutely nothing had been done about them. And if Betty Hydell hadn't called him one day, they would have continued rotting in a taped-up box in a storeroom. On page after page Casso detailed the cops' betrayals. Another Lucchese capo, Sal Avellino, was told that a mobster known as Finnegan was talking to law enforcement. Casso asked Kaplan to have the cops check it out. It took the cops several weeks, but eventually they confirmed it: Finnegan was a rat.

The cops informed Kaplan that Genovese associate Pete Savino was wearing a wire. Casso and Vic Amuso tried to figure out who might get hurt by that wire. It turned out that Sonny Morrissey, who represented the Lucchese family in several meetings with Savino, probably had the most to lose. Casso and Amuso were worried that Morrissey might flip, putting them in jeopardy. Pete Chiodo got the contract. Morrissey was killed and buried in New Jersey. It turned out that Morrissey didn't die easy. According to Casso, after being shot, Morrissey swore he wasn't a rat—then pleaded with Chiodo to kill him quick, to "take him out of his misery."

Casso's stories went on and on. When Caracappa

learned that James Bishop, the former head of Painters Union Local 37, who served as union liaison with the Luccheses, was cooperating with both the NYPD and the New York DA's office, he immediately alerted Kaplan. In May 1990, Bishop was shot eight times while behind the wheel of his Lincoln Town Car—the car was still moving and the shooters had to leap out of the way to avoid being run down by a dead man.

As Dades continued reading, he began to wonder if Eppolito and Caracappa were cops who went bad, or bad guys who became cops. They were officially employed by the city, but there was no question who they were working for. They were traitors to every man and woman in law enforcement. After mobster Bruno Facciolo was murdered—he was found with a canary stuffed in his mouth—in the summer of 1990, the cops told Kaplan that Louis Facciola, Al Visconti, and Larry Taylor had been picked up on a wire making plans to whack several members of the Lucchese family to get even for that killing. Casso and Vic Amuso responded by putting out contracts on all three of them. After Visconti and Taylor had been killed, the cops told Kaplan that the NYPD had tried to convince Facciola to save his own life by cooperating. Facciola refused—and got whacked.

In addition to the range and number of crimes described by Casso, Dades was also surprised by his audacity. Casso admitted that he had ignored mob tradition by trying to kill a family member of another mobster, but his 302s also described an attempt to assassinate federal prosecutor Charlie Rose. That was exactly the kind of crime the Mafia had scrupulously avoided to prevent massive government retaliation. And the "crime" supposedly committed by Rose? Casso blamed him for leaking an embarrassing item about his wife to the press and decided to get even. Naturally, the only people Casso trusted to get Rose's address were the cops. It was amazing, Tommy thought, that the only people a crazed Mafia capo trusted were New York City detectives. He just shook his head in disbelief. For ten years this stuff had been collecting dust. Just reading it made him feel dirty. He wanted to get these guys.

Casso was captured before he could make his move against Rose, but supposedly he did get an address for the prosecutor in the Hamptons. One of his people waited at the house for the prosecutor to show up, but for whatever reasons Rose never got there. That was truly fortunate—it turned out to be the wrong Charlie Rose. It was the wrong address: This was the home of the TV show host, not the prosecutor.

Casso's 302s also solved several mysteries for Dades. On Christmas Day 1986, a kid named Nicky Guido had been assassinated mob-style while sitting in his newly purchased red Nissan Maxima in front of his house in Brooklyn. The NYPD did a thorough investigation, trying to find a link between Guido and the mob, but there was nothing there. Guido had no known mob connections, he didn't appear to have any debts, he wasn't a witness to any crimes, yet the mob had killed him. It made no sense—until Casso explained what had happened: A guy named Nicky Guido was one of the three men who had screwed up the hit on Casso. The cops got an address for a Nicky Guido on Court Street in Brooklyn. That made sense because Guido's father supposedly worked on the docks.

On Christmas Day, Georgie Zappola, Frankie

Lastorino, and Joey Testa went to the house, figuring Guido would be home on the holiday. They waited until a young man got into the driver's seat of the red car. Another man, an older guy—it turned out to be his uncle Anthony—eased into the passenger seat. All the pieces fit perfectly. They pumped nine bullets into the body of an innocent kid.

Casso found out they'd whacked the wrong Nicky Guido from the newspapers. According to the story in the papers, this Nicky Guido was an installer for the telephone company. The murder of Nicky Guido had been a simple mistake. The two cops had provided the wrong address. No one knew what the intended victim looked like, so they had killed an innocent person.

The 302s also included a litany of Casso's greatest hits, including killings that were planned and never carried out, attempts that failed, and the many more that succeeded. He began with the most high-profile miss, his attempt to kill John Gotti for the unsanctioned murder of mob boss Paul Castellano. In an effort to hide his involvement in the plot, he decided to blow up Gotti in his car, the method of execution favored by the Sicilian Mafia. In addition to Gotti, Casso intended to kill his underboss, Frank DeCicco. On Sunday morning, April 13, 1986, a little less than four months after Castellano's death, Casso went after Gotti.

He'd found out Gotti was going to be at the Veterans and Friends Social Club in Bensonhurst. Vic Amuso and his brother Bobby went with him. The bomber was a drug dealer named Herbie "Blue Eyes" Pate, who supposedly had been a munitions expert in the army. The explosive was C-4, which makes a very big bang.

Pate was waiting in Bensonhurst in his own car. Eventually he joined the three men in Bobby Amuso's Chrysler. He had a shopping bag with him, filled with groceries; Italian bread was sticking out of the top of the bag. They sat there for a long time, waiting until DeCicco showed up. DeCicco parked and went into the club. Herbie switched off the safety on his bomb and began walking down the street. As he passed DeCicco's car he appeared to drop something. As he bent down to pick it up, he slipped the bomb under DeCicco's car and went back to his own car.

Tommy knew from his own experience what the waiting feels like. You just sit there, in the freezing cold, in the stifling heat, trying to keep your mind occupied, worrying that you might have to take a piss and miss the target, thinking a thousand thoughts about nothing. Half of the job is waiting, on both ends of the law. Finally DeCicco and another man—from that distance it could have been Gotti—slipped out of the club and into the car. Herbie Blue Eyes pulled alongside DeCicco's car and hit the button. The car disintegrated.

Turned out it wasn't Gotti in the car. He hadn't yet become known as "the Teflon Don," but still, he was pretty lucky. Casso never lost interest in getting even with Gotti, but after that failed hit it became too tough to get close to him. Ironically, Casso told the FBI in this 302, it wasn't the mob who made it almost impossible to get near him—it was the fact that wherever Gotti went he had the FBI watching him.

For Tommy, much of this read like some kind of Stephen King novel—cops using their badges to facilitate murders. But as he continued reading, the story became even more horrific. Eppolito and Caracappa weren't only accessories to many murders, they didn't just provide information—they were cold-blooded killers.

The cops had pulled the trigger. In this 302 Casso admitted that he and Vic Amuso were very concerned that if eventually they were able to kill Gotti, or if their role in the murder of Frank DeCicco was discovered, Gotti's associates Eddie Lino and Bobby Borriello would "look to avenge his murder."

As Tommy later discovered, that wasn't the complete truth. Apparently, while being tortured by Gaspipe, Jimmy Hydell had told him that Mickey Boy Paradiso, Bobby Borriello, Sammy "the Bull" Gravano, and Eddie Lino had set up the hit on Casso. They had gotten permission up the line, Hydell said, although he didn't know exactly who had first come up with the idea. And if he did know, the name died with him.

Eddie Lino and Bobby Borriello had big-time reputations. They were heavy hitters and chances were they'd be coming back for more. So Casso decided they had to go.

Casso claimed that he had spoken to Chin Gigante's brother, Ralph, several different times about his plan to kill Gotti, Lino, and Borriello. He wasn't looking to start a war, just repay a debt. After the three men had been whacked the Chin would have to meet with the Gambinos to explain that the three men were killed in retaliation for the unsanctioned murder of Paulie Castellano. But first Casso had to find a way to get those killings done without his own involvement being known. He asked Kaplan to find out if the cops wanted the contract on Eddie Lino. They were the perfect hit team because their badges would allow them to get close to him.

Eppolito and Caracappa accepted the contract to kill Eddie Lino. It would be an easy job, they told Kaplan, because they knew all about Lino from the streets. Casso agreed to pay them $75,000.

At Kaplan's request Casso provided a dark sedan similar to an unmarked police car for the cops to use in the hit. It was the type of car that any wiseguy would recognize instantly. He left two guns in a paper bag in the trunk.

Apparently Eppolito and Caracappa spent some time watching Lino. Their first plan was to kill him in his house. Casso claimed he didn't know the details, but it was easy for Tommy to envision the scenario. Two detectives knocked on Lino's front door and showed him their badges. We want to ask you a few questions, Eddie. He opens the door for them. End of story. But whatever their reason, the cops decided that was too complicated. They needed to get Lino away from people. So they tailed him to the parkway and pulled him over. NYPD detective Stephen Caracappa murdered him, then calmly walked away.

There were some things about that hit that Casso didn't know but Tommy remembered very well. At the crime scene police found a man's Pulsar wristwatch on the ground. The watch didn't belong to Lino. The assumption was that it belonged to his killer. Forensic examiners found several strands of brown hair caught in the casing. But until a suspect was identified and a hairs comparison could be made, those hairs had no value.

Casso also didn't know that there was a witness to Lino's killing, a guy just crossing the street. This witness described the shooter as "skinny, with dark hair" and watched him race away from the scene. This witness supposedly looked inside the vehicle and saw the blood-spattered body of Eddie Lino. Given the fact that it was dark and that eyewitnesses are often unreliable, Tommy knew that information was of limited use to detectives investigating the killing and would be even less valuable in a courtroom.

As Tommy Dades read this stuff he shook his head. He knew about a lot of it, maybe even most of it, but reading it was just unbelievable. If they had put these stories on *The Sopranos* nobody would have believed them. For example, Gas admitted that he had killed a mob architect named Anthony Fava, the man who had designed Casso's million-dollar waterfront house in Mill Basin, Brooklyn, because he knew too much about the Lucchese family business. Another wiseguy, Joe Brewster De Dominico, was whacked for turning down a contract from Greg Scarpa.

Casso even killed because he was a good neighbor. When his next-door neighbor told Casso's wife that their daughter's former boyfriend had raped her and asked for protection, Casso took care of the problem. Pete Chiodo killed the ex-boyfriend.

In addition to providing evidence about the two cops' massive betrayal of their badges, the wealth of information in Casso's 302s filled in a lot of blanks concerning other cases. Casso told his FBI questioners that the two men were responsible for the theft of the French Connection heroin from the NYPD Property Office. This was in the late 1970s. One of the thieves was a cop, another cop, so he knew how things worked. It was unbelievably simple: This skell put on a police uniform and signed the drugs out of the property office. Nobody questioned him. And then sold them.

Gas told the FBI how the money from the infamous Lufthansa robbery was split. He confessed to extorting substantial sums from the Palm restaurant and several Tony Roma franchises, a school bus company, garbage collectors, and hotels. He talked about the huge profits made in the drug business and explained how the Lucchese family became a police force for Russian mobs operating a multimillion-dollar gasoline tax scam.

Long before Dades had finished reading Casso's 302s he despised Detectives Louis Eppolito and Stephen Caracappa. He believed most of what Casso had said was true. He'd gotten the details right, particularly concerning those cases in which Dades had been involved or those people that he had known. Not every word was right—in Tommy's career he'd never met an informant who confessed everything he knew or told 100 percent of the truth—but this was close enough for him to believe Casso's claims about the cops were true.

As Dades sat alone in a windowless office reading this material he was only a few months away from retirement. The ending of his career was bittersweet; a mess that he'd gotten himself into with a woman had led to an Internal Affairs investigation. He'd been vindicated, but the way he'd been treated had soured him on the department. In almost twenty years he'd never taken a sick day; he'd had his leg broken commandeering a car to chase a drug dealer—when the driver ran him over; his nose had been just about ripped off his face when he got slammed by an attaché case with a steel tip while making a narcotics bust; he'd been stabbed with a hypo, thrown on tile floors, shot at, punched in the face—and never put in a disability claim. Yet when this woman made an easily disproved claim against him, they treated him like a lying felon.

If that hadn't happened he would have stayed on the job for a few more years, no question about that, but he knew they were watching him now. And he couldn't risk losing his pension, his health insurance, all the benefits he'd earned. He still had a wife—just barely, but they were still together—and two beautiful kids. So it was for them he knew he had to put in his papers.

He knew the politics of the department as well as he knew the rules of the streets. He'd seen good cops get screwed out of the security they'd earned for committing minor transgressions. If the department wanted to get you, you were got. So he was leaving angry at the department—but not with the cops, not with the people he had worked with and knew.

Those people he loved. And the final thing he wanted to do on the job was clean out the stink. As he explains, "No one who hasn't done this job can begin to understand it. When you do it day after day you establish friendships and you become part of a family. Every day you put your life in the hands of your partners; you trust them not because you know so much about them, but because they're wearing the uniform. I never stopped to think about it, I never realized it, until it became time to leave. It's just . . . no matter where you go in this city there's a precinct there, and you know you can walk in there and be welcomed. It's an extraordinary sense of comfort.

"I loved the job and I loved the people I worked with. That was my family.

"Eppolito and Caracappa had betrayed them all. Every single one of them. Everybody knows the movie cliché, some actor with a deep voice warning, 'This time it's personal.' Well, I didn't care if it was a cliché or not; for me this time it really was personal. I'd been doing the job for almost twenty years. I don't know how many guys I put in jail. I know I was involved with at least fifty murders, probably more. I never added up the numbers, but I had to be responsible for a few thousand years of sentences. But that had always been part of my job. They were the bad guys and we were the good guys. This was a very different thing. These guys had betrayed my family. I didn't care what it took, but I was going to get them."

Tommy Dades hadn't set out to be a cop. It just sort of happened to him. After he returned from Vegas with his friend, his grandfather got him a job driving a delivery truck for the *Daily News*. He started there as a seventeen-year-old and stayed five years. When he was twenty he took all the civil service exams. "I passed them all," he remembers. "I would have taken any of those jobs. If sanitation had called me first, right now I'd be a retired sanitation worker. But the police department called first. I swore into the police academy on July 16, 1984.

"Mostly I became a cop because it was a decent-paying job with good security. I didn't know anything about the history or traditions of the NYPD and none of that really mattered to me. I didn't take the job to protect society. It was a good job. That was it; that's what it meant to me.

"During those first few years on the job there were times I thought maybe I'd made a big mistake not waiting for the fire department or corrections or sanitation. I remember leaving the academy and walking a foot post on Surf Avenue and West Thirty-second Street in the dead of winter. I would stand there in the snow for five hours in January—there wasn't a soul on the streets—freezing like there was no tomorrow. I was miserable, just waiting for the night to end. I didn't know enough to go inside and get warm. I was a rookie; I was afraid to hide. On the real cold nights my mother would bring me thermoses. She'd come out there in the cold to find me and stay with me for a little while. I spent a lot of nights wondering, *What the hell am I doing? This is not what I envisioned.*"

After spending about two years in uniform Officer Dades got a temporary transfer to narcotics to work as an undercover. It was in narcotics that the job became his passion. "I was out of my mind; I was a wild man. I was commandeering cabs, jumping out of windows—when I heard they were making pot deals in the cemetery behind Trinity Church I'd hide inside until I saw them and then I'd leap out the window and grab them. I pulled my gun a zillion times. I used to use theatrical makeup to make track marks on my arms; I'd put carbon under my eyes, put on some old clothes, and head down to the Lower East Side looking to buy heroin. If I was playing a money guy in a big case I'd wear a nice suit, a flashy tie, expensive jewelry, and I'd drive an Eldorado. In the morning I was a junkie, in the afternoon I was a kilo dealer. One time I was playing the money man, working with a great undercover named John Massoni. We were making a deal for three or four kilos with some Colombians. We met them in a bar—and we had a hundred thousand dollars in a suitcase. You bet you're aware of everything going on around you. If somebody took an extra-deep breath, I heard it. The Colombians came in carrying gift-wrapped boxes containing kilos of coke. My job was to walk over to them and hand John the suitcase. He'd make the exchange.

We'd leave and once we were out of there the arrest team moved in on them. We were having a great time and doing a great job."

It was also the most dangerous job he'd ever done. "The only time I was ever scared on the job was when I went into the Coney Island projects to buy a nickel bag. I did that all the time. My field team, my backup, couldn't come anywhere near the projects. I was wearing a mike but it never worked because it was cheap equipment, so the field team didn't know where I was. I'd go into an apartment with nine locks on the door. There was nothing anybody could do to help. If I got in trouble, by the time my backup figured it out I was already dead.

"I never took elevators in those buildings because I didn't want to be trapped if someone tried to rob me. I'd walk up the steps. All the lights had been busted; all you smelled was piss. On each landing I'd see people sitting with their crack pipes. I carried a .380 automatic; in the winter I'd keep it out of my pocket with my finger on the trigger. This is only a little more than three years after I was driving a newspaper delivery truck.

"You had to be careful and you had to be lucky. There were guys getting guns put to their heads and forced to snort coke. At that point you have to do what you have to do. That didn't happen to me. People would see my gun and I'd play off it. 'So what? What the fuck you looking at?' As a white guy in those neighborhoods I did real good. I had a great time. We had so many small buys and at least five major cases involved half a key [kilo] or more. Every time I got over I had this big adrenaline rush. If you don't feel alive at those moments, if you don't feel your heart pounding, you might as well be dead.

"I'd never experienced anything quite like it. It wasn't just the success. It was the camaraderie; every day we were putting our lives up for grabs and you couldn't do that unless you had complete trust in the people you were working with. From those guys you learn the meaning of trust and loyalty and sacrifice. The badge represents all of that and the pride you take in wearing it is unbelievable."

After three years Dades was transferred to the Sixty-eighth Precinct detective squad. The NYPD offers a variety of training courses for young detectives. "Investigating Homicides" was two weeks long. "Sex Crimes" was one week. It all helped—by the conclusion of each course he could fill out all the proper paperwork—but the real training was done on the job, given by the people who had been doing it. "I worked with legends," Tommy says, "men with thirty years or more on the job. You'd sit around listening to these guys tell their stories and you'd learn more in an afternoon than you could reading three textbooks. They made me understand that I was becoming a part of something that mattered."

They spent as much time talking to him about the past, about their experiences, about the legends of the department, as they did teaching him how to pay an informer and keep a secret. They taught him the skills to succeed, but more importantly they imbued in him an understanding of the tradition that he would carry forward. He was one of the elite, a detective in the greatest police department in the world.

That was an impressive thing to be, and Tommy Dades took tremendous pride in his accomplishment. He knew where he came from; a street kid from a single-parent home, a kid with a ninth-grade education, had made it all the way to detective. And he knew what it had taken to get there. He knew that the only people in the world who had experienced it all, every bit of it, from the incredible joy of breaking a big case to the seemingly endless petty hassles of dealing with the bureaucracy, were the guys who wore the same uniform. These were the guys who knew what it felt like to stand alone in the cold on a deserted street at two o'clock in the morning, guys who were willing to trust their partners with their lives on a regular basis. These were the men and women who knew exactly what it felt like to have to tell a parent their kid is dead or to have to stand and take it when somebody is shouting in your face and the nicest thing they're calling you is a pig; at one time or another most of them had cleaned up vomit in the backseat of the squad car, tried to reason with a belligerent drunk claiming to know powerful people, seen death in too many shapes, and felt absolute fear—yet kept moving forward. These were the only people who knew everything he had experienced in his twenty years—these were his friends, his partners, his comrades, his brothers and sisters in life, a family held together by the badge, and he loved them for it.

Eppolito and Caracappa had treated all of them like they were garbage. They had crapped on that badge. They had used it to facilitate murders. They had taken hundreds of thousands of dollars to betray the same cops who would have risked their own lives to help save them—and then they probably laughed at the stupid suckers taking home $880 a week and turning down a free cup of coffee.

So this time, this time it really was personal.

As Dades read this material he realized there was only one person who could corroborate Casso's claims, one person who knew the full extent of the cops' cooperation with the Mafia, and that was Burt Kaplan. Casso had never met them; he'd only seen them once. But Kaplan? Kaplan and the cops were practically partners. The cops used to go to Kaplan's house for meetings, and when Kaplan got nervous about that he started going to their houses.

One thing was obvious: If Gaspipe's 302s were the Bible they would follow throughout the investigation, flipping Burt Kaplan was the Holy Grail. Nobody, not even Casso, knew more about Eppolito and Caracappa than Kaplan. He was their contact; he relayed Casso's requests to them and reported the information they provided to Casso.

Tommy knew almost nothing about Kaplan. He'd heard the name for the first time in the mid-1990s when Frank Drew, a DEA agent with whom Tommy had worked on several cases, accidentally picked up Kaplan during the investigation of a drug dealer. Initially, he hadn't been considered a major player, just another wannabe earning a living by hustling drugs.

But Dades began learning a lot more about Burt Kaplan in September 1996 when Kaplan was arrested for marijuana trafficking, a crime for which he was eventually sentenced to twenty-seven years. The U.S. Attorney handling Kaplan's prosecution, Judy Lieb, had called Tommy to ask him some questions about the homicides committed by Sammy "the Bull" Gravano. Apparently Lieb suspected Kaplan had a connection to Gravano.

Pretty much everybody in the NYPD knew that Tommy Dades was the guy to see if you wanted to know about Sammy the Bull. His interest in Gravano had begun in 1990, when he caught a mob hit on a guy named Eddie Garafola that was credited to Sammy. From that moment on he studied Gravano like Warren Buffett studies annual reports. He memorized the names of his victims and the dates they died and the motives for every one of the nineteen murders Gravano was accused of committing. He knew Sammy's associates and hangouts, and in at least a few cases, he knew where the bodies were buried. Tommy got to know the two FBI agents who flipped Sammy and they put the detective and the killer together on the phone. Somehow, Dades and Gravano eventually became friendly. The oddest couple.

But one morning, as Dades sat in Leib's office describing in detail the many murders of Sammy Gravano, she began talking about Burt Kaplan. Kaplan was with Gaspipe Casso, she explained, and her office was trying to flip him. "You know he's better than Casso regarding those two detectives," she said.

Tommy recalls, "I didn't know the details of what happened after that, just that Kaplan had refused to cooperate. Instead of flipping on Casso and the cops, he had decided to spend the rest of his life in prison. You couldn't argue that he wasn't a stand-up guy, but he was standing up for the wrong people, a homicidal maniac and two dirty cops. I didn't know how much pressure the Feds actually had put on the old man to testify. Maybe the last thing the government wanted to do right at that time was prove Gaspipe Casso was telling the truth. That could have caused some really embarrassing problems for both the Feds and the NYPD. Maybe they figured that it was better for everybody if Casso stayed buried."

Kaplan was the shovel. Tommy wondered what the Feds had really offered him. On some level Tommy had to admire Kaplan's misguided loyalty; even Casso had flipped faster than a short-order hamburger when his life was on the line. If everything the government said was true, Kaplan had chosen to die in a cage to protect the guy who'd ratted him out. If he'd refused to cooperate way back when to save himself, there was little reason to believe he'd ever change his mind. There certainly was no question that Mark Feldman believed Kaplan was a dead end, otherwise he wouldn't have been so certain this investigation was going to fail.

But Tommy Dades has always been an optimist. He wanted to learn the details for himself. Maybe there was something somebody somewhere had missed. It wouldn't be the first time. He began by calling DEA agent Frankie Drew, who'd arrested "the old man" initially, to begin his education in the world of Burt Kaplan.

As Drew explained, he had stumbled over Kaplan during the Frankie Puglise investigation. Not only hadn't Kaplan been a target, his name hadn't even been in the program. Puglise was a Bonanno/Lucchese associate running a large cocaine and marijuana operation. The DEA agents were listening to wiretaps and eventually they heard several references to a guy who just didn't fit the wiseguy script. He was referred to only as "the old man," but it was clear he was a major supplier. He brought in tons of product. What caught the attention of the agents was the fact that Puglise showed "the old man" respect. That was a big thing, an associate showing respect to some nameless supplier; it meant he was somebody important.

That was Kaplan. Coincidentally, the U.S. Attorney's office knew all about Burt Kaplan from Casso's

302s. When they learned he had been arrested on drug charges they tried to nail him, figuring if they put enough pressure on him he would flip. As Judy Leib had told Dades, if Kaplan had agreed to cooperate he would have been a better witness than Casso. They convicted him on cocaine, marijuana, and money laundering charges and the judge hit him with twenty-seven years. After his conviction the DEA, the FBI, and NYPD Internal Affairs all offered him a ticket out, figuring because of his age, because he wasn't a made guy, he'd accept the offer, but he had turned them down. As Drew told him, the guy was a real hard case.

But there was one more thing the DEA agent Frankie Drew remembered. The Puglise investigation had been compromised. On one of the phone taps someone had mentioned receiving a warning from the "crystal ball." The agents had no idea what that meant, but after that conversation everything changed. Phones went dead, meetings were canceled, people basically disappeared. It was obvious somebody had been tipped off.

One of the men eventually convicted in this case, Bobby Molino, flipped and told investigators that he had seen Puglise speaking with Kaplan, and after they finished, Puglise had come over to Molino and told him, "We're hot." Somehow Kaplan had found out all about the investigation; maybe he didn't know the details, but he had told Puglise that undercover DEA agents were buying drugs, and that their phones were tapped. "We never figured out how Kaplan found out about it," Drew told Dades. "And he wasn't interested in talking to us. The guy didn't flip seven years ago, why's he gonna go now?"

Tommy knew that eventually he was going to have to take a shot at flipping Kaplan. He asked Drew for the names of people who were around Kaplan way back when, people he might approach who had some information on the case. Anything that might help him. Drew gave him the names of guys who had already flipped and might have some additional information about Kaplan, as well as some of his own contacts who could help.

"Look," Tommy told him, "I'm doing this case and I'd like to keep it within the DEA because you were the guys who got Kaplan. If he flips it's only right it goes back to you and not the police department, not the FBI, not anybody. So give me the name of a big boss I can call in New York and in Vegas. Let me see what they want to do."

"Call Timmy Moran in Vegas. John Gilbriet's the guy you want to speak to in New York. They'll get you whatever you need."

Tommy added those names to the long to-do list he was making.

Like an old engine slowly grinding into life, the cold case was starting to chug along. At that moment it was only Dades, Ponzi, Oldham, and the assistant DA Vecchione. It was just four men, a pile of paper, and a whole lot of hope and determination.

Meanwhile, in Vegas, Louis Eppolito and Steve Caracappa apparently had absolutely no knowledge of the investigation taking place back in Brooklyn. Both retired detectives had settled into comfortable lives. Eppolito lived with his wife, three children, and mother-in-law in his home on Silver Bear Way. No one was certain where his money was coming from, but he reportedly had been paid a substantial sum by the elderly benefactor of former stripper Sandy Murphy—who had been convicted with her lover of killing her wealthy live-in boyfriend, casino owner Ted Binion—to write a screenplay showing that she was innocent. Sandy Murphy's sensational trial had been televised by Court TV. Supposedly Eppolito had visited Murphy in prison at least thirty times while researching the story. Eventually both Murphy and her lover's murder convictions were overturned, but they were convicted of trying to steal $7 million in silver bars and coins Binion had buried in the desert. It was the perfect TV movie story: Vegas, strippers, sex, murder, and money.

Eppolito was also commissioned by at least two older women to write screenplays of their life stories and get them produced. That sounded like a hustle. And one of those women, Jane McCormick, complained to the media that she'd borrowed $45,000 to pay Eppolito to write a screenplay detailing her past as a Vegas casino hostess and stripper who partied with Frank Sinatra and his Rat Pack. The screenplay was called *Reflections in the Mirror,* but it never got made. "I was a sucker enough to go for it," she admitted. "He put up a good front, a good game, and took my money." Apparently she didn't like the screenplay: "He couldn't even spell, his English stunk, and he got a lot of the facts wrong."

Caracappa was living a much quieter life with his wife, his daughter, and two cats across the street from his former partner on Silver Bear Way. After serving as assistant chief of security for a private company running the prison in which, perhaps coincidentally, Sandy Murphy was incarcerated, he opened his own private investigation business, Argus West. Friendly neighbors reported that he got up early each morning to go to work and usually was in bed so early that "his wife was always complaining."

Not surprisingly, Eppolito and Caracappa had remained close friends. As far as their neighbors knew, the two were simply retired detectives from New York who were leading the good life in Vegas. But Eppolito remained cautious that his past might still have reach. At one point he was recorded telling a cooperating government witness that he never spoke on the telephone, because he was fearful that the Feds had tapped his phone. No one knew if that was simply another example of Eppolito trying to impress a potential backer for one of his movie projects or if in fact he actually had learned about the investigation.

That just didn't seem possible. There was no identification on the door of the small office where Tommy worked and nobody mentioned the investigation outside of that office. The door was always locked when no one was there, and Tommy held the key. There was a good reason for these precautions: Too many previous investigations involving these two guys had been compromised. The fact was that there still were a lot of cops on the job who had worked with Eppolito and Caracappa. Eppolito in particular was one of those boisterous guys with as many friends as enemies. He was a good-time guy and a lot of people liked him. Caracappa reportedly came back to New York each year for the reunion of the Major Case Squad. There was nothing to be gained by alerting the two cops that the investigation was revving up.

There was no reason to believe that Eppolito and Caracappa knew what was going on in Brooklyn, but still, these guys had the longest reach into the department Dades had ever seen.

In the office on the eighteenth floor Dades continued poring over all the materials he and Ponzi had collected. Usually he got to work by five A.M., beating the rush-hour traffic from his home on Staten Island. He'd bring a bagel, a cup of coffee, and a banana and sit there through the morning.

Joe Ponzi was doing pretty much the same thing in his office. It had been a while since Ponzi had had the opportunity to be actively involved as an investigator in a big case. At night he'd speak with his father, the cops' former commanding officer, sometimes asking questions but more often dropping a few hints about their progress. During the day Dades and Ponzi spoke on the phone numerous times, comparing notes, asking questions, compiling lists of additional documents that might be useful and people they wanted to interview.

Tommy spent endless hours listening to the tapes produced by the wiretaps in the Annette DiBiase investigation; the goal then had been to get Bering to talk about his former girlfriend with Hydell, who had killed her. Rather than simply reading the transcripts Tommy wanted to hear Bob Bering, Philly Boy Paradiso (Mickey Boy's brother), and Jimmy Hydell discuss the crime business. Among those tapes was a recording made the day Hydell disappeared and he wanted to hear the inflections that words on paper could never convey.

Then he went through the folders of every homicide Casso had mentioned involving the cops. He wanted to know if there had been any witnesses and what they might have seen; he wanted to compare these murders to other mob hits. He read the bios of every perp even peripherally involved in the case.

He read both Eppolito and Caracappa's thick NYPD personnel files, hundreds of pages that charted their careers from the day they took the oath until the day they handed in their badges. In an Internal Affairs file he found the reports from the Rosario Gambino case, in which Eppolito's prints had been found on copies of police documents in Gambino's house, but he also found references to additional complaints people had made to IAD about Eppolito and Caracappa. He assumed they were the kind of complaints every active cop inevitably receives and made a note to follow up. You never know.

He reread Eppolito's book. And when he finished reading all of these documents once, he read many of them again, this time reading them with the additional knowledge he had gained from all the other reports. The first read through he just absorbed the information; the second time he was trying to make connections, to make sense out of seemingly random events. This second time information that hadn't fit anywhere the first time he read the reports slowly began to make sense. And always, somewhere in his mind, were Casso's 302s.

Tommy had always operated on his belief that the more he learned, the more power he had. *Knowledge is power,* his mother always told him. *Remember that.* So once he learned something, it stayed filed in his mind.

He also began making phone calls, speaking to people who had worked with the cops, just trying to gather as much information as possible. At the beginning of an investigation there is no single area of focus; it's like trying to light a torch with damp matches. You just keep striking and striking until you get that first spark, then you pay close attention until it becomes a fire, and then you use it to light your path.

Ironically, while forensic science, with all its amazing tools of detection, has enchanted the public, the detectives' most valuable tool remains the telephone. Tommy Dades practically lived on the phone. His cell phone rang all day and deep into the night. So after going through all the written material once, twice, sometimes three times, he finally picked up the phone.

One of the first people he called was former Chief Richard Nicastro, who had been running the Detective Bureau when Eppolito had gotten jammed up with Rosario Gambino. What had really happened there, Tommy wanted to know; how did Eppolito beat that one?

Nicastro had been Eppolito and Caracappa's ultimate superior. He might remember small things that didn't make it to paper, the little inconsistencies and oddities that a good detective never forgets. In the department Nicastro had always been well respected; people considered him a straight shooter. Eppolito didn't share those good thoughts though; in his autobiography he had some pretty nasty things to say about Nicastro. He claimed that after his acquittal he'd had a confrontation with Nicastro, who made remarks about his family and poked him in the chest. Eppolito wrote that he had warned him, "If he poked his finger into my chest one more time I was going to smash his face flat."

Mike Vecchione had heard a rumor that in the wake of former Police Commissioner Benjamin Ward in 2002, Nicastro had given a ride to Hugh Mo, the trial commissioner who had acquitted Eppolito. And out of nowhere Nicastro looked at Mo and said, "I told you back then that you made a mistake. You found that guy not guilty on some technicality. I told you he was dirty." The rumor did not include Mo's response.

Tommy wanted to know if Nicastro still felt that way about Eppolito and if there was anything he remembered about that hearing that wasn't in the reports. When Tommy reached Nicastro the retired Chief politely refused to speak to him, asking, "Who do you know that I can call?"

"How about Chief Allee?" Dades owed a lot of his success to former Chief of Detectives Bill Allee. Tommy had worked for Allee through a lot of ranks and he had been instrumental in his promotions. Within a day Allee had called Nicastro and vouched for Dades.

Tommy was pretty blunt the next time he spoke with Nicastro: "I want to talk to you about Louis Eppolito. I'm starting to look at him and I'd like to know what you know about him."

Nicastro didn't hesitate. "He's a no-good cocksucker."

Well, Dades thought, *looks like that rumor is true.*

CHAPTER 5

The first hint of a problem came from an innocuous request. While going through the two cops' personnel folders, Tommy Dades had found several references to civilian complaints that had been made against them and investigated by Internal Affairs. According to the brief notations, several of these cases involved the sale of confidential documents. The files didn't include a lot of details, but one of these charges involved a woman whose husband was in jail. She claimed to have paid Eppolito and Caracappa several hundred dollars to get a look at her husband's FBI file.

The thing that intrigued Dades was that most of these complaints had been lodged against Eppolito and Caracappa while they were assigned to different squads. That was unusual. Proving they were working together when they had different assignments potentially was very important. Tommy wanted to read the complete reports. In particular he wanted the names of the complainants so he could find them and interview them. Getting hold of these files might be a little complicated, but it wasn't impossible.

It was sort of odd that while Internal Affairs' entire Rosario Gambino file was included in the documents Dades had picked up from the Feds, none of these other files were there. They had to exist, he knew that; he had log numbers that proved it. And they covered the same sort of crime, selling access to confidential law enforcement documents. For some reason though, nobody had followed up on it. That in itself seemed strange to Dades. If you could prove a pattern of theft, that the guy had committed this crime before, that would constitute reasonable evidence of guilt. So why hadn't the prosecutors used all the evidence they had? Why didn't they conduct a thorough investigation? He couldn't help thinking that if they'd nailed Eppolito the first time they had him, for selling documents to Rosario Gambino, a lot of people who were murdered would still be walking around.

For Tommy, the bigger problem was dealing with Internal Affairs. The NYPD's Internal Affairs Unit polices the police department. IA is a quasi-secret unit that conducts investigations into the potentially illegal actions of police officers. This is the unit that brought the charges Vecchione had both prosecuted earlier in his career and later defended cops against in departmental hearings. Dades wouldn't call anybody there; basically, he despised them.

It went back to the stupidest thing Tommy had done in his entire career; while his marriage was crumbling, he had an affair. Not just a simple affair— Tommy never did things the easy way—but an affair with the girlfriend of a bank burglar Tommy had arrested after he had been indicted for murder (later he was acquitted). That was the mess that pushed him into retirement. This woman had filed recent assault charges against her boyfriend and would have been a witness against him. So Tommy's relationship with her could have destroyed the DA's case. The affair started less than a month after Dades's mother had died and lasted eight months. When Vecchione and Ponzi found out about it they were furious. Beyond furious. Both men continually berated Dades, but for a long time he just couldn't break it off. Finally, though, he did.

And when he did, this woman accused him of rape. She claimed that the first night they were together he had raped her—after which she voluntarily stayed with him for months. It was a lie. A few days after filing the complaint she admitted that the boyfriend had returned and forced her to do it, then she acknowledged it wasn't true. But the damage was done. Rather than examining Dades's record throughout his career and the circumstances of the accusation, Internal Affairs launched a full investigation.

Dades was furious. He knew he was guilty of gross stupidity, but he hadn't committed any crimes. The fact that his record had been absolutely clean for eighteen years made no difference to IA; they treated him like a felon. He became embittered at the department. At one point while he was being interviewed by an IA officer he lost his temper and practically dived over a table at her. They had to drag him out of the hearing room. Obviously that didn't help his case.

"I was humiliated. Throughout my career I was honorable in everything that I did and in return they tortured me and made me feel like a criminal. Look, it was an incredibly dumb thing for me to do. I know that, I admit it. I can't explain why I did it and I don't want to make any excuses. It was a mistake and I'm sorry it happened.

"But even after beating my case, I knew I was wearing a bull's-eye. If this hadn't happened I probably would have stayed on the job. But it woke me up. My pension, my medical benefits could go out the window in two seconds for something I didn't even do. I figured I better secure it while I had the opportunity. So I did."

Maybe even worse than dealing with IA, Tommy had to admit his infidelity to his wife. His marriage had been in trouble for a while; things happen between people, but even Ro knew he was not capable of committing a horrendous crime like rape.

Vecchione did what he could to help. As it happened, he was prosecuting the assault and had interviewed Tommy's accuser several times. He also knew that Dades's affair with her would pretty much make it impossible for him to testify in a trial. He was livid about that and he, Ponzi, and Dades argued often, sometimes loudly. Tommy considered the investigation an insult to his entire career. "How can they believe someone like her?" he wondered.

Vecchione told him. "They don't, but once the allegation was made they had an obligation to investigate. You know, Tommy, fucking around with her was an incredibly stupid mistake. She's a witness in this case. You arrested her baby's father. Having an affair with her was an unbelievably dumb thing to do."

But Mike also knew that the rape accusation was bullshit. So when he was contacted by officers at IAB he gave them his assessment of the case. "This is just about revenge," he explained. "This woman is a liar. She's just trying to get in good stead with her baby's father. I'll bet you anything he told her to make the complaint against Tommy."

When IA finally decided that there was no basis for charges to be filed, they referred the case to the department advocate's office, where Dades could be charged with conduct unbecoming an officer. It took the advocate's office another three months to drop the whole case. Tommy walked away clean but not unscarred. He'd made some enemies inside Internal Affairs. That was the main reason he had decided to retire after getting his twenty years in.

The boyfriend eventually accepted a deal and pled guilty. He is serving a state sentence, to be followed by a federal sentence; in all he'll spend about ten years in prison.

So there was a pretty good reason Dades couldn't make the request to Internal Affairs for the missing files. At a meeting of the small team in Vecchione's office in mid-October Tommy brought up the IA documents he wanted to see. Both Ponzi and Oldham had contacts in IA, but at the investigative level. Because Vecchione's division is in charge of investigating police corruption, police brutality, and crimes committed by police officers, he had established a good relationship with the Chief of Internal Affairs, Charles Campisi. Unlike Dades, Vecchione had considerable respect for IA, believing there were some excellent investigators working there. In particular he had great confidence in Campisi.

Vecchione called him. "Listen, Charlie," he told him, "I have something to discuss with you that I think you got to keep just between the two of us. I wouldn't ask you to do that if it wasn't important. I know you have a boss but I got to tell you, for now I'd appreciate you keeping it to yourself." While IA essentially operates independently of the normal police reporting structure, Campisi was still responsible to Police Commissioner Ray Kelly.

"Okay," Campisi agreed. "What's up?"

Vecchione laid it out. "We have some new information about a Brooklyn homicide, a wiseguy named Jimmy Hydell, which took place fifteen, sixteen years ago. Thing is, we think that it may have involved two New York City detectives, Louie Eppolito and Steve Caracappa, who you probably know about. I have to tell you, Charlie, we think we've got some pretty strong evidence against these guys and we've opened up an investigation."

Campisi took a deep breath. He knew the stakes. "What do you need from us?"

"We know that the IAB did some investigations on both of these guys when Eppolito was in the trial room. We've got some log numbers from other complaints and we want to see the complete files. I can't imagine you don't have a dossier on both of them because they've been under suspicion forever."

"I've never seen anything on them, Mike," he replied. Vecchione heard the doubt in Campisi's voice. "But the files have to be somewhere. Let me put somebody on this."

Mike cautioned him that it had to be somebody he trusted.

"I'll have somebody personally go through the storehouse and look for the files. If they're there, you'll get them."

"You need a subpoena?" Mike asked.

"No, no, that's okay. You can have whatever we got."

Vecchione hung up confident Dades would get the

files. At the next meeting he assured everybody that Campisi was taking care of it himself. "Don't worry," he said. "We'll get them." But Campisi never called back. Vecchione waited almost a week before calling him again.

Campisi was apologetic. "Mike," he said, "you're not going to believe this, but we've searched everywhere that those folders could be and we can't find them."

Vecchione was incredulous. That didn't seem possible. After the Gambino case Eppolito in particular was a known guy. He was high profile; people had to be looking at him every time he took a breath. So when complaints were made about Louie and his partner the alarms must have gone off. Files like that just don't disappear. "What are you talking about, Charlie? How can they not be there?"

Campisi explained. At the time Eppolito and later Caracappa were being investigated the NYPD was divided into seven divisions for management purposes. Each of those seven divisions ran its own satellite Internal Affairs unit, all of which were supervised by a headquarters division. "Brooklyn South did these investigations back then. When the system was centralized all the smaller units were supposed to have transported all their files to bureau. Do I know for sure that every file made it from the units? Mike, the truth is I don't know where these files are." He added without too much hope that there was one storage facility still to be checked—but a couple of days later he reported that the files weren't there either.

Internal Affairs had absolutely no files on Eppolito or Caracappa, two of the most controversial cops in recent memory.

Dades wasn't the slightest bit surprised at the news. "That's just bullshit," he angrily told Vecchione. "How can there be nothing? You tell me. I told you that these guys were gonna fuck us."

Vecchione didn't agree. "C'mon, Tommy, nobody's fucking anybody. Just relax. Believe me, I know Campisi. I'm telling you, the guy's a fair guy. If he had this stuff he'd give it to us. He doesn't have it; what do you want him to do?"

"I've been telling you right from the beginning," Dades said, "these guys are gonna fuck us every way they can. Listen to me, Mike, if the Feds can take this case away from us, they're going to."

"They can't, Tommy," Mike reassured him. "There's no way."

None of these files was ever located. No one knows precisely what was in them. It's probable they were simply misplaced—they might still be sitting in a file cabinet somewhere collecting dust—but it's also possible that somebody friendly with the two cops found them and destroyed them.

To Tommy though, this was a reminder that they were taking on the system and they shouldn't expect to receive a lot of help. As anyone who has ever worked inside the system knows, the first objective of the system is always to protect the system. This was an old case, long forgotten; it wouldn't do anybody any good to dredge it up again. And as it turned out, this was only the first of the many dead ends the investigators would explore. There was nothing for Dades to do but go back to work, chasing another lead.

And it was only a few days later that he caught a real big one. The majority of cold cases are solved through existing paperwork. Somebody picks up on a detail that previously had been overlooked. At that point the small task force was focusing almost exclusively on the Jimmy Hydell murder. Vecchione's plan was to nail Eppolito and Caracappa for one killing, then investigate their other crimes. The Hydell case offered the greatest opportunity to put them away. Betty Hydell could connect the cops to her son, which would corroborate Casso.

Following Hydell, there was a loose agreement that they'd go after the Eddie Lino killing. Lino was a lot more difficult in many respects. But Gaspipe was on record saying that the cops had actually killed Lino and there was an eyewitness who had seen someone fitting Caracappa's description walking away from Lino's car. They would try to find that witness again; who even knew if he was still alive or around or even remembered what he'd seen, but it was a link that might lead to others.

Among the piles of documents Tommy examined were numerous computer runs done by Eppolito and Caracappa. "It was just the regular work you gotta do," he explains. "Back in the 1980s if a cop wanted to access the police department's computers they had to type in their name and tax ID number. The actual reports were printed on the old kind of computer paper, attached sheets of pinfed computer paper that folded onto itself. I went through all the printouts in Eppolito's file first and I didn't find anything that connected him to these crimes, so then I started going through Caracappa's file.

"Caracappa was a member of the Major Case Squad, so he was in the perfect position to look at all the confidential information on wiseguys. It was legitimately part of his job. And that's exactly what he'd done. As I went through his file I began to see the names of wiseguys who had been killed that Caracappa had run under his ID number. I was trying to find some kind of connection between the dates he ran the files and the dates these guys got killed. But the timing was off. I was positive there was a tie-in, I knew there was an explanation, I just couldn't figure it out. I kept telling myself, 'You had to make a mistake somewhere. I know you did and I'm gonna find it.'"

Tommy had set up a timeline. A crime line, actually. Casso had been shot on September 14, 1986. Everything sprang from that day. Within a few days Gaspipe had learned from Kaplan's sources inside the department that Hydell had been one of his assailants. A couple of weeks after that Jimmy Hydell had been kidnapped, tortured until he admitted who sponsored the attempt and identified the other people who had been with him, and then killed by Casso.

One of the shooters was a wiseguy named Nicky Guido. In the pile of computer printouts run by Detective Stephen Caracappa, Dades discovered that on November 11, 1986, he had run the name Nicholas Guido through the NYPD database. On the surface that made sense; the police had learned the mob associate Guido had been part of the hit team that attacked Casso, and they would want to know everything possible about him, so Caracappa might simply have been doing his job. But unlike the other homicides, in this case the timeline was perfect: Guido was ID'd, Caracappa ran his name and got his information, Guido was murdered. The only problem with this scenario was that the wrong Nicky Guido had been killed.

Right around the time Dades found this file he had

a conversation with George Terra, a top investigator in Ponzi's office. George Terra was another one of those old-timers, the experienced guys who didn't need a scorecard to know all the players. Joe Ponzi liked to tell people that Terra was so cunning that the fox who bit *him* had died. Terra had been working aspects of this case almost from the very beginning, first as an NYPD detective who broke the Annette DiBiase murder and was a key member of the task force that finally located and arrested Gaspipe Casso in his New Jersey hideout, and after his retirement as an investigator in Joe Hynes's office. In fact, many of the tapes that Dades had spent hours listening to had come from an investigation run by Terra.

Those tapes had allowed Dades to get to know a dead man. They practically were Jimmy Hydell's autobiography. Terra told Tommy the history of the tapes: One afternoon the DA's office unexpectedly had gotten a call from Philly Boy Paradiso, who was sitting in jail. This was less than a year *before* the attack on Casso. Philly Boy had taken a good long look at his future and decided to cooperate. He told Terra that he could give him the Annette DiBiase kidnapping/murder.

It was Jimmy Hydell, he said. Hydell had insinuated to him that he had killed her. He didn't straight-out admit it, Paradiso told Terra, he just sort of suggested it. The DA agreed to a deal: Philly would wear a wire and try to get Hydell's confession on tape. Terra and the two FBI agents in their small task force would work with him. During the next few months Philly Boy and Hydell were together every day. But instead of talking about DiBiase, Hydell began discussing his personal hit parade. Hydell told him about the murder of Joseph Trinetto, who made the fatal mistake of living with Bob Bering's ex-wife. Trinetto came out of the house one morning and found his tire was flat. While he was changing it in his driveway someone put a couple of bullets in his head. And Hydell told Paradiso about the murder of bar owner Giacomo DeAngelo, who was machine-gunned to death in front of his house. But then he began talking about Casso—and disappeared.

As Terra told Dades, "We put Philly with Hydell every single day. Jimmy doesn't talk too much but as time goes by we're putting together little bits and pieces of who got killed and why. Then comes the day, October eighteen, 1986. Jimmy disappears. All we know is that he went to meet somebody over by the VA hospital at Dyker Park. There are U-shaped concrete bleachers and that's where he was supposed to meet somebody. We don't know who. His car was there. His change of clothes was there, but he's gone.

"According to Philly," Terra continued, "nobody knew what happened to him. So now we put Philly with Jimmy's younger brother, Frankie. We're trying to find out what happened to Jimmy and we're trying to find out what happened with the Casso shooting. Frankie kept saying that Casso had something to do with a bond deal, $40,000 worth of bonds . . ."

Terra had come all the way back to Tommy's starting point, Frankie Hydell. The murder of Frankie Hydell had led to Dades forming a relationship with Betty Hydell, and Betty's information had started this entire investigation. Bigger pieces were beginning to fit together. Tommy had a long list of questions he wanted to ask Terra. He never had to ask them; Terra handed him the key to the lockbox.

Like Dades, George Terra was an organized crime expert. He told Tommy that after each of the Casso killings he'd done computer searches about the victims. When Nicky Guido was killed, he said, he'd done a group search. He had gotten a computer printout of all the Nicholas Guidos living in Brooklyn. There were eight or nine of them, he remembered, but only one of them lived in downtown Brooklyn. That Nicky Guido, the one who lived near the mobsters, had been the victim—but he was not the Gambino associate.

But then Terra had gone further. He discovered that several Gambinos supposedly lived in upstate New York, in Sullivan County. It turned out there was a reason for that. More than a century earlier—long before the establishment of the child protective services—the New York State legislature had permitted the establishment of societies dedicated to the prevention of child abuse. Members of these societies were given all the powers of peace officers; they could make arrests, file charges, even take custody of children. But most important for the Gambinos, they were legally permitted to carry concealed weapons without having to obtain a permit. This was one of those archaic laws that had survived mostly because few people knew about it. Somehow, the Gambinos found out about it and took full advantage. The Sullivan Society had been incorporated in 1982, and most of its twelve members had ties to organized crime. Gambino associate Nicky Guido was a member of the Sullivan Society. And while he apparently was living in New Jersey, his legal address was in upstate New York.

Any doubt Terra might have had that this Nicky Guido was one of the shooters was resolved when he found out that he had been arrested at the Vista Hotel in Manhattan on a gun possession charge—along with Jimmy Hydell. The case was dismissed—it wasn't even part of Guido's record—but it was all the proof George Terra needed to know he'd identified the right Nicky Guido. And then he realized what must have happened—the shooters had killed the wrong Nicky Guido.

Terra was so certain of his information that he'd gone to the Seventy-sixth Precinct on Union Street and told detectives there that Nicky Guido had been murdered by mistake, that he was the wrong Nicky Guido. They looked at him like he was crazy, he told Tommy, and paid no attention to him.

But Dades knew it all squared. Armed with this knowledge, Dades went back to look a little more closely at Caracappa's computer search for Nicholas Guido. Maybe, just maybe, Caracappa had made the same mistake. As he remembers, "I looked at the date of birth of the Nicky Guido that had been killed, the innocent kid. He was born on February 2, 1960. I thought, *Please let that be the birth date of the Nicky Guido that Caracappa ran.* I got out the Nicky Guido homicide folder and checked the computer run. It took me a little while to find the birth date. And there it was, February 2, 1960. Caracappa had assumed because this Nicky Guido lived in the right area that he had to be the target. Caracappa had identified the wrong Nicky Guido. The Nicky Guido who had been part of the team that shot Casso had been born on January 29, 1957. He was about three years older than the victim and lived somewhere in Jersey.

"I just held that piece of paper in my hand, looking at it. I gotcha, you fuck. I gotcha. Gaspipe wanted to know where to find Nicky Guido. You gave him this kid's address by mistake and a couple of weeks later he got killed. That's no coincidence."

Tommy just sat there, staring at the sheet of paper. This was the first piece of physical evidence that connected either of the cops to the murders. It proved that Caracappa had been actively looking for Nicky Guido—just as Casso had told the FBI. It had been sitting in that file for sixteen years. Who knows how many other people had searched through that file without grasping its significance? Dades knew it wasn't proof beyond a reasonable doubt. Caracappa could claim he was simply running names because that was the job of his unit; he could say he was sloppy; he could try to explain it a dozen ways, but Dades knew it was going to be very difficult for anyone to believe that the connection between Caracappa's mistake and the murder of Nicky Guido was just an innocent coincidence.

Dades was absolutely elated. "In that instant," he recalls, "the investigation changed fundamentally. It wasn't just speculation anymore. I went out into the hallway waving the paper and started yelling down the hall to George Terra, 'We got him, George. We fucking got him! It's the wrong birth date. We got him!' Nobody else knew what I was screaming about, but they knew that I'd found something important."

Terra immediately came running into the office. Tommy showed him the computer run and the birth dates. Terra was smiling and nodding. "That totally fits with what I looked at on the computer back then," he said.

He called Ponzi; he didn't wait for him to say hello. "We got him. Caracappa gave Casso the wrong Nicky Guido. That's why they killed the kid."

Ponzi got it. "Are you sure?"

"I'm holding the paper in my hand."

Dades walked into Vecchione's office, a big smile on his face. Mike was in the middle of his breakfast. "You're not gonna believe this," Tommy said, waving the printout. "Look at this, look at this. We got him. We got him in black and white."

He walked around Vecchione's desk and laid down the paper in front of him. Mike looked at it, not quite understanding what he was looking at. "What do you got?"

"Look at this," Tommy said, pointing to the birth date on the printout. "Nicky Guido, the kid who got killed, remember we could never figure out why he was killed 'cause he wasn't a wiseguy? This is it, this is why. Caracappa got the wrong guy. He ran the name on the computer, but he came up with the wrong guy. It's the wrong address."

"Geez," Vecchione said. He stared at the sheet of paper through the eyes of an experienced prosecutor, trying to find the holes that a good defense lawyer would exploit. "This is unbelievable, Tommy," he said. He was ecstatic. His mind started racing; within seconds he was already in the middle of the trial, already dealing with the first legal hurdle. His plan was to indict Eppolito and Caracappa for the Hydell murder. Getting this paper admitted as evidence in that trial would be complicated because it had nothing to do with Hydell's killing. If either cop dared take the stand he could bring it in during his cross-examination—but at that point Vecchione believed there was little chance that would happen. More likely he would have to make a Molineux motion to get it in. Basically, this allows a prosecutor to introduce evidence of crimes that are similar to the crime for which the defendant is being tried or goes to prove his identity. It allows a prosecutor to show a pattern; this is the same way this guy committed this crime, this crime, and that crime. Somehow, Vecchione knew, he'd manage to get it in.

Joe Ponzi was equally excited. He looked at this evidence from the detective's point of view; what does this give us and where do we go from here? This was a promising beginning; it was the first solid proof that these guys were dirty. It was enough to get everybody excited, maybe even to get additional resources if that became necessary. They knew now they were following the right path.

Finally Dades called federal prosecutor Mark Feldman. "Mark," he said, "you're not gonna believe what we found . . ." Feldman was intrigued by the discovery. More than anyone else, Feldman knew about the real Nicky Guido—in 1989 he had put Nicky Guido in prison for the attempted murder of Anthony Casso.

After the missed hit on Casso, Bob Bering had taken the car that they'd used to a body shop and had it repainted. Eventually George Terra was able to put the car and the bill for the paint job and Bering together. When he confronted Bering with the bill, Bering flipped and implicated Nicky Guido. Terra's an auto crimes guy; he knows how to search every DMV in America for a name. He found Guido living in Pinellas County, Florida. He put a wire on Bering and flew him south, and Bering got Guido on tape confessing to his involvement in the hit attempt. Casso took the stand during the trial—and took the Fifth Amendment. This was a matter he intended to settle himself. It made no difference; Feldman got Guido convicted of assault 1 and sent him to jail for eight-plus.

So Feldman went all the way back with the Nicky Guido story. At this point in the Mafia cops investigation though, he was simply an interested observer. The Feds had been unable to make the case against the detectives seven years earlier; it was a state case now. But as a good friend of both Dades and Ponzi, as well as one of the best wiseguy prosecutors in the business, at that moment Feldman was probably pleased for Tommy, for Ponzi, and for justice. But it's also possible he might have been just a little envious. This was a no-lose situation for the Brooklyn DA's office: If Dades's small team could accomplish what the FBI couldn't, nailing Eppolito and Caracappa, careers were going to be made. It was a big-time get. And if they couldn't make it stick? Well, only a few people would know they even tried and certainly no one would blame them for failing. That was the beauty of a cold case.

One thing did change abruptly following the discovery of this evidence: Dades's somewhat fanciful quest evolved quickly into a serious investigation. Over the next couple of months several people joined the team. Bill Oldham had long been lobbying to add Assistant U.S. Attorney Robert Henoch from the Eastern District, explaining that Henoch would serve as Mark Feldman's representative. When Dades wondered exactly why he was needed, Oldham explained, "This is going to be a state trial and Henoch used to be a Manhattan DA."

Tommy was incredulous. "Are you kidding me?" he said. "We got Vecchione. He's got more experience than anybody in state court. If that's your reason, then we don't need him."

Oldham persisted. Feldman just didn't have the

time to focus on this investigation, particularly in the early stages. If any legal work had to be done on the federal level, Henoch could take care of it right away. He could save everybody a lot of time. So Robert Henoch joined the team. And as time passed, Dades began to appreciate Henoch's tenacity, and the two men became friends.

Ponzi assigned two additional detectives from Joe Hynes's office, Robert "Bobby I" Intartaglia and Doug Le Vien. Bobby I had retired from the NYPD after twenty-eight years and had been with the DA's office for nine years. Like the other detectives on the team, Intartaglia had known most of the wiseguys in this case for almost two decades. In the 1980s he'd spent several years investigating a burglary crew known as the Bypass Gang, which specialized in bypassing alarm systems to rob banks and jewelry stores. That was a particularly frustrating investigation; it seemed like every time he got close to making a solid case something went wrong. In October 1987, his key informant, a member of the crew named John "Otto" Heidel, had been murdered. A year later his second informant, Dominick Costa, was shot five times in front of his own house but miraculously survived. Robberies that the squad had been tipped off about were canceled for no apparent reason at the last minute. Meets that had been scheduled didn't take place. After a while it became obvious to Bobby I that his investigation had been compromised. The worst fear of a good cop had come true: The mob had a source deep inside the NYPD. Bobby I launched an internal investigation, but he was never able to find the leak. To keep the Bypass Gang investigation alive he changed his procedures: He stopped talking about the case on department telephones, he limited his communications to a small group, and he carefully protected his paperwork. It took him almost six years, but eventually he put nineteen members of the Bypass Gang in prison.

He was thrilled when Vecchione told him about the mob cops investigation and asked him to join the task force. As Bobby I began reviewing the progress they'd made, a lot of old questions suddenly had new answers. As a member of the Major Case Squad, Detective Steve Caracappa had had access to all of Intartaglia's paperwork in the Bypass Gang investigation. It was obvious now. Caracappa was the mole, the spy, the bastard. The skell. Now it was Intartaglia's chance to get even.

Doug Le Vien, a special assistant to Hynes, had a storied career in the NYPD. In the 1970s he'd successfully worked undercover, posing as a corrupt cop to infiltrate the Luccheses. He'd then served on the President's Commission on Organized Crime before joining Hynes's office. Le Vien and Vecchione went all the way back to the old neighborhood in Brooklyn, where they had been classmates in grammar school. Coincidentally, decades later, as both men struggled through difficult divorces, they worked in adjoining offices. They ended up spending a lot of time together, drinking and talking about their divorces and divorce lawyers, which caused them to drink even more. They even traveled together to Italy as part of a group of single men who rented a villa in Bologna. When Vecchione was putting together the task force, Le Vien was an obvious choice. It was a spot for which he had unique qualifications: In the introduction to *Mafia Cop,* Eppolito's coauthor, Bob Drury, wrote, "I am forever beholden to Detective (Ret.) Doug Le Vien, the 'fixer' who smoothed my research path too many times to recall." So Le Vien knew the story well, he knew most of the people involved, and he knew this was perhaps the last big case of his long career.

Vecchione also asked one of his assistants, Jim Kilduff, to handle much of the legal paperwork. Kilduff participated in several meetings but eventually left the DA's office and was replaced by Senior Assistant DA Josh Hanshaft.

On top of the whole pyramid was Brooklyn DA Charles "Joe" Hynes. When the cold case began heating up Vecchione had laid it out for his boss. Charles Hynes, who had hired Vecchione in 1992—and three months later made him Chief of the Homicide Bureau, the job he held until becoming Chief of Rackets in 2001—was known for giving people he trusted a long rope, and he gave Vecchione permission to stretch it out as long as necessary.

Almost nine months had passed since Betty Hydell had told Tommy Dades she could identify Eppolito and Caracappa. The team of veteran investigators was in place, the paperwork was beginning to pile up, they had the scent—and if they all did their jobs and had a little luck, they were going to break the biggest scandal in NYPD history.

CHAPTER 6

The task force met in secret in a conference room just outside Vecchione's office. Unlike the lavish meeting rooms of private industry, with highly polished mahogany tables and comfortable high-backed chairs, warm lighting, carefully chosen art on the walls, and all the amenities of power looking out over the grandeur of the city, this room was strictly government-issue. Eight unmatched metal chairs that had been pulled from other offices were scattered around a white coffee-stained faux-Formica rectangular table in the bright, fluorescently lit windowless room. The white walls were bare. It was a space for work.

As Dades glanced around the conference room that first morning he took a long and deep breath. *Here we go again,* he thought. It had been almost ten years since he and DEA agent Eric Stangbey had put together an officially unauthorized task force consisting of gung-ho federal drug busters and dedicated New York City cops. Dades and Stangbey just happened to meet one day, found they liked each other and had much in common, and decided to work together. Just that simple. What made their plan work was the enthusiastic cooperation of their bosses. In particular, U.S. Attorney Jim Walden had been unusually supportive. Normally a U.S. Attorney doesn't deal directly with city cops—but Dades and Walden worked together almost daily for five years. The team solved several murders and put forty members of the Lucchese crime family behind steel, and Dades ended up with a wall full of plaques and commendations given to him by the FBI, the DEA, and the U.S. Attorney, Eastern District.

Most often, though, combined agency task forces don't work. But the Mafia cops team was a real odd one because of the way it had been banged together. No one remembered anything quite like it; it consisted of a city detective, investigators and attorneys from the Brooklyn DA's office, and investigators and at least one attorney from the federal prosecutor's office. There were a lot of people with significant accomplishments—and sizable egos—in that room. Tommy knew the investigation could go very well—but if a turf war broke out it also could fall apart pretty quickly.

Certainly Mark Feldman was a key player. Tommy liked Feldman, and he trusted him, but Feldman wasn't Jim Walden. He played much more by the rules. And unlike Walden, who settled any agency disputes right down the middle, if people started angling for power Dades knew which way Feldman was going to fall—and it wasn't in his direction.

The first meeting started well enough. There was unanimous agreement that the task force would focus on the Jimmy Hydell murder. And everybody understood the importance of secrecy. They were about ten minutes in when things started falling apart. Dades started asking Henoch what he figured were some pretty simple questions about the way the investigation would proceed: If Burt Kaplan flipped, would they get to talk to him? Could Vecchione put him in front of a grand jury?

Simple questions, but Henoch was noncommittal, saying, "Well, I don't really have the power to make that decision."

Dades was furious. He had worked with the U.S. Attorney's office more often than he'd worked with the Brooklyn DA, yet Henoch was treating him like some inexperienced kid. "Listen to me, there's no fucking way you were sent here by Feldman without having discussed that. It had to be discussed."

Henoch repeated his answer. Dades persisted and finally exploded. "If you can't answer a fucking question," he yelled, "what the hell are you here for?"

Ponzi glared at Dades. His meaning was clear: *Don't start.*

Henoch said evenly, "We're here to set the up the guidelines on how this investigation is going to proceed."

When Tommy began responding, Henoch interrupted him, trying to take control. Vecchione jumped to Tommy's defense, telling Henoch, "Just hold on. Let *me* tell *you* what the story is." Vecchione backed up Dades completely. "We've got a deal with Feldman," he explained. "We're going to get this case first and then if you can do anything with it you're going to go after us."

Henoch grimaced, telling Vecchione, "I don't know anything about that. Maybe that's the deal you have with Feldman, but nobody told me anything . . ."

Tommy threw up his hands. "Oh man, this is bullshit! I'm fucking useless here." He walked out of the room.

Ponzi went after him and grabbed him in the hallway. "What is wrong with you, Tommy?" he asked. "What was that all about?"

"Don't you see what they're doing, Joe?" Tommy responded. "They're jerking us off. We're gonna spend more time arguing over who, what, when, and where with the people who're supposed to be our partners than we will investigating the case."

"Oh, c'mon, Tommy, he's just—"

"I'm telling you, Joe, they're gonna try to take the whole boat away from us. They got Kaplan and Casso and they're not going let us talk to them. If they can make a RICO out of this they're not going to let us do anything. You watch."

Ponzi was adamant that wasn't going to happen. "C'mon, Tommy, we got a deal with Feldman," he said firmly. "He's my friend. I can't imagine him going back on his word. I'm telling you, just give this a little time. We're not even near Kaplan yet. When we get to the point we need him, I'm sure things are going to work out."

Dades didn't agree. With people starting to stake out jurisdiction in the first minutes of the first meeting, he didn't see how the situation was going to get much better.

Vecchione was a realist. He was certain the Feds would instantly grab the case if possible, but he just didn't think it would be possible. "Look at it like this, Tommy," he said. "Right now Feldman can't make any kind of case. Gaspipe and all the wiseguys Eppolito and Caracappa worked with are gone. And both of those guys are retired out in Vegas, so they don't have access to information that anybody cares about anymore. They've got nothing to sell and nobody to sell it to. Unless they've been incredibly stupid—and I don't think these guys lasted so long by being stupid—it's going to be really difficult for Feldman to show a continuing conspiracy. If he can't prove that they're still doing bad things he's time-barred; there's a five-year statute of limitations on a RICO charge and there's no way he can make that. So Kaplan's got no value to him. If the old man changes his mind, Feldman'll have to give him to us. What else is he gonna do with him?"

Twenty years as a New York City cop had taught Dades several very important lessons about dealing with the federal government: The first one was that the Feds always win. Always. The media stories about the competition between local police forces and government agencies were generally accurate. The Feds had a habit of marching in and taking over. Whatever has to be done for them to get what they want somehow gets done. Promises don't get kept. Lies get told. Which led to the second lesson: You couldn't believe what they told you. The Feds owned Casso and Kaplan. They weren't going to give up access to them without extracting some type of payment. Knowing that, he responded to Vecchione, with very little confidence, "I hope you're right."

The way Tommy figured it, some Feds were better than others. As long as he had to work with them, in this investigation he much preferred that the DEA be the lead agency rather than the FBI. "Lead agency" was a relatively important designation. The lead agency gets to call the shots. The lead agency is the core of the operation; everybody reports to them and they get to make most of the decisions. Dades thought it was only fair that the DEA get the lead position because they had originally locked up Kaplan. They had extensive knowledge about the whole case. And he already had a good working relationship with several of the DEA agents who had been involved in Kaplan's case; while there were several FBI agents he had loved working with—Matt Tormey, Gary Pontecorvo, and Jimmy DeStefano, for example—there were others he'd worked with previously and didn't want to work with again.

Mark Feldman, who would designate the lead federal agency, was known to favor the FBI. Dades asked him specifically to keep them out of it, pointing out that the FBI had a reputation for jumping into a case, doing as little as possible, and then taking credit for all the success. "These guys on the Lucchese squad don't know this case," he said. "[DEA agent] Frank Drew was the one who put Kaplan away. If anybody deserves the right to run this from your side, it's the DEA."

This wasn't the usual kind of DEA operation. Technically, it wasn't even a drug case. Feldman tried to reassure Dades that the FBI would commit the necessary resources. "Honestly, Tommy, you don't need worry about it. It'll work out."

Dades argued that in addition to Kaplan the DEA had a legitimate stake in the case. Several agency drug investigations had been compromised. Their informers had been whacked.

Feldman and Dades had been friends for ten years. They'd worked together often enough for Feldman to know that Dades could be as persistent—and as irritating—as a summer cough. Finally, he suggested a compromise. It's impossible to know his reasoning; maybe he still believed the case was a long shot or maybe he'd bought Dades's argument. He told Dades that if the DEA guaranteed 100 percent dedication to the case, he'd allow them to take the lead. But they had to guarantee dedication and cooperation.

Dades had his deal—now all he had to do was convince the DEA to accept it. None of the agents with whom he'd previously worked were in the kind of management position to make that decision. The natural choice was John Peluso, the assistant special agent in charge of the DEA's Manhattan office. Peluso was a well-respected veteran of the South American drug wars, but Dades believed he was the wrong choice for this job. He told Vecchione, "Peluso don't know the difference between a wiseguy and a Jamaican posse."

Instead, he reached out to DEA agent Timmy Moran, who was working in Las Vegas. Moran flew to New York to meet with Mark Feldman. Dades picked him up at the airport, drove him to the meeting, and then drove him right back. Moran was in New York long enough to agree that the DEA would dedicate its complete resources to the operation. Timmy Moran became the face of the DEA, returning to Vegas to begin taking a good long look at Eppolito and Caracappa.

Moran learned almost immediately that the two cops had forged some good contacts within the Las Vegas Police Department. He didn't know who they knew or how well they knew them. He didn't know which Vegas cops could be trusted with confidential information. So he warned Dades that if the team in New York intended to keep the investigation secret they had to stay far away from the LVPD.

Timmy Moran did something else: He took a leisurely drive past Eppolito's house one afternoon just to look the place over. It was basic procedure, the kind of thing any good cop would do at the beginning of an investigation. Get to know your subjects. Moran noted there were several cars in Eppolito's driveway and wrote down the license plates. When he got back to his office he ran the plates through the DEA's computer system. All standard stuff. You just never know.

Minutes after getting the results he called Dades and said, "You're not gonna believe this one, Tommy."

Tommy was sitting at his desk in the Intel Division. His retirement papers had already been filed and he had only a few weeks left in his NYPD career. He'd already started cleaning out his desk. "What ya got?"

A slow drive past Eppolito's house, a license plate number in a computer, and just like that the entire investigation got turned upside down. "There was a car in Eppolito's driveway when I went by there," Moran told him. "When I ran the plate bells started ringing. You ready for this? The car belongs to a member of the Cali cartel."

Dades took a long, deep breath. Eppolito was still in business.

The Cali, Colombia, drug cartel was the major leagues of drug operations. The DEA originally had been pulled into this investigation by Dades, as much to keep the FBI from grabbing control as to put two dirty cops in prison. But this discovery changed everything. For the DEA this was no longer just about Eppolito and Caracappa; this was a pretty good indication that the Cali cartel was operating in Vegas. Almost immediately Moran and the FBI began setting up a major undercover operation.

The bureau recruited fifty-nine-year-old Steven T.

Corso Jr. to try to get close to Eppolito. Corso was kind of a strange choice to be dropped into the middle of a major criminal investigation. He had been a partner in a prestigious New York accounting firm until 2002, when he'd been caught by the FBI with his whole arm in the till. Corso turned out to be a degenerate gambler, and to support his habit he'd stolen more than $5 million from his clients. Corso's only shot at getting out from under was to roll over. Rather than go to prison, he'd agreed to work as a confidential witness for the bureau under federal protection. The FBI had planted him in Las Vegas, where he'd opened an accounting office and became known around town as a guy who knew how to make numbers jump. That proved to be the perfect bait for wiseguy types who were looking for an edge. Few of those tough guys believed a certified public accountant would have the cojones to wear a wire for the FBI and DEA against legitimate mobsters. The IRS? Okay, maybe that was believable.

It turned out Corso was a natural. In fact, he had just finished participating in an FBI investigation of the boxing industry, in particular the operation of promoter Bob Arum, when he was approached by the DEA. The plan was irresistible. Corso would befriend Eppolito and eventually offer to sell his screenplays to rich investors. It was artistic justice: Eppolito had scammed women into paying him to write screenplays by promising to get the movies produced; now the government was going to try to get Eppolito by proposing to get those same screenplays produced.

At one of Louie Eppolito's early meetings with Corso he proudly boasted about his mob connections. He claimed that he had been told by John Gotti's attorney, Bruce Cutler, that on his deathbed Gotti professed to have trusted only three people. "He says, 'My family, as a whole; my father; and Louie Eppolito because he went through so much as a cop.' He says, 'I knew Louie. We hung together . . . The cops always said the cock-sucker's a wiseguy with a badge. Always. But this guy never broke. Never wavered.'"

Corso was professionally impressed—and record-ing every single word Eppolito said.

Dades and Vecchione didn't know the details of the FBI's Vegas operation. But what they knew was enough: Louie Eppolito was dealing with a member of the Cali cartel. Maybe it was completely innocent, maybe these guys were just tennis buddies—and maybe Tommy could still get a good price on the Brooklyn Bridge. They did some figuring: The last killing that Casso credited to Eppolito and Caracappa took place in 1992. For their crimes to qualify under the RICO Act as a continuing conspiracy the Feds would have to prove that at least one criminal act had occurred within the past five years. If the Vegas part of the investigation produced evidence of a crime connected to Casso or the Luccheses, the Feds theoretically could bring RICO charges against the cops.

Eventually Joe Ponzi learned about Corso's prog-ress from the DEA. He informed Vecchione that the DEA had a confidential informer "who may be into these guys on some stuff. He's wired and apparently he's getting some very good information."

As a prosecutor with a passion for justice who had spent most of his life trying to make sure bad things happened to bad people, Vecchione was happy to learn the Vegas operation was going well, but as the guy who wanted to personally put two scumbags in a small cage for the rest of their lives he was pretty pissed off. He could almost hear the Feds smiling as they greased the gangplank for the state.

Dades didn't need to say I told you so. He'd been telling everybody that it was going to go that way since the investigation started. But even Tommy had to laugh at the irony. It was his own insistence that the DEA get involved that had made the possible probable.

The tree that had grown in Brooklyn had planted roots in Vegas. That created a lot of interesting possibilities: The Feds could make a drug case against the cops in Vegas but not be able to connect it to Casso, meaning there would have to be two completely independent indictments. Or they might be able to link the cases—but even that wouldn't do any good if they couldn't make both cases. And whatever was happening in Vegas, in Brooklyn the investigation was a lot of evidence away from a sure thing.

It had taken Dades several months to put together most of the pieces of the Jimmy Hydell murder. Starting at the end, Hydell was killed because of his participation in the hit on Gaspipe Casso; there was no question about that. But why the attempt was made on Casso was tough for everyone to figure out. Dades still believed it was in retaliation for Casso going after John Gotti and blowing up his guy Frank DeCicco, but on the DiBiase tapes Philly Boy Paradiso had claimed it was because of a bad debt, something about some missing bonds. There was another rumor floating around that Gambino captain Angelo Ruggiero owed Casso a lot of money from gambling losses and decided to whack him rather than pay his debt. And another informer claimed that Casso was hit because he had made some "denigrating remarks" about Ruggiero and threatened to kill Gambino soldier Bobby Boriello.

The actual reason Mickey Boy Paradiso ordered the hit could have been any one or even several of those reasons. It didn't matter, whatever it was; it was Paradiso who put together the team of shooters including Jimmy Hydell, Nicky Guido, and Bob Bering. Their driver was a guy named Dominick Lattori. None of these people were made guys. And obviously they hadn't spent a lot of time planning the job. It was amateur hour. Not much more than a shoot-and-pray. The hit team pulled their car alongside Casso's car and opened up on him. They hit him twice, but police reports from that night state that he escaped by running through a parking lot into a Chinese restaurant, then ran through the kitchen and out the back.

The police reports also included the information that the car Casso was driving was registered to a convicted drug dealer named Burt Kaplan. And in the glove compartment the police found an NYPD computer printout identifying the license plate number of a car that had been tailing Casso as an unmarked police car. That was the first physical evidence that Casso—or Kaplan—had a source inside the NYPD.

Casso claimed in one of his 302s that Kaplan had handed him a manila envelope containing the police report of the attempt, which included the names and some photographs of members of the hit team. Supposedly the information was a gift to Casso from the cops, a way of proving to him that they were the answer to his prayers.

Maybe, but there was another possibility too. Jimmy Hydell's sister, Lizzie, told Dades that her brother had come home all upset and she'd overheard him talking excitedly about the attack on Casso. Also in the house at that time was the guy she was dating, a kid named Frankie Sapanaro. Frankie Sapanaro's father and uncle were both soldiers in the Colombo family. Through an informer inside the Colombos, Dades was able to confirm his hunch that Frankie Sapanaro had gone home that night and told his father what he'd heard. Nobody was saying that Frankie did anything wrong, or even considered the consequences of this information. His father had done the so-called right thing; he'd given up Jimmy Hydell to Casso. Loyalty was more important than love.

However Casso learned about it, the information about what happened next had come from numerous different sources. Detective George Terra flipped Bob Bering, who informed him that Jimmy Hydell knew he had been fingered as one of the shooters. Hydell told Bering he had to meet some wiseguys in Dyker Park, Brooklyn. Apparently Jimmy had been told the whole problem could be "squashed," but Bering described him as "real nervous about it."

After Frankie Hydell became an informant for Dades, he told him that just after Jimmy had left his house on Staten Island to go to the meeting, Eppolito and Caracappa had mistakenly picked Frankie up. Betty Hydell told Tommy that when Frankie told her about that, she got in her own car and had her confrontation with the two cops. She identified Eppolito after seeing him appear on *The Sally Jesse Raphael Show* to promote his book.

Dades later confirmed through NYPD records that Eppolito and Caracappa were no longer partners at that time, making the fact that Betty saw them together much more significant. They certainly had no police business bringing them together.

Frankie said that as he drove toward the Verrazano

Bridge less than an hour later he saw the two cops again. He didn't know if they had seen him, but they definitely were not following him. They were on their way to Brooklyn.

Later that day, Betty eventually told Dades, she got a phone call from Jimmy. Nothing special, he told her, he was just checking in. Betty didn't remember anything unusual about the call, nothing to make her anxious, and absolutely nothing to indicate he was worried about the next few hours. Tommy figured that was probably the last phone call Jimmy Hydell ever made. What Betty had never told anyone—until she told Tommy— was that a couple of days later, after Jimmy had disappeared, she made an effort to find him. She had no way of knowing he was dead; no body was found, and it was possible he knew that detectives were close to solving the Annette DiBiase murder and had gone on the lam. Betty Hydell successfully traced Jimmy's phone call. Through telephone company records, she learned that he'd made that call from a pay phone on Bay Eighth Street, near Dyker Park. Dades hoped she'd saved the phone company printout, but it was lost.

Dades then learned from FBI reports how Hydell had been lured to the meeting. An FBI agent specializing in organized crime had testified in a bail revocation hearing for Mickey Boy Paradiso in 1987 that informers had told him, "There was a meeting to take place on October 18, 1986, where Mr. Paradiso was scheduled to represent an individual known to us [the FBI] as James Hydell, who is the alleged shooter of Anthony 'Gaspipe' Casso. The meeting was to take place in the vicinity of a frankfurter stand located on Bay Eighth Street in the Dyker Park section of Brooklyn. Mr. Paradiso was supposed to meet with two other members of the Gambino family in addition to a representative of the Lucchese family, where they would resolve the issue regarding Mr. Hydell shooting Mr. Casso."

From the tapes of Bob Bering's debriefing by George Terra, Dades learned that Hydell had tried to get himself some protection at that meeting. Hydell knew that Detective Al Guarneri was in charge of the Annette DiBiase murder investigation. He knew Guarneri from the neighborhood. Guarneri had become completely obsessed with the DiBiase case. During that time period he generated something like 350 DD5s, reports of actions taken during an investigation. He had worked on it day and night for ten months, both on and off duty. "I lived and breathed this case," he told Pulitzer Prize–winning reporter Mike McAlary. It's clear that Guarneri believed Hydell and Bering were involved in her disappearance—and that both of them knew that Guarneri was tracking them.

Dades took what he knew and tried to figure out what was going on in Jimmy Hydell's mind that day. He had to be aware this meeting might be a trap. Apparently he arrived there early enough to give his mother a call. Maybe that was his way of saying goodbye. Just in case. But chances are he was also looking for protection—so like any Joe Citizen, he turned to the police. He would use Al Guarneri to shield him from the wiseguys. If he was being set up, the presence of cops would prevent the wiseguys from killing him.

Bering admitted that Jimmy Hydell had told him to call Al Guarneri at the 6-2 and tell him that Hydell was going to be at a meeting in Dyker Park and he was probably going to get hit. Hydell obviously fig-ured Guarneri would come running. Bering called the Sixty-second Precinct. Guarneri later told reporters that he wasn't working that day, but someone from the Sixty-second called him and told him Bering was looking for him. Guarneri returned the call and pre-sumably Bering passed along the message.

There are information gaps in every investigation. Usually they can be filled in by putting together causes and events, what had to happen to enable the next ac-tion to take place. It's a leap of information, sort of the way a nerve impulse will leap across a synapse from one neuron to another. The question that Dades couldn't answer was how Eppolito and Caracappa found out that Hydell was going to a meeting in Dyker Park. So again he had to speculate based on the facts he did know.

The wild card in the murderous deck—that Jimmy Hydell could not possibly have known—was that Al Guarneri's brother-in-law was Detective Louis Ep-polito. And he also could not possibly have known that Eppolito was working for Gaspipe Casso. So what might have happened—this is one of those jumps cops make to fill in some blanks—was that Bering called Guarneri, and Guarneri called Eppolito. Dades be-lieved that Guarneri knew that Eppolito was looking for Hydell—they were relatives, they talked—and that it was also highly probable that Guarneri didn't know and didn't care why Louie was looking for Hydell. Ep-polito was an active cop, Hydell was an active bad guy; they were a legitimate match. Tommy's supposition was that Guarneri got Bering's phone call and com-pletely innocently reached out to Eppolito by beeper, and when they got connected he told him Hydell was going to be in Dyker Park.

Maybe it happened that way, maybe not, but however it happened, Eppolito and Caracappa found out about Hydell's meeting and raced across the Verrazano to get there before the wiseguys. Frankie Hydell saw them on their way.

Jimmy Hydell was already at the park when the two cops got there. As Casso later admitted, while he was incarcerated in New York City's Metropolitan Correctional Institute he had spent a lot of time with a Colombo family shooter named Chickie DeMartino. Dades knew DeMartino well—working with FBI agents James DeStefano and Gary Pontecorvo, he had arrested him for an attempted murder. Wiseguys in the joint together spend a lot of time talking business. According to Casso, during one of their conversations, DeMartino suddenly started talking about Jimmy Hydell. He told Casso he had been sitting on Jimmy and was going to kill him, although he didn't give a reason. Casso may have been amused when he heard that.

Talk about your coincidences—here were two wiseguys looking to whack the same guy! Sometimes it's amazing what two men will have in common. But clearly, whatever happened at the park, it wasn't going to be Jimmy Hydell's day.

DeMartino told Casso he was sitting in his car watching Hydell, getting ready to make his move, when two men approached Hydell and put him in their car. DeMartino told Casso that he figured the two men were either cops or FBI agents, because their car looked like an unmarked police car.

Obviously that made great sense to Dades. Hydell had alerted the cops, so he certainly wouldn't have been surprised when two detectives showed up and flashed their badges. In fact, he was probably thrilled.

But not as happy as Eppolito and Caracappa. This was precisely how their badges made their crimes so simple. That badge made it easy to get a real suspicious guy in a car—"Hey, Jimmy, you're under arrest for whatever," or "Hey, Hydell, get in the car; we want to ask you a few questions."

Jimmy Hydell probably believed he was saving his own life by getting into the car. Dades also believed the cops must have handcuffed Hydell; it was standard procedure when you were putting somebody in the backseat of a car, and Hydell would have understood that and accepted it.

Casso said that once the cops had Hydell in their car, they drove him to an auto repair garage on Nostrand Avenue owned by someone they trusted. Gaspipe did not know the exact location of the garage.

Casso had been told by Kaplan that when the cops got to the garage Eppolito physically picked up Hydell and hog-tied him, then threw him in the trunk of another car, a car that had been provided by Kaplan.

Dades had learned from several sources—informers as well as Casso's 302s—that Eppolito and Caracappa then brought Hydell to the parking lot of a Toys "R" Us on Flatbush Avenue in the trunk of the car. The cops had sent a prearranged code to Kaplan's beeper informing him that they had Hydell and were bringing him to the planned meeting place. It was there, Casso told the FBI, that he saw the cops for the first and only time. From the parking lot Casso and his friend, Lucchese underboss Vic Amuso, drove the car to an unidentified house nearby belonging to a wiseguy and took Hydell into the finished basement.

60 Minutes had done a story about Casso in 1998 after his plea agreement fell apart. Although during that interview Casso told correspondent Ed Bradley that he "had cops on his payroll," for legal reasons that show's producers had edited out that information. But Casso did describe the Hydell killing on camera, telling Bradley, "I took him to a place that I had prearranged, somebody's house that I could use. I brought him there, sat him down. I wanted to know why I was shot and who else was involved, who gave the orders to shoot."

Bradley asked him, about killing Hydell, "Was it just one shot to the head?"

"I didn't shoot him in the head. I didn't shoot him in somebody else's house. You make a mess. I shot him a couple of times. I didn't torture him or anything like that. I shot him a couple of times, the kid died."

"What's a couple?" asked Bradley.

"I don't know, more than a couple. I don't know the exact amount. Maybe I shot him ten times, twelve times . . . It could've been fifteen."

"Why?"

"Because of the hatred I had for him. I wanted to beat him with the gun after it was empty. He just tried to kill me. He doesn't deserve anything. That's the law anyway . . . That's the law of the Mafia."

Tommy watched this clip over and over, and every time he did he found himself thinking about Betty Hydell. Long ago Betty had accepted the fact that her son was dead, but she wanted to know why and how and who. She wanted to find his body. In the twelve years between Jimmy's disappearance and broadcast of this show in 1998 she had spoken with the FBI numerous times. The bureau's response was always the same: *We have no new information about the disappearance of Jimmy Hydell.*

As she discovered watching *60 Minutes,* it turned out they knew everything. It was while watching this program that Betty learned for the first time how her son had died. It was brutal for her, and for her daughter, Lizzie, but it also confirmed Betty's suspicion that just about everybody in law enforcement was lying to her. That had left her feeling there was no one she could trust, no one who cared.

So Dades—and the task force—knew the whole story of Jimmy Hydell's murder. They knew exactly what Eppolito and Caracappa had done. And now their job was to prove it beyond a reasonable a doubt.

CHAPTER 7

The task force met each Tuesday morning. While some of the meetings continued to be held in the Brooklyn DA's office, perhaps symbolically the other meetings were held two blocks away at the Eastern District. These meetings generally lasted about two hours, during which everyone reported what they'd learned the previous week and got their assignments for the following week. The meetings were conducted very professionally—and equally dispassionately.

Every joint task force eventually takes on its own identity. Sometimes it becomes a cohesive unit, working smoothly and efficiently as the loyalty of its members shifts gradually from their assigning agencies to this makeshift team. The common goal, putting bad guys in a cage, becomes a powerful engine for unity. Dades knew the exhilarating feeling, the excitement, that resulted when everybody finally got it together to experience the legendary Three Musketeers bravado, all for one, one for all.

Sometimes, though, it doesn't work so well. Sometimes agency rivalries can't be overcome and disparate personalities cause friction. It's the difference between harmony and a cacophony. This task force was one of those other times. Rather than one for all, it was more like one for one. In contrast to the unified front always presented to the media, as this investigation progressed, there existed a wide and ever-present breach between the state and the Feds that just couldn't be crossed. While they shared a common objective, neither side ever learned to trust the motives of the other side. And even within the two camps, there were personality conflicts.

This particular joint task force was practically an all-star team of veteran cops and lawyers. Each of them had enjoyed considerable success in his career. These were powerful guys who knew how to navigate the system. Several of them were close to retirement and knew well that nailing two murderous detectives would create a great wave of media attention they might ride into the future. So in addition to putting away two skells, there was the potential for personal enhancement. There were some strong personalities in that room, and at times tempers got raised. According to Dades, Bill Oldham often tried to dominate these meetings. "Who knows why?" Dades wondered. "Maybe because he worked for the Feds and thought they owned the case. Bill Oldham was a good guy; he was a thorough, productive investigator and as dedicated to justice as anybody on the team. But truthfully we had our differences. He'd always bring something to eat to the meetings. Other people would have a cup of coffee, but he was the only one eating at these meetings. McDonald's, a bagel, a muffin, sushi, he was always eating something and he'd sit there stuffing down food as we tried to work. The real problem was that sometimes he got so enthusiastic that he tried to dominate the meetings. Like everybody else, he wanted to see the justice done, but he had his own issues. There were a lot of really accomplished people in that room and some of them resented him."

Mike Vecchione attended only those meetings that took place in the DA's office conference room. As the Feds gradually began to impose their rules over the investigation, his relationship with Mark Feldman, always respectful but never particularly friendly, grew substantially worse. Dades, too, had started to become disenchanted with Feldman. He had long considered the prosecutor a friend, but it had become obvious to him that Feldman put their relationship second to business. What made that more difficult to accept was Tommy's deep belief that this case would best be prosecuted by the state, who could go after the cops for at least eight individual murders in addition to a shopping list of criminal acts, while the Feds basically had a single RICO charge to make.

Among the few things the members of this task force had in common were their law enforcement experience and their dedication to this investigation. Everybody wanted to put these two dirty cops away. So no matter how badly their personalities clashed, the real work, the daily drudgery, got done. This was an unusually difficult investigation, made considerably more difficult from the very beginning by the continued emphasis on secrecy. There were people out there who might have pertinent information whom Henoch would not allow investigators to approach because he was afraid they would "spill the beans." Tommy pointed out that there weren't any beans to be spilled, reminding Henoch forcefully that the crimes being investigated had been committed more than a decade earlier and there was nothing Eppolito and Caracappa could do to erase them. They couldn't change history.

It turned out that the Feds were worried that if Casso's cops found out that the investigation was active they'd stop doing whatever illegal deals they were doing in Vegas. Dades thought that was pretty much a bullshit excuse. He wanted to shake the trees, get people running, making phone calls. That was a technique he'd used successfully several times before; you get somebody up on a wire, you light a match and find out who he calls and what he says. One time in a murder case Dades and Mike Galletta were working, they had taps on the phones of the two primary suspects. They had a few bits of information, but not nearly enough to make the case. They picked up one of the suspects and during his interrogation dropped the few details they'd learned, then warned the suspect he was crazy not to flip because it was getting late fast and if he walked out of the office the deal was off the table. Dades and Galletta knew that as soon as the suspect left the office he would have to report the entire conversation to his capo in the family. That's exactly what happened. Dades and Galletta listened on the tap as he told his boss, "They questioned me about [so and so] and they're getting hot. They know a lot of stuff. I don't know what to do."

The capo told him to calm down and shut up, reassuring him that there were certain incriminating details only the two of them knew.

The information they got from that phone call was crucial to making the case against the two mobsters.

When faced with additional evidence the first suspect finally flipped. The evidence was so overwhelming both men pled guilty.

Dades wanted to try the same technique in this case. He wanted to plant a story in the newspapers that would rattle Eppolito and Caracappa. He wanted to see how they reacted, what they did, who they called, and who called them as a result of the story. But he was overruled. The U.S. Attorney didn't want anybody knowing that this particular cold case was being thawed.

That decision hampered the investigation. For example, Dades realized pretty quickly that several wiseguys who might have information about the case were living happily in the Feds' Witness Protection Program. These were people who had worked with or knew Casso—some of them may have even benefited from information provided by the two cops. Getting to them required cooperation from the Feds and going through some red tape. The U.S. Attorney finally agreed to let him speak with several of these men, but with one condition: He couldn't tell them precisely why he was speaking to them.

Basically, when an individual flips he agrees to co-operate with law enforcement agencies for a specific length of time. During that time he is required by his agreement to answer any and all questions to the best of his knowledge. The law enforcement agency owns his past. But at the end of that time period his obligation ends. He doesn't have to speak to anyone. He doesn't have to answer any questions. That's the way most agreements read; but in practice, most of these guys love talking about their former lives, back when they were somebodies. Often they're living ordinary lives under made-up identities, working mundane jobs, unable to talk about their good old days. In their new lives recounting their greatest hits just doesn't make good cocktail party chatter. So these occasional conversations with law enforcement at least temporarily allow them to talk about who they were way back when.

"Among the people I wanted to speak to," Dades explains, "were a former Lucchese family captain named Fat Pete Chiodo, a three-hundred-pound wiseguy who had flipped after he got shot nine times during a botched hit in a gas station, and Little Al D'Arco, who had been the acting boss of the Lucchese family while Casso and Vic Amuso were on the run. D'Arco was later demoted for messing up the hit on Chiodo. I also wanted to speak to D'Arco's son Joe; he was another made guy and he was involved in the Anthony Dilapi hit. I thought there was a good chance the D'Arcos would talk because the family had turned on them, and I knew that Pete Chiodo had no love for the family because Casso had made an attempt on his sister's life to punish him for testifying."

D'Arco was the first mob boss in history to testify against his Mafia family and then go into the Witness Protection Program. What made Al and Joe D'Arco particularly interesting to Dades was the fact that Joe D'Arco had been the triggerman in the Anthony Dilapi murder. Dilapi was the wiseguy who was hiding from Casso and Vic Amuso in California. To find out where Dilapi was hiding, Caracappa had written to his parole officer, claiming the NYPD wanted to speak with him because his name had come out in an investigation. Caracappa got the address and passed it along to Kaplan, but Dilapi managed to get away—so

Caracappa again wrote to Dilapi's parole officer, again under the guise of NYPD business, to get his new address. As a result, Joe D'Arco was able to find Anthony Dilapi and kill him.

Like Casso and Kaplan, Chiodo and both D'Arcos were the property of the federal government. Nobody got to speak with them unless the U.S. Attorney approved it, arranged it, and supervised the interview. For example, Dades's request to speak with the younger D'Arco was turned down. He never found out why. It just wasn't approved. Arrangements to interview Chiodo and Al D'Arco were made through the offices of the federal prosecutor and the Federal Marshal Service, which runs the Witness Protection Program. After Dades's request for those two interviews had been approved, a time and location was designated for each of the calls to actually take place.

Dades sat in an office in the Southern District with Bobby I and several other people while a marshal actually placed the phone calls. The New York end of the interview was conducted by speakerphone. "I pretty much followed the same script for both phone calls," Dades recalls. " 'Listen,' I told them, trying to ask them questions without giving them any information, 'this is what we're doing here. We're looking at law enforcement leaks and law enforcement corruption that involved Gaspipe Casso. We know that he was getting inside information from somewhere, but we don't know where. You know anything at all about that?' "

Both Chiodo and D'Arco seemed to be cooperative. Fat Pete verbally shrugged his shoulders. He didn't know nothing about any of that kinda stuff. D'Arco admitted that he knew Casso had very reliable sources, but he had never asked him where the information was coming from. "He would just come back from wherever and say that he had got some information from his guys. You know, it was always pretty good. But where he got it, who knows?"

D'Arco said that when Casso gave them Dilapi's location he'd told them, "The cops got where he was." Three men had been sent out to California—his son among them—and "they killed him [Dilapi] in his garage."

The conversations took a lot longer to arrange than they lasted. Without being able to refer specifically to leaks or sources or even names, Dades felt like a guy playing poker blindfolded. These calls, and other similar conversations, confirmed what the task force already knew: Casso had been extremely careful about protecting his source. Even in a world in which any wall might have ears, or at least an embedded listening device, Casso—and Kaplan—had been remarkably successful at keeping this secret.

Dades also began visiting as many of the places described by Casso as possible. He wanted to see the crime scenes so that he might visualize the crime. After more than thirteen years he didn't expect to find any physical evidence, but that wasn't his objective. He liked to roam around these places by himself, collecting information, seeing how the shadows stretched through the day. He wanted to know if there were trees there that might have provided cover, or a building or an overpass nearby from which someone might have seen something, or if the streets ran north or south. You just never know what you need to know.

He started at Dyker Park. He was almost positive he knew the precise spot where the cops had picked up Hydell. It was a comfortable place for a quiet meeting: It was in the shadows, you could easily see anybody approaching, and there weren't a lot of people passing by. He sat there in his car for a long time, looking at air, wondering what Hydell thought when he saw the cops walking toward him. Had he been relieved? Did he think he was safe? Did he know Eppolito or Caracappa?

He walked down the street, looking for the pay telephone from which Jimmy Hydell had called his mother. It wasn't there. Maybe it never was there, maybe it was in a completely different location, but that was something he would never be able to determine. Betty had lost the number and location she'd obtained from the phone company and he knew too well from previous investigations that the company wouldn't have kept such records.

From there he drove to the Toys "R" Us parking lot on Flatbush Avenue where the two cops had handed Hydell over to Casso and Amuso. He drove to the back end of it. He knew that area pretty well too. It was a secluded place where he had often met informants. This was where Casso had seen Eppolito for the only time. There were a few cars in the lot, and an adult and two young kids were walking toward the store. Dades just looked around, taking it all in, etching it into his memory.

He also would have gone to see the garage where Hydell had been transferred from the backseat of the cops' car to the trunk of the second car, and the house where Casso had killed Hydell, but they hadn't identified either place yet. They knew the garage was somewhere on Nostrand Avenue and they had a pretty good idea where the house was—and they knew it belonged to a wiseguy. They were confident they'd figure out the exact locations pretty soon.

So Tommy headed for the Belt Parkway, to the spot where the two cops had pulled over Eddie Lino and Caracappa had shot him to death. Like all the other places he would visit, he knew there would be little to see, unless he could look into the past. He drove along the service road, stopping just before he reached Ocean Parkway. He walked around, feeling the place more than looking for something that wasn't there.

There are three types of evidence: physical evidence, meaning the smoking gun or, with the assistance of a good forensic lab, the smoke; circumstantial evidence, where facts and logic lead to an inescapable conclusion; and eyewitness testimony.

Tommy had already found the computer readout, but with a lot of luck, the task force might discover another little bit of physical evidence. Maybe a sheet of paper that might have been stuck in a file and forgotten or a note somebody wrote, or even evidence saved from one of the murders that could be connected to the cops, but it wasn't going to be much.

There already was a lot of circumstantial evidence, but a good defense lawyer can create an alternate reality, poking holes in a prosecutor's case, raising maybes to possibilities to doubts.

So almost from their first meeting, Vecchione, Dades, Joe Ponzi, everybody on the task force, knew their ability to convict the two cops would probably depend on gaining the cooperation of Gaspipe Casso, Burt Kaplan, or maybe even a wiseguy named Tommy Galpine. Galpine was a younger guy who had worked for Kaplan. Among his many jobs, at times he served as the liaison between Casso and Kaplan, carrying cash from Casso to Kaplan to pay the cops. And while he was a minor player, apparently he knew all about Louis Eppolito and Steve Caracappa.

This little piece of information had appeared as easily as a magician's rabbit. Apparently someone had interviewed Galpine's girlfriend while working another case. Dades didn't know how they found the girlfriend, just that they did and she told her story. According to this story, she was with Galpine in a popular Chinese restaurant in Brooklyn. During their meal Galpine looked up at a black and white photograph hanging on the wall above her head. It was a signed head shot, the kind of picture that covers the walls of every deli and Italian restaurant in New York. But this was a head shot of a burly Louie Eppolito. "See that guy?" Galpine bragged to his girlfriend. She turned to look and he explained, "That's one of our cops."

So it was known that Galpine knew. The task force decided to approach Casso first, mostly because he was already in New York, sitting in a cell in the Metropolitan Detention Center in Brooklyn, waiting to testify in another case. He was right there, just down the block, easy to get to. More importantly, he was already talking. In another case he had agreed to speak to Suffolk County detectives investigating the source of a leak that had led directly to the killing of two courageous businessmen, Robert Kubecka and Donald Barstow, who were helping detectives infiltrate the mob-controlled trash collection industry. Vecchione was actually mildly optimistic that Gaspipe would cooperate with this investigation; he knew that Casso had absolutely nothing to lose—he had been sentenced to spend his next thirteen lives in prison—and perhaps his freedom to gain. He'd already spilled once; why not do it again? If he could prove he had been telling the truth seven years earlier he might be able to get his plea agreement reinstated.

Kaplan would be the second choice. Everybody knew the One-Eyed Jew would be a tough nut to crack. The hope was that he was growing older without any chance of getting out of prison and might want to see one more sunset without bars in front of it before he died. Nobody would have bet on it though.

They would approach Tommy Galpine only as the third resort. Galpine had been convicted of dealing drugs and was serving a sixteen-year sentence in federal prison. But Galpine had remained a true believer, totally loyal to Kaplan. Vecchione believed he wouldn't talk unless Kaplan flipped. The only real hope for a prison cell conversion was that down the line he would remember he was a lot younger than his onetime boss. Kaplan was old enough to know he wasn't going to live that many years in prison; Galpine wasn't that lucky.

So that was it. While the task force was doing grunt work, Vecchione started to talk lawyer. "We agreed that I would pitch Casso first, Kaplan second, and only then Tommy Galpine," Vecchione says. "Gaspipe Casso was represented by an attorney named John D. B. Lewis. I didn't know him, but I'd learned that he shared office space down in Greenwich Village with O. J. Simpson defense lawyers Barry Scheck and Peter Neufeld. Lewis had filed Casso's final appeal after the government canceled his plea agreement, claiming in his papers that the entire arrangement, as well as Casso's role as an informer, had been compromised by the defense attorney selected by prosecutors to represent him. That attorney was a former prosecutor who apparently didn't like certain elements of the plea deal. He had tried to withdraw from the case, but when he did, prosecutors threatened to bring ethical and disciplinary charges against him. That made it impossible for him to withdraw—resulting in a serious conflict of interest. I thought it was an interesting argument that had some legal merit—the U.S. Attorney had forced Casso to keep an attorney who didn't want to be there—but the judge had tossed it out. After reading those papers it was obvious Lewis was a very good lawyer."

D. B. Lewis was one of those rare New York lawyers who actually answered his own telephone. He picked it up on the second ring. Mike Vecchione introduced himself and explained briefly the purpose of his call: He was Casso's last hope.

"We're looking at prosecuting Louis Eppolito and Steve Caracappa," Vecchione said simply. "And we could use your client's help." Secrecy certainly didn't matter here. Besides, who was Gaspipe going to tell? "I'm going to get these guys," Vecchione continued firmly, "and your guy potentially has a lot to gain by helping me. Let me tell you, I've read his 302s and I believe him. I think he was telling the truth back then. I just don't see how he's got anything to lose by helping us and if he does I'll make sure his cooperation gets in front of a judge."

Lewis was noncommittal but open to the possibility that his client would cooperate with Vecchione. For Lewis, this was probably a little like seeing a tiny light suddenly and unexpectedly go on at the distant end of a collapsed tunnel. It was a sign of life. He told Vecchione he would speak with Casso and get back to him.

Lewis returned the call a few days later. His client would be interested in working with the Brooklyn DA's office, he said, and he was very happy to know that they believed him. Then he added—Vecchione would never forget his exact words—"And he wanted me to tell you you've got the right guys."

Vecchione knew that—he didn't have even a wisp of a doubt—but still, when Lewis said that, he couldn't help smiling. *Casso wants to talk about it,* he thought. *We're gonna get them.*

The two lawyers began negotiating the ground rules, working out exactly what Casso would get in return for his testimony. Vecchione had spent years making similar deals. Generally it was pretty straightforward: Here's what I want in return for here's what I can guarantee to deliver, and here's what else I can try to do. Usually he promised as little as possible and never anything that he couldn't produce. He had been doing lawyer business for a long time.

Mike Vecchione had graduated with the first class of Hofstra University's law school still believing in the majesty of the law. He liked to tell people that everything he knew about the law he'd learned on TV, that he was a graduate of Perry Mason University. But that wasn't true; in fact he learned from reading about the great men who shaped American jurisprudence— Cardozo and Brandeis and Learned Hand, Oliver Holmes and Charles Hughes—and studying the great cases that formed the spine of our democracy. He continued to believe all of it right up to his very first day in criminal court as a member of the bar. "I'll never forget that day. I was so proud, standing right in front of the bench, wearing my brand-new suit. I was officially part of the great American tradition of jurisprudence. And then the judge, wearing the solemn robes of his office, cleared his throat, opened a top drawer in his desk, and spit right into it. And then closed the drawer.

"Well, so much for majesty."

In the years since then Vecchione had learned that while the law was a lot more than spit in a drawer, most of the time it was less than the noble words of the great justices. In real life most lawyering—even in criminal law—took place in somebody's office, reading voluminous files, conducting endless interviews, and making deals. It was a lot of negotiation—much of it aimed at staying out of the courtroom. Vecchione figured he would offer Casso some form of letter affirming that his cooperation had played a significant role in a very important case. Casso was in federal detention, so there wasn't too much Vecchione could do for him. But he was surprised at Lewis's first condition.

"Here's what we need," Lewis began. "The bottom line is you have to get the Feds to give him immunity for anything connected to the Hydell murder."

"You're kidding me," Mike responded. That was an odd request. "That's got to be covered by the pleas that he took." Casso had pled guilty to fifteen killings when he made his agreement. His admissions didn't disappear when the deal fell apart, and it was those crimes for which he had been sentenced to spend the next several hundred years in prison.

Lewis was agreeable. "Yeah, I think it is too. But do me a favor, go ahead and check to confirm that it is."

Even if it wasn't covered in his plea agreement, Vecchione continued, it didn't seem like it would be much of a roadblock. "We can probably get that for you from Feldman. He's with us on this."

Vecchione could almost hear the laughter in Lewis's response. "Boy, I got to tell you, Mike, I think you're underestimating how tough they're going to be. Even if they tell you they're going to do it, they have to put it on paper, because I just don't believe anything any of them say. Believe me, they have no interest in helping my guy."

Vecchione tried to reassure him. "Feldman's not going to let two crooked cops walk away over something minor like this. The U.S. Attorney is our partner in this investigation. Feldman'll go along with it." *He might not like it,* Mike thought, *but eventually he'll understand the value of cooperating.*

"Maybe you're right," Lewis said without conviction. "Maybe because of this case they'll do it but, Mike, I got to tell you, I don't have a lot of hope that this is going to work out. You haven't spoken to Feldman about this yet. I believe everything you say and it's probably good for my client. But I'm telling you, Feldman isn't going to let this happen."

Vecchione called Mark Feldman, who could easily find out precisely what crimes had been included in the agreement, and told him what he was trying to do. Feldman was incredulous. "Are you kidding me?" Feldman responded, his voice rising. "What do you want to use that scumbag for? Casso's a lying piece of shit."

Initially Vecchione assumed this was just Feldman letting off steam. There was no chance he hadn't been aware that eventually the task force was going to need to talk to Casso. "I don't know, Mark," he said. "The guy's right on the money. You know it as well as I do. Eventually we're gonna need him to make the case."

"Oh, come on, Mike. Nobody's gonna believe this guy. Why do you want to use him?"

"He's got the information we need, Mark," Vecchione insisted. "And I know he's telling the truth because we've already corroborated some of the things he said in his 302."

Feldman was insistent. "The guy is a piece of shit and we have no use for him."

"Bottom line, Mark, is that we do. And since it's our case, I want to use him." Vecchione explained that Casso's lawyer wanted immunity from the Feds for the Jimmy Hydell murder. "We're prepared to give it to him," he said, "but he's still gotta have it from you."

Feldman sighed. It seemed obvious to Vecchione that he still thought the whole investigation was a waste of time. "All right," he agreed, "let me see if it's covered by his plea deal. If it is then you can satisfy his guy and go ahead and do whatever you want to do."

They spoke again a few days later. "You know what, Mike?" Feldman told him, surprise in his voice. "It isn't in there. He's not covered for it."

That was just a matter of doing the paperwork, Vecchione figured. This was a no-brainer; they had everything to gain and absolutely nothing to lose. He had believed Feldman would be jumping for joy at the opportunity to get these cops. "Well, it doesn't really matter, does it? Let's be realistic here. Casso's looking at thirteen life sentences, he's got four hundred and fifty-five years. Even if he gets some consideration, what difference is it gonna make? He's not going to walk out tomorrow or next week. The greater good here is to get those two cops. So what difference does it make if you give Casso immunity on Hydell?"

Feldman said evenly, leaving no doubt about his

intention, "I wouldn't give that motherfucker anything. He's a piece of shit and I'm not giving him
anything."

Mike was stunned. "What are you talking about,
Mark? You're not giving Casso anything and look
what you're getting. How can you not make this deal?"

Feldman was adamant. He wasn't going to give
Casso one damn thing. Period.

"I don't get it, Mark; what's the big deal here?"
Vecchione continued. "I don't understand. How can
you guys get hurt by this? Any cases you got that
might be jeopardized by Casso have been done almost
ten years. How can we let two New York City detectives who have killed people get away with it? This is
horrendous." It was unnecessary for him to add that
John Gotti was dead. And no matter what Casso said
or did, there was no appeal from the grave.

"Look, Mike, that's our position. We're not giving
anything to Casso. That's it." Feldman's attitude made
no sense to Vecchione. This was the kind of deal any
prosecutor would make. Trying to make sense of Feldman's motives, he took another look at the segment *60
Minutes* had done with Casso. And as he watched the
piece, he began to speculate on the source of Feldman's absolute refusal to even consider negotiating.

In the middle of the piece Ed Bradley interviewed a
bulldog prosecutor named Valerie Caproni, who at
that time was the head of the Criminal Division of the
U.S. Attorney's Office, Eastern Division. Vecchione
knew Caproni well. After the Brooklyn DA's office
had failed to convict Lemrick Nelson Jr. for the stabbing death of an Orthodox Jew named Yankel Rosenbaum during riots in Crown Heights, he and Hynes

had gone to Washington and met with Attorney General Janet Reno to request a federal prosecution of Nelson. Caproni's office had successfully prosecuted Nelson for violating Rosenbaum's civil rights and he was sentenced to ten years in prison. The thing Vecchione remembered most about Caproni was how much she hated to lose—she didn't yield an inch without a fierce battle. She appeared in the *60 Minutes* segment on Casso, telling Ed Bradley, "He [Casso] was involved in a conspiracy to murder a federal judge. He was involved in a conspiracy to murder a federal prosecutor. He murdered and authorized the murder of witnesses. These sorts of crimes are beyond the pale."

Vecchione was astonished that the piece had gotten made. He guessed that the Attorney General's office and the Bureau of Prisons hadn't conferred about it, because there was no way the Feds could have benefited from it. The segment revealed no new information. Apparently Casso had mentioned the two cops in his interview but it had been edited out—at the time it was done Eppolito and Caracappa were not being investigated and any accusation of criminal conduct could have resulted in a huge slander suit against CBS. But the segment was still a strong accusation of malfeasance against the government.

What attracted his attention wasn't so much what Caproni said as the way she said it. Firm. Unyielding. A roadblock of granite. It became obvious to Vecchione as he watched Caproni over and over how much the Feds had to lose if they gave Casso's testimony any countenance. Only a few months earlier Caproni had become the FBI's general counsel, the head lawyer. It would not do her, or Feldman, or Henoch, or any of them a bit of good if it turned out the Feds had failed to prosecute two of the dirtiest cops in history to protect their case against John Gotti. The best thing that could happen for all of them was that this prosecution disappear. And as long as the Feds controlled Casso and Kaplan, they had the ability to make that magic.

Vecchione sat at his desk long into the evening, wondering if that might actually be true. Had the Feds really buried the case against the cops? Was that possible? He no longer held many illusions about the law, as at that moment he was deeply involved in the prosecution of a judge for taking kickbacks in return for assigning a lawyer to profitable cases, but this? This was very hard to accept.

He called D. B. Lewis once again. Maybe there was some way around this dilemma. "You were right," he admitted. "I've really gotten a lot of resistance."

"I told you that was going to happen," Lewis said. "They hate my client."

Vecchione didn't want Lewis to know about his suspicions. So he told him simply that he wasn't convinced Casso's plea agreement had been terminated for the announced reasons and that he was doing some more checking.

He tried to treat this as if it was simply a difficult negotiation, believing that it made too much sense for everybody not to work it out eventually, but his frustration level rose with each conversation. He had always taken great pride in his ability to move juries with stirring summations. He'd made courtrooms cry with emotional appeals. But Feldman wouldn't be moved. Vecchione spoke with him once again, by this time fighting to maintain his composure. "Let's talk about this, Mark," he said as impassively as possible. He laid out for him the whole strategy, reminding him how much work had already been put into this case and how close they were to making a major break-through. "I just don't understand this. Why would we let this case go by the boards when I can take Casso to the grand jury, get an indictment, then God knows what'll happen? Maybe the world'll open up for us. Maybe one of them, maybe Caracappa, will flip. Who knows? C'mon, Mark, let's take the first step. Let's get the murder indictment and go from there."

Feldman just wouldn't budge. "I won't give Casso anything," he responded as calmly as any poker player holding all the cards in the deck. "We will give him nothing." He paused and then finally allowed the first ray of hope to shine through. "I'll tell you what though, here's the best I can do for you. You can tell D. B. Lewis that we're not interested in his client."

Vecchione took a deep, calming breath. A guaran-tee not to prosecute Casso would have the same effect as official immunity, but with fewer potential political implications. Nobody's butt would be on the line. "That's terrific, Mark," he said with as much enthusi-asm as he could manage. "If that's your position, how about putting it down on paper or at least talking to Lewis and telling him that? Maybe that'll be enough for him."

The clouds of reality obliterated that small ray of hope. "I'm not going to talk to anybody about Casso," he insisted. "I don't want to talk about him at all. I don't care about Casso and we're not giving him any-thing."

Mike Vecchione hung up the phone and gathered

himself. Then he picked it up again to take another shot with Lewis. There are times when persistence wins out. "Just look at this for a minute," he told Lewis. "We're going to convict these guys. We have the evidence. If your guy goes along with us he's going to get credit for it. Let me make your guy look good. We're an agency with credibility who believes your guy. We've corroborated enough of his story to make me understand he was truthful in what he said. I'm willing to put that in papers afterward. I'm willing to outline for you in motion papers what his cooperation was, why we believed him. It's like I told you, I'm going to convict these guys and he's going to be the center of our case. That'll give you not only the papers, but you'll have a conviction based on his testimony. He can go back and say to a judge, 'See what I did? I'm not a liar.' If the state comes along and says we believe him, it's got to help your guy."

Lewis sighed. "I think that's terrific. But you have to understand our position . . ."

Mike just sat there, shaking his head. Casso was doing thirteen life sentences. Did it really make a difference if the government gave him immunity on the Hydell murder? So what if he got convicted of that crime; how much more time could he do?

That's when Vecchione made up his mind that he was going to indict Casso for his role in the Jimmy Hydell murder. He was going to put him with Eppolito and Caracappa. "I had Gaspipe's confession on *60 Minutes*," he says. "I had the ability to corroborate the crime; we got that from Betty Hydell. And we were starting to put together several other pieces to make the case."

Meanwhile, Tommy Dades was making his own

effort to get to Casso. His situation was considerably different than Vecchione's. Mike needed him to testify in a courtroom; all Dades wanted from him was information. He figured Casso, or his attorney, would recognize the benefits that might accrue from cooperating with him. If Casso could convince Dades that he was essential to making the case against Eppolito and Caracappa, he might be able to negotiate a substantially better deal with the lawyers—and maybe even get Feldman to compromise.

Two different mornings Dades went to work believing he'd be meeting with Casso later that day. The first time, he discovered that Feldman had placed a block on Casso. Gaspipe had been brought to New York as a potential witness in a federal case, so no one could speak with him without Feldman's permission.

Dades called Feldman, who agreed to let him speak to Casso—but only after the current trial was done. This was simple for Feldman, who told Dades, "You want to go talk to him, go talk to him." As Feldman had promised, when the trial ended—Casso didn't testify—he lifted the block. Again Tommy planned to go see Casso, but this time it was D. B. Lewis who wouldn't let his client speak to anyone.

At about this same time the two Suffolk County detectives were meeting with Casso to talk about the trash-hauling murders. These detectives conferred with Dades, who suggested questions they might ask. The problem, Dades discovered, was that Casso was lying to those detectives. In several instances he completely contradicted statements in his own 302. He never even mentioned Burt Kaplan's name—until Dades told the detectives to ask him directly about Kaplan's role. Only then did he remember his good friend Kaplan. As Dades told the Suffolk cops, "He admitted the truth was the truth."

As far as Dades was concerned, that was it for Casso. The guy was no good and wasn't smart enough to change, even when he had a last long shot at walking out one day. Gaspipe was still trying to play more angles than a billiards champion. Maybe he wasn't lying; maybe he'd been lying so long he no longer remembered what was truth. And maybe Pam Anderson was born with that body. It didn't matter anymore; Dades wasn't going to waste his time trying to chase Casso's lies.

This was just another incredibly frustrating dead end for Dades, who was struggling through a rough time both professionally and privately. He felt like his life was spinning and he couldn't right himself. He was losing everything that mattered. Terrorism was the new hot thing in law enforcement and no one—particularly his new boss—was paying too much attention to organized crime. And OC was what he knew; in that world he was an expert. He'd already put in his retirement papers, so basically he was marking time until he had completed his full twenty. He'd become a dinosaur.

By now this was pretty much the only case he was working on and it seemed like every avenue was being blocked by the Feds. The continued emphasis on secrecy was making it impossible for him to contact people he felt he needed to interview, and Casso was now done.

Things were going badly at home too. Ro was finding it difficult to forgive him for his affair, and even when things between them had been good he'd felt excluded. Throughout most of his career Ro had gone to her parents' on the big holidays—Christmas, New Year's, Easter, even Father's Day—and he'd been the guy volunteering to work. So he'd ended up alone, eating Chinese food, or going to his aunt's house to wait for Ro to show up with the kids. More than two years had passed since his mother's death and the emptiness she'd left didn't seem to be going away. It didn't seem like things could get a lot worse.

And then they did. One night Tommy was at the home of a close friend, retired Detective First Grade David Parello. The two of them had practically grown up together, right through high school. After retiring Parello had become a private investigator, operating his business out of his basement. Parello had made himself a virtuoso on the computer; he could find any public record in the country in a few minutes. "I got a good idea," he suggested to Tommy. "Let's look up some of our old girlfriends and see where they ended up."

Tommy had a different idea. When he heard the words coming out of his mouth even he was surprised. He didn't even know the thought had been hiding in his mind. "Why don't we throw my last name in there and see if we can find my father?"

"You're kidding?" Parello asked.

Tommy shrugged. "I don't think so."

"Okay," Parello agreed, "let's try it." Dades had spent his whole life not thinking about his father. "My mother and I were so close you figured that sometime we would have talked about my father," he says. "I was thirty-nine years old when she died and in all those years maybe the conversations we had about him added up to an hour. I never asked about him and she never said much."

He didn't know where he was, what he was doing, even if he was alive. And he'd never cared. He wasn't the slightest bit curious. At least that's what he'd convinced himself of. He knew his parents had been married for three years but together for only one of them. He knew his father's name was Peter Dades and he knew he had served in the marines for more than a decade, that he'd been in action in Vietnam and was stationed for a time in Germany. He knew he had been born in Athens, Greece, but he didn't know where in America he had lived. He had several photographs of him his mother had kept—coincidentally in one of them his father was standing in front of an army headquarters building on Fifty-eighth Street and Second Avenue, precisely the same building Tommy had worked in while assigned to Intel. And he remembered one additional minor fact: While going through some paperwork after his mother's death, he had found a transfer of title of a car from New York to Minnesota in 1962. It was an odd piece of paper for his mother to have kept, and it stuck in his mind.

Parello did a group search for the name Dades. Numerous Dadeses popped up, so they began by focusing on Dadeses in the state of Minnesota. They eliminated those people too young or too old, further narrowing the search. And within minutes they found a Peter Thomas Dades within the appropriate age group. "That's got to be him," Tommy said, staring at the screen. Perhaps the most interesting thing to him was that he still felt no emotions at all. He didn't feel happy or nervous, curious, or even satisfied. Nothing. That lack of feeling was pretty amazing.

There were no phone numbers listed for this Peter Thomas Dades. Tommy wrote down the numbers of several Dadeses in the same city. It wasn't a particularly common name, so he assumed one of these people would know about Peter Thomas Dades. The next day he called the first name on his list. When an older woman answered he said, "Excuse me, I'm looking for a man named Peter Thomas Dades who lives in the city. Do you know him?"

She did, she admitted somewhat suspiciously.

"Look," Tommy continued. "I don't want to get you scared, but I'm not crazy. I believe that he's my father. My name is Tommy Dades and I live in New York."

The woman was intrigued but noncommittal. "Are you sure?" she asked.

No, he wasn't, he admitted. "But let me ask you a few questions," he said. Was Pete in the military? Yes. Was he in the marine corps? Yes. Was he born in Athens? Yes. Did he ever live in Brooklyn?

"Yes."

It was him; Tommy knew it. Peter Thomas Dades. On a whim, he'd found his father. The woman began opening up to him, explaining that Pete Dades was her brother. Tommy asked if she had a phone number for him. Her answered surprised him. "No, I don't really talk to him anymore." She hesitated. "But I probably can get it for you."

The following day his phone rang at home. A much younger-sounding woman asked, "Is this Tommy Dades?" Yeah, he answered; who's this? "I'd rather not say."

"Well, if you're not going to tell me who you are this conversation isn't going to go too far."

After a brief pause, she said, "I'm your aunt Elaine." Tommy had always known he had an aunt by that name. She asked him a few questions to confirm his identity, then admitted, "I know all about you, Tommy." Then she began telling him about his father. Incredibly, he was a private investigator, having worked previously in the District Attorney's office. He had met a woman while stationed in Germany, divorced Tommy's mother, and married her. They had two children, a girl named Maria and a son, a son he had named Thomas Peter Dades.

For the first time Tommy felt something about his father—something bad. He felt like somebody had reached into his gut, grabbed hold of his stomach, and was twisting it inside out. His father had given his second son the same name, Tommy. There was no mistaking the meaning of that. As far as his father was concerned, he had ceased to exist. Once again, he had been abandoned. Then his aunt told him, "I'll give you his number, but I'm not going to call him for you. You're going to have to decide on your own if you really want to speak to him. I have to warn you, he's not a very nice guy. And, truthfully, I can't understand why you're doing it."

Anger? Loneliness? A need to move his life out of neutral? Or maybe just because there was no good reason not to. It wasn't a good answer, he understood that, but it was the only one he had.

He went to the gym that night and started hitting the heavy bag. When everything around him was falling apart the gym was the one place he felt he belonged. In the gym he was welcomed and appreciated for the person he was. He loved the sport of boxing. It was a world in which the rules were clear: Hit the other guy more than he hits you. There were no shades of gray, no bureaucracy, no tantalizing clues leading to solutions just around the next corner and next corner. Just hit the other guy more than he hits you. And no wives who felt betrayed, or mothers who had died, or fathers who . . . He hit the bag hard that night.

Tommy dialed his father's number the next morning. The answering machine clicked on. For the first time in his life Tommy heard his father's voice. He left a message: "This is your son. Tommy. I'm just calling to say hello to you. You can call me at . . ."

His father returned his call that night—and left his own message: "I don't know who this is, but I got a call from you. I think you probably have the wrong guy. But if you want to call back, call me tomorrow morning at . . ."

They spoke the next day. Tommy had never imagined the sound of his father's voice, so nothing about the sound of it surprised him. Nor did his cold words. "I'm sorry," Peter Thomas said, "but I think you're mistaken. I don't think you got the right person."

"I'm not mistaken. I know exactly who you are," Tommy said firmly. "If you want to deny who you are to me, go ahead, that's your business. But if you do . . . then I think you're a coward. Look, I'm not calling you looking for anything, I'm just calling out of curiosity. My mother passed away a little while ago; I probably never would have looked for you if she hadn't died. I just basically called you on a whim. If you don't believe who I am, go buy a book called *Mob over Miami*. It's about a case I broke. There's a picture of me and my name in the book. You'll see, I do look like you. Then call me back."

Several days passed without any response. At times Tommy wondered if he'd hear from his father again. He'd already made the decision that he would never call him again. He'd done as much as possible. But even as he concentrated on the investigation the question hung somewhere in his mind, like the slightly out-of-focus background of a snapshot.

At work he continued trying to pin down the location of the garage in which Eppolito took Hydell out of the first car and put him in the trunk of a second car, and the house in which Casso killed him. That switch inside the garage had taken place during the day; it was quite possible—even probable—that there was a witness or witnesses to it. Find the garage and maybe find a witness. And who knows what type of physical evidence might still be found in the house? In another mob execution that took place in a basement, years after the shooting, detectives had found a bullet that had gone through a plasterboard wall and lain untouched on the floor behind that wall, long after the hole it made had been patched and painted over. You just never know.

But still, Tommy wasn't surprised when Peter Dades called him back. "Sir, you really are my son," he said quite formally. Sir. The strange use of that word said much about him. "I don't know what to say to you." And so they started talking. He asked about Tommy's mother and his grandparents, about other members of the family.

They were dead, Tommy told him. He then asked about Tommy's life. Tommy told him about his wife and his own kids, about his career. He told him about the cases he'd solved and the awards he'd won, from the FBI, the DEA, even a Black Achievement Award. "I'm not going to cause you any trouble," Tommy said. "I want you to know that. I don't want anything from you. If you think that's why I called you, you're wrong. I'm doing fine myself. I drive a brand-new car. I'm going to send you pictures of my house; we even have a built-in pool. Maybe once we get past that you can be a little more cordial to me."

Peter Thomas Dades was less forthcoming with the details of his own life. He had a son and a daughter, he said. He said he was still with his wife, then suggested they were living apart. It was a discussion of the facts of their lives, devoid of warmth. It was a small step taken vaguely in the direction of a relationship.

They began corresponding through letters rather than on the phone. They exchanged photographs. Tommy received photographs taken on his parents' wedding day. They were well preserved; someone had handled them carefully. He got photographs taken during the Vietnam War and taken more recently.

Those conversations they did have most often ended curtly. Peter usually spoke in generalities, avoiding anything truly personal. At one point though, he did say that sometime in the future they would meet and he'd talk more about certain things. But on another occasion he said snappishly, "You know, I don't owe you any explanation. Two people got married, they got divorced, and that's it."

Tommy couldn't let that one go. This was as close to real anger as he'd come since making that first phone call. "Hey, I'm a father. It's not like you just had a wife and you didn't get along so you parted ways. How do you have a son and . . . and you're a PI, you had the ability to find me. Weren't you curious about your kid?"

"No," he said.

"Okay, that's fine, at least you're being honest."

Tommy also spoke to other members of his family. His grandmother, who was in a nursing home, welcomed him. He spoke often to his aunt Elaine and established a warm relationship with her. His half brother and half sister both told him that as far as being raised by their father went, he "didn't miss anything." And he even spoke with his father's wife. "I hope you're not mad at me for all this," he said to her.

"No, no, not at all. I'm happy to talk to you." She was quite open and friendly, telling him, "I wanted him to find you for a long time. We had so many fights about it. I used to ask him how he could have a son and not want to know what his story is." They all thought Tommy was crippled, she said, because in the one baby picture they had he had braces on his legs.

Tommy laughed at that. "No, I'm fine. I was born bow-legged; that's what that was," he explained. "They were just straightening out my legs."

Time passed, but both at work and in his personal life, Dades felt like he was standing still. He was making little progress in the investigation and in his relationships with his father and with Ro. It was like he was running just to stay on top of the quicksand; he was working hard and getting nowhere. He'd never worked a case as frustrating as this one. Usually, the object of an investigation is identifying the perp. The evidence is the trail that gets you there. This one was entirely different. This one started with a witness providing key evidence against the killers. They were starting near the end and backtracking to find evidence. And they had seventeen years of catching up to do.

But that was barely a blink of time compared to the catching up he had to do with his father, and he had him walking blind through an emotional minefield. He was almost always comfortable when conducting an investigation. Whatever the situation, he'd been there before. But his relationship with his father was different. He had no emotional resources on which to draw, no experience, no one to talk to about it. Finally, one Saturday, Dades was in his office speaking with his father when Peter made a derogatory comment about his ex-wife, Tommy's mother. He started to tell a story about a night she did something that caused him to get beaten up. Tommy exploded, letting loose all his frustration, screaming at him, "Who do you think you are to speak about my mother like that! You don't have the right. You left her like a dog and shut the lights off. She had to go live with her parents. She almost died giving birth to me. My mother was a wonderful woman who had a miserable life and you had a lot to do with that. Her whole life, she never said a single derogatory word about you. So who do you think you are to judge her . . ."

The conversation ended abruptly and angrily, but not the relationship. It seemed obvious Peter was as ambivalent about it as his son. Peter wrote a letter telling Tommy, basically, "Leave me alone, I don't want to be bothered with you again."

And then he called, telling his son to disregard the last part of the letter—the part in which he warned Tommy not to contact him again.

Sometimes Peter Dades made Gaspipe Casso seem logical.

Tommy wrote back, for the first time sending him pictures of his own children and telling his father, "You have two beautiful, smart grandchildren."

Peter Dades didn't write back. He didn't call. Once again, he disappeared from his son's life. He cut off all contact without any explanation.

Eventually a family member explained that Peter had wanted nothing to do with Tommy after he learned Tommy was talking to another member of the family. It was a complicated story. There was nothing Tommy could do about it but finally let loose his hatred for his father, the man he'd just found. He went through a period in which he felt embarrassed to have the man's genes in him and accepted the fact that contacting him had been a great mistake—except for the aunt and grandmother he found.

In every aspect of his life he was becoming more and more isolated.

His closest friends, Vecchione, Ponzi, Parello, and all the others, tried to help, but there really wasn't too much anyone else could do beyond showing up and offering support. This was a stew of his own making. So as he had done other times in his past when the problems of his life threatened to become overwhelming, he dived deep into the job.

In the investigation Vecchione continued to believe that somehow, some way, he would eventually get access to Casso and that his testimony would help hang the cops. Other people were telling him to forget about Gaspipe, that even if he agreed to testify Vecchione couldn't risk putting him on the stand. According to the government of the United States of America, Casso was a no-good liar. It would be very difficult to convince a jury that the federal government had that wrong, that instead of believing two highly decorated detectives they should believe a stone-cold killer who'd confessed to seventy crimes, including fifteen murders.

Well, it wouldn't be easy. But Vecchione had been both a prosecutor and a defense attorney. He'd questioned and cross-examined just about every type of witness imaginable. He'd convicted numerous killers, and in many of those cases he'd depended on the testimony of even-more-violent killers. And he'd won the vast majority of those cases. He'd faced the jury and told them that his witness was a lowlife—and then reminded them that the only people bad guys would commit crimes in front of, or confess to, were people from their world. In that world the only people who could be trusted were thieves and killers. He had no doubt that if Casso went for a deal, he would find some way to squeeze the full value from his testimony.

Of course, that "if" remained the problem. Mark Feldman was intractable. But at the same time he was telling Vecchione he wouldn't give Casso immunity for the Hydell murder, he was telling Dades and Ponzi that he was keeping Casso in New York so they could interview him as soon as an agreement was concluded. That was real cute, Vecchione thought, real cute. For his friends he was playing the good guy, saying he was keeping Casso close by so they could get in and see him, while at the same time knowing that he wasn't going to agree to any deal. Vecchione finally decided to approach Feldman's boss, Chief of the Criminal Division Dan Alonso. He called Feldman to inform him he was going over his head, to his boss, and he didn't want to do so without telling him. Turned out it didn't matter; before Vecchione spoke with Alonso, he was told not to bother, because Alonso was not going to do anything for him. Another brick wall.

Vecchione didn't want to give up. He discussed the situation with his own boss, Brooklyn DA Joe Hynes, who confirmed that Feldman had him in a box. "What is, is," Hynes said. "We can't make them do something they don't want to do."

That left Casso's lawyer, D. B. Lewis. Vecchione spoke with him several more times, trying to convince him that this was his client's only shot at changing the equation. "I don't understand the problem," he said. "Your guy's already confessed to Hydell's murder on national television. If the Feds were going to prosecute him for it, they would have done it a long time ago. His own words would have hung him. It doesn't make any sense not to talk to me.

"We're giving him a chance to get back into court. Once he gets there who knows what a judge'll do? Right now Casso's got nothing. You know as well as I do that the Feds wouldn't dare prosecute him for testifying against two dirty cops. They already got him for fifteen murders. And this'll give him what he needs, a law enforcement agency verifying what he said was true. Once he gives us what we need, we're gonna go out and corroborate a lot of it, something nobody else has done. We've already corroborated some of it." Vecchione gave him no details about the investigation beyond what was absolutely necessary and perhaps even hinted they had more than they actually did.

Lewis replied that he would talk to Casso "and make every attempt to get him in."

It didn't work. Lewis reported to Vecchione that without a written guarantee of immunity on the Hydell killing from both the Feds and the state Casso wouldn't speak to him.

Vecchione's own feeling was that Lewis was being too much of a lawyer, that he was hurting his client. The entire situation seemed crazy to him—Feldman refusing to grant immunity for a crime he had no intention of prosecuting; Casso—or Lewis—turning down the only shot he had at a reduced sentence. Vecchione made one final plea to Lewis: "Do me a favor. Let me come into the jail and speak to him. You be right there, but just give me one shot. One shot, that's all, to see if I can convince him."

Vecchione was confident that he, Dades, and Ponzi could persuade Casso to talk to them. Each of them had spent much of their career convincing reluctant witnesses to do just that. But they never got the chance. According to Lewis, until his client had immunity he wasn't interested in meeting with anyone working the two cops case. Years later, though, Vecchione was told by someone in prison with Casso that Gaspipe had wanted to speak to him. In fact, long after it would have done any good, Casso wrote to Vecchione and had a second lawyer call him to confirm that he wanted to take his last shot. But it all came too late, much too late.

Just like Dades, Mike Vecchione was incredibly frustrated—and really pissed off. Casso was done; he was out of the equation. That left only one path to the cops. Vecchione turned the page and took a good, long look at the One-Eyed Jew.

CHAPTER 8

As the investigation expanded into new and promising directions, trying to maintain secrecy was like trying to catch the wind in a strainer. While there was no direct evidence that anyone outside the task force had learned about it, all of a sudden inexplicable things began happening.

On a beautiful afternoon in late fall 2003, Mike Vecchione was in his office making last-minute preparations for the surrender of Brooklyn's Democratic political boss Clarence Norman. For Vecchione, this was the culmination of a long undercover operation. Another crooked politician was going to take a fall. The media was going to love this one. This was a front-page indictment.

So when Vecchione's phone rang he just assumed it concerned the last-minute details of Norman's arraignment. To his surprise, it was his sister. "Mike," she said anxiously. "You'd better get right home."

His first thought was his eighty-three-year-old

father, with whom he lived in the house in Queens. "What's the matter? Is Dad okay?"

"No no no, he's fine. But somebody broke into the house. They wrecked it."

"I raced out to Queens," says Vecchione. "After my divorce I'd moved into my parents' small home until I could get resettled. It was just a temporary stop; I didn't expect to be there more than a few months. Then my mother died unexpectedly and my father had a quadruple bypass and was diagnosed with prostate cancer. There was no way I could leave my father there alone. Ten years later I was still living there.

"My father lived on the main floor, while I had a small bedroom and office upstairs. It wasn't terrible; the house was close enough to my ex-wife and my two sons to enable me to get over there easily and often. It wasn't perfect, but it had worked out well for all of us—until I got that phone call.

"I didn't know what to expect. By the time I got home the cops were already there. Somebody had really wanted to get in—they'd taken a big chance by kicking in the side door in daylight. I began walking through the house, and I couldn't believe what I was seeing. Whoever it was had ransacked my bedroom and my office. They'd pried open locked desk drawers and dumped them on the floor, pulled out every bureau drawer and thrown the clothes around the room, they'd ripped apart the closet and stripped the bed, they'd knocked over the bookcases and cabinets. My whole life had been dumped on the floor. I couldn't believe it—and then the situation got worse. A day earlier I'd cashed a large check to cover my son's high school tuition and my Christmas gifts. That money was gone, I figured.

"And then I went down into the finished basement. What they'd done down there was even worse. They'd stuffed up the toilet with paper, then defecated in it and flushed it over and over and over and then left it running. The basement floor was flooded with fecal-polluted water.

"But truthfully, it was what I discovered on the first floor, my father's floor, that really shook me up. There was almost no damage at all and nothing had been taken. My father's coin collection, his jewelry, none of that had been touched. The thieves had barely touched anything in his bedroom. So it was pretty obvious that this wasn't an ordinary robbery—somebody was sending me a message.

"My father had been at work—he does fine-jewelry enameling—so he was okay. The whole thing was just overwhelming. I sat down on the living room couch, and I cried."

And then he returned to his office to accept the surrender of Clarence Norman, who arrived trailed by a large entourage of supporters, reporters, and cameramen. Norman treated it like a political rally, stopping outside the building to make a brief speech, then cavalierly marching inside.

As the shock dissipated over the next few days, Vecchione began considering the facts. And they were chilling. This did not have the hallmarks of a random break-in. Whoever had done this presumably had been watching the house. They appeared to know that Mike lived on the upper floor. Obviously they knew when no one was at home. The fact that they had gone through all his papers might mean they were looking for something specific, but he doubted that. No one could possibly believe he kept important papers at home. His first reaction was that this break-in was somehow connected to the Norman indictment. A basic fuck-you-very-much gesture. That was the logical conclusion. It had taken place the day Norman was to be arrested.

It didn't occur to him that this might have something to do with the Eppolito and Caracappa investigation until he had a conversation with his close friend Assistant District Attorney Joe Petrosino. Petrosino, who lived only a couple of miles away from Vecchione in Queens, is in charge of prosecuting all vehicular crimes for Hynes's office. That includes everything from drunk driving to hit-and-runs. When Petrosino heard about the robbery he told Vecchione about some similar problems he'd had.

Petrosino recently had prosecuted two egregious drunk-driving cases involving cops. He hadn't given either officer any kind of break. And as a result strange things began happening around his house. All four tires on his car were flattened. Garbage was thrown on the front lawn. Beer bottles filled with urine were left out in front. Someone wrote in the dust on the back of his car "We know you." The telephone rang at odd hours and threatening messages were left for him. Eventually Internal Affairs got involved. Security cameras were installed around his house; his phones were wired. On several occasions the cameras got pictures of a dark car stopping in front of the house, but no one was ever identified.

Vecchione still tended to believe that the break-in had something to do with Clarence Norman—Norman had been indicted, and a month later additional charges were lodged against him—rather than the cops. Others around him didn't share that belief. If

Eppolito and Caracappa had found out they were being investigated, who knew how they would respond? These were well-connected men, mob guys, and if Casso was telling the truth, they were murderers with nothing to lose.

Normally, the mob doesn't go after cops and prosecutors. It's one of those unspoken rules of organized crime warfare. Besides, the promise of payback is too tough. Hit a cop or a prosecutor and all the rules are off. Anything goes. But as Vecchione knew, Casso and the cops played by their own rules. As Casso admitted in his 302, he had already plotted against a prosecutor, against Eastern District ADA Charlie Rose. So Vecchione didn't kid himself; his title offered him little protection from the mob.

There wasn't too much he could do about it except clean up the house. It took industrial cleaners several weeks to return the basement to a livable condition. But overall, he figured, he was lucky. His father hadn't been home and so was never in danger; the thieves had failed to find most of the cash he had at home and hadn't touched his father's belongings. And whatever warning they were trying to send to him, it didn't work. Threats didn't make him back down. Ever.

Within a couple of weeks all that remained of the break-in were some anxious memories and the stains on the basement walls. And then he got the second threat. He knew where this one came from; it was from a murderer he'd put in prison. This one was pretty straightforward: "I'm gonna kill Vecchione," he'd told an informer. Even that threat didn't really worry him. Just about everybody on the right side of the law has received death threats at some time during their career. Vecchione had gotten his share. One of

Vecchione's first major trials was the prosecution of two mob guys who were being tried for killing another lowlife. Unfortunately, his key witness was slightly insane. At various times this guy had told people he was a doctor and that he'd driven in the Indianapolis 500, which were both completely untrue. But he had seen the murder and he claimed he could identify the two defendants. Vecchione knew his witness would have some trouble surviving a cross-examination, but he also believed he could support the key elements of his testimony with other evidence.

One night, as Vecchione and this witness left the office and walked out onto the sweeping steps of the municipal building, the witness told him, "Uh, you know, Mike, maybe you'd better not stand too close to me."

Vecchione looked at him quizzically. "What? Are you kidding me?"

He shook his head. "Don't stand too close. There's a lot of people that don't like me." He pointed to his right. "You go that way, I'll go the other way."

"You're kidding, right?"

He wasn't kidding at all. As Vecchione was to learn, he was in a business in which sudden and sometimes unexpected death was part of the job description. So he just never worried about it.

Vecchione took this threat from prison less seriously than some of his colleagues. Imprisoned tough guys are always boasting about what they are going to do to the cop or prosecutor who put them away, but very rarely do those threats become reality. Every once in a while, though, you do get a skell like John Pappa, who sat in his car in front of Dades's home waiting to kill him. But just in case this threat to Vecchione was real, security in the DA's office was immediately increased—and the DA assigned detectives to guard him around the clock.

Dades tried to determine the seriousness of this threat. It had been made by a wiseguy he and Vecchione had convicted of homicide in the skull case. He went out to the detention center on Rikers Island and wired up the informant who had told authorities about the threat, then put him with the killer who'd supposedly made it. But the informer couldn't get him to repeat it.

It was a third seemingly unrelated event that changed Vecchione's life. This one was simple and direct: Very early one morning a few weeks later someone smashed in the rear window of his car. No other cars on the street were touched. And when technicians were replacing the window they discovered a stash of marijuana that someone had hidden in the ceiling of the car. It seemed probable that "someone" had smashed the window so the drugs would be discovered—and maybe destroy Vecchione's career. But Vecchione had spent too many years building his reputation for anyone to believe the pot belonged to him. Either these incidents were simply an unpleasant coincidence or somebody out there was sending a real strong message. After the burglary, the threat, and the broken rear window, Joe Hynes decided Vecchione needed real protection once again.

For the first time in his career Mike Vecchione admitted he was scared, but for his father rather than for himself. He was confident he could handle pretty much any situation, but his father was eighty-three years old and frail. Vecchione still didn't know for certain that these events were even connected to a specific case, but he could no longer ignore that possibility. Hynes reassigned bodyguards to both Vecchione and his father. The DA office's technical unit installed security cameras inside and around the house. The NYPD equipped the house with a state-of-the-art panic alarm. This is a fail-safe system hardwired into the telephone lines. If someone cut the phone lines a signal would instantly be sent to the nearest police precinct. The techies also put a panic button next to his bed and gave him a button device on a neck chain to wear when he was in the house. "If anything out of the ordinary happens," one of the men installing the system explained, "you just hit this button."

Mike asked, "What happens then?"

The cop told him, "The whole world will respond. You'll get everybody, the precinct, the borough, emergency service, special operations, they'll all respond immediately. So do us a favor, be real careful with it."

Vecchione smiled at the thought. "Oh, I don't think you need to worry about that." Knowing the panic button was there when his father was at home alone made him feel more secure. The worst aspect of the protection, for him, was the bodyguards. It was ironic; he'd spent much of his career dealing with scum and had never felt like he was in danger. Now he was prosecuting politicans and cops and something very strange was going on. He didn't want bodyguards, but Hynes insisted. They began protecting him at a most inopportune time—just as a new relationship was beginning to get serious.

He had started dating an assistant ADA from Manhattan about six months earlier—and to his surprise had fallen in love with her. At the beginning of this investigation he had been very circumspect about it.

He hadn't said a word about it to her. It had nothing to do with trust; he just believed he should keep it inside the task force. But as it began occupying more time in his life, he couldn't keep it a secret. The fact that she was an excellent lawyer as well as an experienced prosecutor made him feel comfortable discussing it with her. It wasn't light dinner conversation, but he did keep her informed about the investigation's progress. She actually proved very helpful. The only people in his own office who knew about it—he believed—were the members of the task force and Joe Hynes. At times while directing the investigation he had to make legal decisions and wanted someone to provide a little counsel. She proved to be the perfect person for that job.

It was only when Mike showed up for a date accompanied by bodyguards that she became very concerned about his safety. Mike tried to treat the whole thing as little more than a misunderstanding. He didn't want to alarm her. But the constant presence of two burly detectives made that almost impossible. "Why are you taking this so lightly?" she demanded. "This isn't a joke."

He didn't have a good answer to that question. And the more he considered it, the more he began to understand that maybe he should be taking this situation a lot more seriously. It seemed like somebody had a real gripe against him. There was no telling how far it might go.

The bodyguards interfered with their relationship. One beautiful New York night, for example, Mike and his date went to a quiet restaurant on Columbus Avenue. They sat across from each other at a small table, speaking in low voices, low enough so the two big, armed DA investigators sitting nearby couldn't hear them. Vecchione's date lived nearby, so as he began to walk her home he told the cops, "We're okay, you know. You don't need to come with us. We're just gonna walk a couple of blocks."

To which one of them responded, "Nothing's going to happen to you on our watch. We were ordered to guard you, so we're going to guard you." They walked slowly back to her apartment, just the four of them, chatting pleasantly. And then Vecchione and his bodyguards drove back to his home in Queens.

Fortunately, Dades and Vecchione balanced each other. Their personal battles came at different times, enabling each to provide support for the other one when it was needed. Both of them had the ability to focus completely on a problem, eliminating the surrounding static. So no matter what was going on in their personal lives, they didn't bring their home life to the office. Meanwhile, Joe Ponzi remained steadfast, an anchor for his friends, his own life stable. But there still were the frequent conversations with his father, who had commanded Eppolito and Caracappa, who knew them both, and who still found it so hard to believe that two cops he had trusted could be so completely corrupt.

Joe had to be extremely careful not to reveal to his father any information about the progress of the investigation. Confidential means confidential. It was hard for him, but his father was a cop, so he knew how it worked and didn't ask questions. But on those occasions when the conversation would end up focused on Eppolito and Caracappa, it was Larry Ponzi who shared his memories. "When Steve was working undercover for me," Larry told Joe, "he had a ponytail, he had a beard, so I called him into my office one day and I asked, 'What are you trying to do, look like Serpico?' "

Joe finally asked him, "What do you think? Think they could have done all this?"

Larry Ponzi shook his head and responded, "Honestly, I got to tell you, I just don't see it. Tell me Eppolito beat somebody within an inch of his life, tell me he's got more civilian complaints than any cop who ever lived, tell me that maybe he was taking money from somebody or that he dangled some guy out a window and I'd say, that could be, this was a guy who liked to live big. But this other stuff, to be on the pad for the boss of the Lucchese family and to be a hands-on participant in whacks? No, that just couldn't be. No."

At the weekly meetings Vecchione and Henoch continued making assignments. Tommy Dades moved forward in several directions, trying to find routes of investigation that wouldn't be blocked by the Feds' obsession with secrecy.

For example, Casso claimed that he had handed over Hydell's body to two Lucchese soldiers, Frank Lastorino and Joey Testa, for disposal. After that he didn't know what happened to it. Dades wanted to find out exactly how much Lastorino and Testa knew about the killing. Testa was in prison serving several life terms; Lastorino had about eight years left in his sentence but had had some problems and lost his phone privileges. Dades was going to talk to both men. He couldn't offer them any time reduction, but he could make their lives a little easier. If they told him where to find Hydell's body, which might provide some physical evidence to verify another aspect of Casso's story, he could make sure that the remainder of their time in prison was a lot more pleasant. He didn't expect to find much left of Hydell. He guessed the body had been cut up and buried somewhere. But who knew what went into the ground with him? Maybe Eppolito or Caracappa had stuffed a handkerchief in Hydell's mouth and covered it with duct tape. Maybe a tiny piece of that duct tape had been overlooked when they disposed of the body and had a partial fingerprint on it. Maybe some hairs or fibers got caught under his fingernails or in the rope that bound his feet or in the handcuffs that held his hands. It was worth taking a shot at them.

But every time Dades began planning to meet either man, the Feds would block him. Supposedly they were concerned he would reveal too much information about the investigation, that word would get out.

That happened over and over to Dades, Ponzi, to all the investigators. They weren't permitted to do what they'd been doing throughout their careers—talk to people who had information and get it out of them.

Shut out from a primary source, Dades followed the paper trail. As he had done so many times previously, he read and reread the folders in his office, looking for the next bit of information that had been overlooked. For a time he got intrigued by Casso's claim that Eppolito and Caracappa had planned to kill Sammy Gravano in 1988. Supposedly they sat in their car watching Gravano's office at 1809 Stillwell Avenue on and off for three months, waiting for him to make a mistake. But he was always with too many people for them to make a move.

What few people other than Dades knew or remembered was that the NYPD was also watching Gravano at that time. He knew it because his former partner

Patty Pesce spent eight hours a day sitting in an apartment directly above a fish store taking surveillance photographs. If the detectives had been there, it was possible Patty had caught them on police *Candid Camera*. Dades got hold of literally thousands of photographs taken during that period. And he looked through them one by one by one, over and over. He remembers, "I went through them like crazy. I didn't even know exactly what I was looking for—anything that connected Eppolito and Caracappa to that place. Whatever it might be, if it was there, I knew I would find it." He searched the pictures for vehicles or license plate numbers that might be associated with the cops, looking for one or both of them walking down a street carrying a cup of coffee or leaning against the car smoking a cigarette, looking for one-tenth of a second in the past that proved the two cops were there. He spent days going through the photographs—and found nothing. Just another idea that went nowhere.

Dades also remembered reading in some report somewhere that one of the detectives sitting on Sammy had confronted Eppolito and Caracappa. Apparently this unidentified detective didn't know who these two guys were but spotted them sitting there day after day. He probably asked the usual questions: What are you doing here? Where are you from? That detective could put Eppolito and Caracappa together when they weren't supposed to be together, doing exactly what Casso said he had sent them to do. Dades's problem was that he couldn't identify the detective. There were no records he could check, no other cops who knew who it might be. Patty Pesce had no idea who he was. Finding that detective would have been a grand slam, but he just couldn't do it.

The task force continued spending a lot of time trying to identify the garage in which Hydell was transferred to the trunk. They talked about it a lot at their meetings, tossing out ideas, trying to find the right approach. While it seems like a specific garage on Nostrand Avenue would be pretty easy to locate, in fact this was a tough and very tiresome task. Unlike TV cop shows, in which investigations move smoothly and rapidly, with each step bringing the cops just a little closer to the perp, in real life an investigation usually takes months, often nothing happens for long periods of time, and sometimes the biggest enemy to be overcome is boredom. If Bill Oldham wanted to speak to a potential source, for example, sometimes he had to begin by finding someone who knew where that source might be found. A lot of the people living in this world didn't have legitimate jobs where they could be found nine to five Monday to Friday or homes where they spent each night. So to find that someone who knew how to find the source, he might have to backtrack three people. That's the drudgery of a real investigation.

Dades also got in touch with several retired cops who knew the neighborhood. Cops learn the secrets of the places they work. They know what happens behind locked doors and late at night. They know where the power is and the people who make things happen. The one bit of information they had about the garage—this came from an informant—was that at one point the owner was being shaken down by a Lucchese capo named Bruno Facciola. The owner knew Eppolito and Caracappa from the precinct and asked them for help. They turned to Kaplan, who brought it to Casso, and the problem was solved. That's the kind of story that gets known around a precinct. Tommy asked people who had been there at the time if they had ever heard anything about a garage around Nostrand that was having some problems with a wiseguy and got some help from Gaspipe Casso. That was as much information as he could give them. Once again, some people had a vague memory of something like that happening, but nobody had an address for him.

The search for the garage continued.

They had a lot more success finding the house in which Hydell had been murdered. Casso didn't remember the address; all he remembered was that it was close to Toys "R" Us and it was owned by a Mafia soldier. By going through real estate tax bills and other documents the task force was able to narrow it down to three or four locations. But one of them had belonged to a wiseguy named James Gallo who was known to be associated with people around Casso. Finally, they had the house.

Jimmy Hydell had been murdered in the basement of an ordinary house on East Seventy-third Street. New York Real Property records confirmed the house was then owned by James Gallo, who'd sold it two years later. Casso explained that Gallo's house was used because it was close to the Toys "R" Us parking lot, it had a finished basement, and Gallo and his family were away on vacation. Tommy wasn't going to be able to speak with Gallo; he had died a long time ago. But the house, the murder scene, was still there.

East Seventy-third Street was tree lined and quiet. During the day it seemed almost deserted. The house was larger than a Cape Cod but certainly no mansion. A comfortable place with a bloody history.

Nothing in this case came easy. The ownership of

the house was legally murky. Two years after the murder Gallo had sold it to a now elderly woman. This woman had recently resold it, but the new buyers hadn't yet closed on it. The deal was set, but they were waiting to do the final walk-through. The elderly owner proved to be very cooperative, although she was quite surprised to learn what horrors had taken place in her basement. She gave the task force permission to search the place. But the closing date already had been scheduled, so there was some discussion about whether or not the buyers had the right to be notified. Informing them that at least one person— and maybe more—had been murdered in the basement of the house they'd just bought might make them hesitate about closing. Some people get very sensitive about murders in the basement. And if they decided to walk away based on information provided by law enforcement, who knew what might happen? It sounded like it could be the basis of one of those weird lawsuits the papers love to write about. Eventually the situation was explained to the new owners, who also granted permission to search the place.

Just to make certain everything was done completely legally, Vecchione drew up a search warrant allowing investigators, accompanied by forensic scientist Ralph Ristenbat, an employee of the Chief Medical Examiner's office, and his associates, to search the scene. As Dades stipulated, "I am . . . informed by Ralph Ristenbat that, based on his experience and training, he is aware that physical evidence, including blood, bodily fluids, tissue samples, and bone fragments can remain at and be recovered from crime scene areas over 17 years after the crime occurred. He further states that such samples can survive washing and painting of the area, and that samples recovered over 17 years after an incident may be successfully used to conduct DNA testing that can provide evidence relating to the death . . ." The affidavit requested permission to remove "floorboards, ceiling and flooring" to enable examiners to search for evidence.

Only a few years ago most people outside law enforcement had never heard of forensic science. But numerous nonfiction and dramatic television shows have made it the hottest major on college campuses as well as the subject of many books. A forensic scientist identifies physical evidence and attempts to link it to a specific person or persons. Dades had worked often with the NYPD crime scene team but preferred the more meticulous DNA evidence collection team from the Medical Examiner's office at Bellevue Hospital.

The task force knew that chances of finding any physical evidence in the house were slim to nonexistent, but the basement still had to be searched. Even if they found nothing, they had proved that the house Casso described as being close to the Toys "R" Us actually existed, that it was owned by John Gallo, that Gallo was an associate of an organized crime family, and that he was known by and associated with people within Gaspipe Casso's circle. And if during the trial a clever defense lawyer asked Dades if they'd found the crime scene and bothered to search it, the answer would be yes, sir.

No one was currently living in the house. Dades went with Detectives Mike Galletta and Jimmy Harkins and several other investigators from Hynes's office as well as Ralph Ristenbat's team. From the very beginning of this investigation Dades had been running into brick walls—but this time he ran into walls of mirrors.

The basement had been completely renovated since the killing—twice. The entire room was now covered with mirrors. The walls, the ceiling, everything except the floor was mirrored. It was like being in a fun house lacking the fun. The floor was covered with worn tiles, but it was impossible to even guess when they had been installed. Reflected in those mirrors, the small search team was magnified into an army. The mirrors also made the search even more difficult, as it would be necessary to break them to get behind the walls.

Even if the room hadn't been touched since the murder it was unlikely they would find any evidence. Normal life erases most traces of the past. Any evidence that had been left there in 1986 almost definitely had been wiped, washed, vacuumed, swept, or painted away. But still they scoured the room. As the search team went to work Dades stood to the side, imagining ghosts. He wondered where in the room they had put Hydell. Where did they kill him? Toward the back, he guessed; that's the way it was usually done, as far away from any windows as possible.

The searchers swept the floors, reaching as far as possible under the floorboards. They chipped away at several floor tiles. Because oblique lighting casts shadows that enable people to see things unseen under ceiling lighting or lamps, they turned off all the lights and laid their flashlights on the floor, looking for anything unusual. They poked several holes in the walls and searched behind them, looking for patches, a piece of cloth, maybe a bullet hole or even a spent bullet. And they found nothing. Tommy Dades checked the house off his list.

Dades and Ponzi, Bobby I, Oldham, they just kept

going, checking leads, following paths that led into rooms of mirrors, going nowhere. What makes cold cases so tough is that the network of informants that every good detective builds has little value. Dades had maybe fifty informants on the street, multiplied by the number of people each one of those guys could reach out to and question. But this was the next generation of skells. The old-timers, the class of '86, were mostly gone, dead or in prison. Those few guys still around who had been there back when remembered nothing. Maybe they knew the price of every score they'd made, and they remembered the legendary deals and the disputes and the big-time players. But even Tommy and Mike had to admit that Casso had been smart enough to keep the biggest secret of his career to himself—the identities of the Mafia cops.

Burt Kaplan was going to be the key to convicting the cops. That had become apparent to everyone. Dades, Ponzi, and Vecchione would talk about it a lot. How do we approach him? What can we offer him? What would convince him to flip now when he refused offers years earlier, when he easily could have negotiated his get-out-of-jail-free card? Meanwhile, as is often the case, things they didn't even know were happening were about to make all the difference.

CHAPTER 9

In Las Vegas, the current investigation was progressing into the past. The Feds were trying to pull off a pretty complicated trick, attempting to find evidence proving that Eppolito and Caracappa were committing crimes in the present that had a connection to criminal acts committed less than ten years earlier. That was the only possible way to create a RICO charge. Eppolito's subpoenaed telephone records showed that he was in contact with known members of both the Lucchese and Bonanno crime families. And surveillance had videotaped a known Bonanno associate driving a car owned by Eppolito. Most importantly, the DEA's undercover operative, Steve Corso, the gambling accountant posing as an accountant interested in getting involved in the movie business, had successfully forged a relationship with Eppolito. In fact, Eppolito had even given him an autographed copy of his memoir, *Mafia Cop*. Eppolito apparently liked to impress Corso by dropping the names of organized crime celebrities. He secretly had been recorded bragging about his "former and current LCN [La Cosa Nostra] connections," among them Gambino family leader John Gotti. He told the undercover that he was trying to raise money to produce one of his scripts and that he had already received $25,000 from a Bonanno family associate. When asked if he was nervous about taking money from the mob he replied that he "doesn't give a shit."

Meanwhile, the DEA was setting several traps for him. Their belief was that Caracappa was tied to him by history and would be forced to go wherever his garrulous partner led. Caracappa wasn't stupid; he knew that Eppolito's problems would quickly become his, so he couldn't afford to let Eppolito freelance. One DEA plan called for Steven Corso to ask Eppolito to launder $75,000 he'd made in drug deals, enabling the government to follow the money. In the second scenario the undercover told Eppolito that several friends—two of them "famous" players who might be willing to invest in a screenplay Eppolito had written entitled *Murder in Youngstown*—were flying in from Los Angeles for the weekend and wanted to have "a good time." "These guys," Corso told Eppolito, "being young, they like to party. And they do things I have no knowledge about. Basically, that's designer shit, designer drugs . . . They want me to get them either Ecstasy or speed."

Eppolito understood and replied that he would contact "Guido," a friend of his son Anthony—the clear implecation being that he could handle that request. Every word was caught on tape.

Weeks later Anthony Eppolito was videotaped selling an ounce of crystal meth to Corso for $900 and guaranteeing the drugs would be good—proudly adding that he was sure of that because the people who supplied them knew it was for a deal involving Louis Eppolito.

The cooperating witness, Corso, captured Eppolito telling his tales on hundreds of hours of tape in meetings that took place all over Vegas, from fashionable Italian restaurants at places like Caesars Palace and the Venetian to their living rooms. During their many conversations, it became clear that Eppolito may have retired from the NYPD, but he still enjoyed playing the tough-guy role. He bragged to Corso about a fight he'd had with a contractor who was late finishing some work for him. The contractor was holding a hatchet. Eppolito took it from him. "I told him, 'Don't think I won't put this through your fucking head, faggot.' I said, 'You are nothing but a faggot,' . . . I said, 'If you don't finish this job today or tomorrow,' I said, 'I'm gonna personally kill you in front of your friends, then I'm gonna kill your friends.' And he fixed it. I said, 'You're taking kindness for weakness. Don't do that . . . If you ever want to push, I will personally kill you, and I'll do it in front of your mother and father and then I'll kill them.' Got to let them know that you'll kill first . . . that's embedded in me."

At another meeting Eppolito boasted about his mob connections, explaining, "My whole career, every time I'd walk into a club with these guys, cops would be watching . . . They ask me what I'm doing with John Gotti. I've known John since he was a fucking kid . . ."

Corso was appropriately impressed. "So you were respected by everybody?"

"All of them." He was immensely proud of that fact, that he was respected by all of them. Eppolito was performing a great balancing act, living his life on both sides of the law. One night, he told Corso, he was in a late-night place in Brooklyn when a wiseguy walked in, obviously unaware that Eppolito was a cop, and muttered, "I shoulda shot him. I shoulda shot him. I must have stabbed this cocksucker a thousand times. I'm holding his arm, I'm stabbing him in the fucking back, in the neck, in the head . . ."

It was bona fide mob talk, better than any movie, and Corso played the wide-eyed innocent, asking, "If you heard something, even as a cop, that this guy got whacked and it was none of your business, you didn't hear it?"

It's easy to imagine Eppolito's confident smile as he said, "I didn't . . . That's why I was always so respected by them."

As much as Eppolito clearly enjoyed reminiscing about the past, he was struggling to survive in the present. Increasingly desperate to raise money to finance his screenwriting career, Eppolito told Corso he didn't care where the cash came from. "If this is the biggest drug dealer in the United States," he said, "I don't give a fuck. If you said to me, 'Lou, I want to introduce you to Jack Smith, he wants to invest in this film,' [if] he says, 'The seventy-five thousand dollars comes in a fucking shoebox,' that's fine with me. I don't care."

Eppolito gradually was being ensnared. He trusted Corso so completely that he even asked him to prepare his tax returns for him and provided all the essential financial data. As a result, the IRS was brought into the investigation.

For a case that had been in the freezer for almost a decade, Eppolito and Caracappa were attracting a lot of attention. In addition to Brooklyn and the U.S. Attorney, there were now three federal agencies, the DEA, FBI, and IRS, involved in the investigation. But the question still remained: Would the cops reach far enough into the past to enable the Feds to make a RICO stick? Or would Mike Vecchione get to try him and Caracappa for the murder of Jimmy Hydell?

Eppolito was going to jail, it was just a question of how long and who held the keys. His drug dealing was a criminal act; it was enough to put him away. In addition, Corso had uncovered evidence that Eppolito had evaded taxes by not declaring his screenwriting income. But unless those crimes could be connected to the crimes he'd committed years earlier, Vecchione still didn't believe there was enough evidence to support a RICO charge. It was also obvious that Eppolito was still associating with known members of organized crime—he was talking to them on the phone, lending them his car—but talking to criminals wasn't a crime. The basis of a RICO charge wouldn't come from there either.

Several investigators from Brooklyn went out to Vegas to see what was going on. Bobby Intartaglia spent some time out there; so did Oldham. Nobody got the whole picture, but they did get some of the big brushstrokes. In 1994, Kaplan was in his bathtub when he received a phone call from his well-respected criminal attorney, Judd Burstein, telling him that Casso had fired his attorney and agreed to cooperate with the FBI. Kaplan knew exactly what that meant to him. He calmly dried himself off and went on the lam. He went directly to Steve Caracappa's apartment to explain to him what was happening. He was going to disappear and he didn't want Caracappa to think he'd gone bad, meaning cooperated with the law. Eventually he kissed Caracappa good-bye and took off.

He'd flown to San Diego, then spent time in Mexico before going to Las Vegas to meet Eppolito. In Vegas Eppolito had asked Kaplan to arrange a $75,000 loan so he could buy a new house. That wasn't much information, but it meant that both Eppolito and Caracappa had remained in contact with Kaplan. The Feds were positive that Kaplan had earned the money he loaned Eppolito in a marijuana deal, which established at least a tenuous link between the cops and Kaplan's criminal enterprise. It wasn't much, but as it had occurred well within the ten-year span mandated by RICO, it moved the clock forward. Vecchione couldn't believe this was strong enough to support a conspiracy charge, but the Feds were elated. As far as they were concerned this was proof Eppolito and Caracappa were still part of a criminal conspiracy.

Back in New York a much happier event would also become part of the equation. Unknown to the investigators, Burt Kaplan had a daughter with whom he was very close. Ironically, Deborah Kaplan was a judge; she had been elected to the New York State Civil Court bench in 2002 and was eventually assigned to Manhattan's Criminal Court. A friend of Judge Kaplan's once claimed, perhaps facetiously, that Kaplan had become an attorney "to get her father out of jail." Years earlier, when Vecchione had spent a lot more time in the courtroom, he'd dealt with her often. In those days she was a legal aid lawyer, and he remembered her as quiet and competent. But until he'd read it in the newspapers he did not know that her father was mob associate Burt Kaplan. And he certainly did not know that she and her husband had adopted a baby born in Tula, Russia, in November 2002. And it was this baby who changed everything.

Burt Kaplan's criminal life was no secret to his daughter. In 1973, after Judge Jack Weinstein had sentenced Kaplan to four years in prison for selling stolen clothing, camera flash cubes, and hair dryers, twelve-year-old Deborah and her mother appealed to the respected judge to reduce that sentence. They claimed that Deborah had become isolated and depressed because of her father's absence. While Weinstein did not reduce that sentence, he did recommend that Kaplan be paroled early. Almost twenty-five years later, when Kaplan was on trial in 1998 for selling twenty-four tons of marijuana, Deborah Kaplan, by that time a legal aid attorney, testified in her father's defense, attacking the key prosecution witness Monica Galpine as an alcoholic and a liar "not capable of telling the truth." Her testimony apparently had little impact; her father was sentenced to twenty-seven years in prison. That was a tough sentence for an old man convicted of nonviolent crimes. If he did the whole stretch he would be ninety-two years old the next time he took a breath as a free man. He would never live to kiss his grandchild.

But prosecutors who thought it was the hammer they needed to get him to cooperate and provide the information they needed to prosecute Eppolito and Caracappa were disappointed. While all around him onetime wiseguys were making deals to reduce their sentences, the real stand-up guy turned out to be the Jew. Because he wasn't Italian Kaplan could never be "made," never be inducted into the Mafia, but he was a respected associate, and far more than some of the big-time made men, he was faithful to the old ways, to omertà. Silence. Basically, when approached by federal prosecutors he'd suggested politely that they go fuck themselves.

Kaplan was a hard case. But he wasn't only the best shot, as Vecchione told Dades: "I'll tell you, Tommy, he's the only shot we got. Without him, we might as well pack up and go home. There's nothing we can do." The first thing every good cop does at the beginning of an investigation is learn as much as possible about the people involved. You just never know what information is going to be handy. So all of them, Dades, Vecchione, and Joe Ponzi in particular, started learning everything they could find out about this man in the middle.

Burt Kaplan was another Depression kid from Brooklyn, from Bed-Stuy, where his family owned an appliance store on Vanderbilt Avenue. He had started gambling as a kid, poker and the horses mostly, and never stopped. "I couldn't control myself," he once said. "I was doing every bad thing to get money to gamble."

After dropping out of Brooklyn Tech, Kaplan served as a naval radio operator in the early 1950s, stationed in Japan, where he deciphered and analyzed Russian army codes. He often claimed that the National Security Agency had tried to recruit him, but he'd turned down their offer. Instead he returned to work in the family appliance store. His life changed the day he installed an air conditioner in the Grand Mark, a social club run by, coincidently, Jimmy "the Clam" Eppolito—which happened to be around the block from the apartment in which Mike Vecchione had grown up. He began hanging out there, playing in the card games.

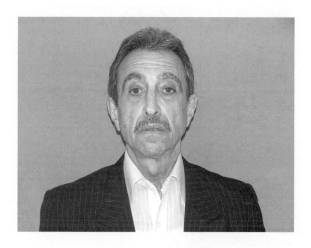

In March 2009, sixty-seven-year-old Steven Caracappa *(seen above in his arrest photo)* was sentenced to life plus eighty years in prison and was fined $4.2 million, actually a lighter sentence than sixty-one-year-old Louis Eppolito *(below),* who received a sentence of life plus one hundred years and a $4.7 million fine.

Thomas Dades at Intelligence Division.

The credit belongs to the man who is actually in the arena, whose face is marred by dust and sweat and blood; who strives valiantly; who errs, and comes up short again and again, because there is no effort without error or shortcoming; but who does actually strive to do the deeds; who knows the great enthusiasms, the great devotions; who spends himself in a worthy cause; who at the best knows in the end the triumph of high achievement, and who at the worst, if he fails, at least fails while daring greatly. —Theodore Roosevelt

Jimmy Harkins, Joseph Ponzi, Thomas Dades, and Mike Galletta, promoted to First Grade.

The parents of Thomas Dades: his beloved mother, Della, and father, Pete.

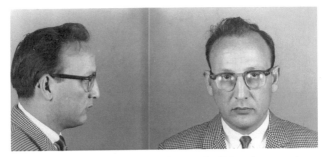

Bert Kaplan *(above and below)*, who was the liaison between the mob and the mafia cops. He testified against them in federal court.

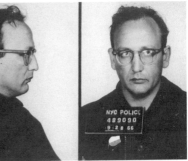

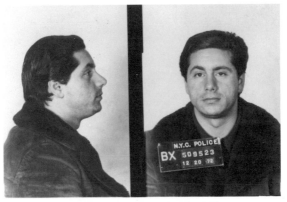

Arrest photo of Anthony "Gaspipe" Casso, Caracappa and Eppolito's mob boss.

Joe Ponzi, Michael Ryan, Mike Vecchione, Joe Alexis, and John Holmes– members of the Rackets Division in the Brooklyn District Attorney's office.

District Attorney Charles J. Hynes *(right)* and Mike.

Michael Galletta, James Harkins, and Tommy Dades on their promotion day, March 2001.

The gun that was on Eppolito's person when he was arrested. On the butt of the gun it says "Mafia Cop Louie Eppolito."

Mike Vecchione receives the Distinguished Alumnus Award in Public Service from Hofstra University Law School.

Anthony Ferrara, unknown male, and Frankie Hydell.
Courtesy of Frankie Hydell

Jimmy Hydell.

Pulled from the Headlines

Detectives Used Badges to Kill For the Mob, Indictments Say

By WILLIAM K. RASHBAUM

Two retired New York City police detectives, onetime partners who had long been suspected of ties to organized crime, were charged by federal prosecutors yesterday with taking part in eight murders on behalf of the Mafia — most while one or both were still active members of the police force.

The charges, detailed in a document unsealed yesterday...

Rat squeals: 'Mafia cops' delivered wiseguy to execution

Blood Ties: 2 Officers' Path to Mob Indictments

By ALAN FEUER and WILLIAM K. RASHBAUM

It looked at first like a classic gangland...

Officer in Murder Case Got Benefit of Doubt in '85

By WILLIAM K. RASHBAUM

It was in March 1984 that F.B.I. agents searched the New Jersey home of a heroin trafficker and made what they felt was a stunning discovery...

'BLOOD TRAITORS TO NYPD BADGE'

Feds slam 'Mafia cops' in wrap-up

DAILY NEWS

MAFIA COP SCANDAL

Family of innocent man slain in mob hit wants rogue cops to ...

ROT IN JAIL

SEE PAGES 6-7

Mike, Tommy, Ponzi, and Arthur Aidala in front of the World Trade Center.

Tommy and Terance Meyers *(far left)*.

The only thing worse than being a degenerate gambler is being bad degenerate gambler. And that was Burt Kaplan. To settle his gambling debts Kaplan began borrowing money from loan sharks, including Lucchese consigliere Christy "Tick" Furnari. Eventually he got into the *schmatte* business, building a legitimate clothing distribution company in Bensonhurst selling designer knock-offs, but his real business was buying and selling anything he could turn over quickly and profitably, from hair dryers that fell off the back of that legendary truck to heroin. He sold counterfeit watches and homemade quaaludes and smuggled tons of marijuana. He got involved with diamond mines; he was wrapped up in some scheme to manufacture clocks that featured Muslim prayers; he even tried to sell a hair lotion in Africa, but when his chemist forgot to put in some chemical the whole shipment turned brown. To square things the chemist offered to make crystal meth for him. So he went into the crystal meth business.

While there were a lot of gaps in Kaplan's story, the big pieces fit together. He was "owned" by Furnari, who took a piece of all the business he did. In 1981, while serving three years in the federal prison camp in Allenwood for manufacturing and distributing quaaludes, Kaplan had apparently met mob associate Frank Santora Jr., who was doing time for a $12 million swindle.

When Santora found out that Kaplan knew Jimmy "the Clam" Eppolito, he offered to introduce him to the Clam's nephew, who also happened to be his cousin, a detective named Louis Eppolito. But Louis was a very special detective, Santora told him; he and his partner had access to confidential police information and were willing "to do business on the side if the price was right." A lot of lives were changed because Kaplan once installed an air conditioner in the Grand Mark.

According to Casso, after getting out of prison Kaplan had established a relationship with the cops. Wiseguys rarely trust cops, but this was an unusual situation. Eppolito had a pedigree. So Kaplan believed the cops could be trusted to be dishonest. The only rule was that everything had to go through Santora. Santora owned them. He carried all the requests for information, brought back the answers, delivered the money, and kept a little taste for himself. Initially it was mostly small jobs—checking out the license plates of cars seen around a social club, getting an address, looking at a report—and it didn't involve any heavy hitting.

The situation changed considerably for Kaplan when Christy Tick went to prison in 1985 and he became the wiseguy version of a valuable free agent. Gaspipe Casso grabbed him for his crew and—always through Santora—Kaplan continued to do business as usual with the two cops he'd never met. It was a big step for Kaplan: Inside the mob Furnari was respected as a serious guy who would do whatever had to be done, while Casso was thought of more as a homicidal maniac. As Lucchese associate Anthony "Tumac" Accetturo once described Casso and underboss Vic Amuso, "They had no training, no honor. All they want to do is kill, kill, get what you can."

Kaplan would later admit, perhaps wistfully, "Mr. Furnari would have never let me get involved in the things that Mr. Casso did."

In early September 1987 Frankie Santora was walking along Bath Avenue with Lucchese associate

Carmine Varriale, who apparently had done something to piss off Casso. Santora was simply with the wrong wiseguy at the worst time. Three shooters caught up with them outside a dry cleaning store and killed both men. Apparently Casso did not know that Santora was Kaplan's mysterious go-between. He once told Kaplan that if he had known about Frankie Santora's relationship with the old man he would have been able to save him.

By then, though, the two cops were comfortable working with Kaplan. Santora's widow arranged for them to get together. Eppolito supposedly told Kaplan, "We like working with you and Casso. You take care of business. If we tell you somebody's cooperating you take care of it." From that night forward Kaplan worked directly with the two cops. Although Eppolito asked many times to meet Casso, Kaplan refused to let that happen. Eppolito told him, "I'll stand on one side of the door and he can stand on the other side."

"That ain't gonna happen," Kaplan told him. The killer cops were his life insurance policy. As long as Casso needed the cops, he needed Kaplan. This relationship was a beautiful thing.

In early May 2004, as the investigation narrowed to Kaplan, Tommy began packing up his career. Once it had been a joke, "twenty and out," but all too quickly it had become a reality. He was going out angry at the department, like a lover scorned. There were a lot of things a retired cop could do to earn, although admittedly none of them offered the excitement of one day on the job. The PAL was opening a boxing gym on Staten Island and he could run that. That was boxing, and he'd be working with kids, teaching, so that had real appeal. Several really good people he'd worked with, like Mike Galletta and Jimmy Harkins, were doing private investigations and offered him work. It was a little civil, a little criminal, mostly checking records and serving subpoenas—divorce cases, insurance fraud. A little of this, little of that; the bills would get paid.

But Vecchione and Ponzi were pushing hard to bring Dades into the Brooklyn DA's office as an investigator. The main difference between that and being an NYPD detective was the job title. There was a hiring freeze in place, so it wasn't easy to find a slot for him. Vecchione pushed, not just because of their friendship, but because Dades was a damn good cop and they were in the middle of the investigation of a lifetime. Ponzi pushed too, and Hynes was completely supportive. Eventually a way was found to open a slot for him. So going out of the NYPD, he was going into the prosecutor's office.

Officially he still had a couple of months left, but he'd accumulated vacation days and sick days and he wanted to get out as quickly as he could. It was a time for change in his life too. Ro had suggested it would be better for both of them if he moved out of the house, so he'd found a one-bedroom basement apartment. It was a new building, a nice place, and the only thing it lacked was everything that mattered to him. After years of marriage, after coming home every night to Ro and their two smart, noisy, wonderful kids, having to walk into an empty apartment every night, the only sound the electronic hum of the refrigerator, was one of the toughest things he'd ever done.

It was a bad time for Tommy Dades. His career was ending, his marriage was screwed up, and getting in touch with his father had turned out to be a big-time mistake. The man had made it obvious he didn't want anything to do with him. The concept of a father rejecting his son was too big for Tommy to understand, so he just accepted it. He was okay with it; he couldn't miss what he'd never had. Besides, he was still in contact with his aunt and a few other newly discovered relatives. When he would speak with his aunt they would make plans to meet, but somehow that never happened.

What he did have were the many friends he'd made on the job, and boxing. It had been almost a year since his last bout, but since then he'd been in the gym for two hours after work five days a week, hitting the heavy bag and the speed bag, jumping rope and sparring. The gym had become his real home, where he was as good as his right hand and hitting those bags again and again and again, harder, harder, let him get it out, all of it, the anger, the frustration that he kept bottled up. In the gym, he could explode.

For Tommy Dades, friends and boxing, those were the constants. And the case of the two skells.

He'd been working the case for more than a year now. He was pretty sure he knew the facts that mattered and he was still confident eventually he or somebody else would prove the two cops were guilty. But there was one thing he couldn't figure out, one thing that just didn't make sense to him.

Why.

Unlike the TV shows on which detectives spend just about the whole hour trying to unravel the always complicated motive behind the crime, most often the motive is pretty obvious: Money, sex, and power pretty much cover most crimes. In fact, neither Dades nor Ponzi nor Vecchione, none of these guys, ever wasted too much time wondering why a crime was committed, but this one was different. Just about every man or woman who has ever pinned on a shield, almost without exception, at one time in their career gets the opportunity to go the wrong way. The offers are there, big and small, a cup of coffee to thousands of dollars. It's a reality of the job. To the credit of law enforcement, most of them turn it down. But having to make that decision, sometimes over and over, is an ingredient in the bond that holds them all together.

But not Louis Eppolito and Steve Caracappa. They went bad early in their careers and never looked back. If even some of these accusations were true, as Tommy Dades believed they were, then he was looking at maybe the two dirtiest cops in the whole history of law enforcement. The worst cops ever. And this time Dades, Ponzi, Vecchione, Bobby I, Le Vien, Oldham— all of them wondered why.

Louis Eppolito was easy to figure. He came from the bottom of the well. His father, Fat the Gangster, and his uncle Jimmy the Clam were made guys in the Gambino family. Jimmy Eppolito was a capo; he learned his lessons from Carlo Gambino. Louis's father, Ralph, used to bang Louis around pretty good, trying to teach him respect and honor. Except he was supposed to honor wiseguys and respect criminal behavior. What Louis Eppolito really learned from Fat the Gangster, as he wrote in *Mafia Cops,* was the difference between the bad guys and the good guys. "My father hated cops with a passion, had no respect whatsoever for them. I guess that stemmed from the days he was buying them off for nickels and dimes."

Growing up, Louis hung out with these guys. He spoke the language, he knew the streets. He'd even been the one to identify the bullet-riddled bodies of his uncle and his cousin, a wannabe they called Jim-Jim, after they'd been whacked. Maybe there was some time in Louis Eppolito's life when he really had intended to join the right team, but if there had been, it didn't last long. He was a natural.

Steve Caracappa was a little tougher to figure. It wasn't in his genes. But by the time he joined the NYPD in 1969 he had something most cops never get: a criminal record. Caracappa had grown up on Brooklyn's streets and dropped out of high school at sixteen. He started working with his father as a laborer. In 1960, he and a partner were indicted on Staten Island for stealing a truckload of construction materials. Apparently the judge in the case gave him a break, reducing the charge to a misdemeanor. Caracappa pleaded guilty and was given probation. In 1966 he joined the army and served a yearlong tour in Vietnam.

Normally, a high school dropout with a record— even a sealed juvenile record—wouldn't have been considered by the NYPD. But in the late 1960s a lot of the young men who might have applied for the job were serving in the military, and at the height of the antiwar movement it was a pretty controversial job. To fill its ranks the NYPD was forced to reduce its standards—and even then Caracappa was initially rejected. Finally though, in 1969, he was accepted.

On paper, he'd had a great career. He'd moved right up the ladder and gotten his gold shield. He'd been given important slots. Several cops who had worked with Caracappa during his career were stunned when Casso fingered him. An officer who had worked with him in narcotics defended him, saying, "On many occasions Steve put his life in danger protecting me when I was involved in making narcotics buys." He was trusted so completely that he helped create the department's Organized Crime Homicide Unit inside the Major Case Squad. Dades looked at his record over and over, trying to pinpoint that place, that event, when he turned. There was no easy answer. It was possible he'd been straight all the way to 1978, when he and Louis Eppolito became partners under Larry Ponzi. But even if that was true, you couldn't blame it on Eppolito. The switch was there all the time; all he did was flip it. Dades finally decided, "I think the both of them just liked the money and enjoyed playing both sides of the fence. I don't think they knew what side they wanted to be on. What else could it be?"

While Brooklyn and the Feds supposedly were working together in late May, U.S. Attorney Roz Mauskopf, the head of the Eastern District, called Vecchione's boss, Joe Hynes. Mauskopf and Hynes knew each other but spoke only occasionally. They just didn't have a lot to talk about. Although the Brooklyn DA's office works regularly with federal investigative agencies like the DEA and postal inspectors, with rare exceptions the U.S. Attorney's office maintained its distance from the local prosecutors. They were the Feds; they had the full power of the government of the United States behind them. They didn't need to make nice. Hynes had long ago accepted this situation as a reality, knowing there was nothing he could do to change it.

But Joe Hynes also knew that the Feds were armed with a much greater array of legal weapons than his office and when he believed that arsenal was needed—as, for example, in the case of Abner Louima, who was sodomized by a cop using a broomstick and who faced substantially more prison time if convicted by the Feds—he would ask the U.S. Attorney to take over the case.

Ironically, Mauskopf was calling to ask Hynes to take over a murder case. A couple of years earlier Mario Fortunato and Carmine Polito had been convicted of a RICO violation for planning a hit on Genovese family associates Sabatino Lombardi and Michael D'Urso, then attempting to fix the jury and lying to the FBI about their involvement in the crime. This wasn't the usual kind of wiseguy hit; it was more about personal business—Polito was a piss-poor gambler who'd borrowed hundreds of thousands of dollars from Lombardi and D'Urso and wanted to wipe out his debts in two shots. Lombardi died immediately. D'Urso had been shot in the back of his head at point-blank range, but somehow he had survived.

Fortunato and Polito appealed their convictions, claiming that however serious their crimes and however many different crimes they may have committed, they still didn't add up to a RICO. They were killers, not conspirators. This was a personal gripe; it had nothing to do with the family business. Incredibly, Judge Roger Miner of the Second Circuit Court of Appeals agreed. In reversing their convictions for "murder in the aid of racketeering" he wrote, "The evidence was insufficient to establish that Polito and Fortunato murdered Lombardi to 'maintain or increase' positions in the Genovese crime family or to establish that the shootings of Lombardi and D'Urso were related to the activities of the Genovese crime family criminal enterprise."

There was nothing more the U.S. Attorney could do. Even if her office could figure out a way to make the RICO charge stick, retrying them would violate their protection from double jeopardy. Fortunately, being tried under the federal RICO statute does not relieve an individual of the underlying charges, in this case murder. So legally the state could try them for the murder of Lombardi and the attempted murder of D'Urso.

"I was really stunned when Hynes told me about this phone call," Vecchione remembers. "Here the Feds were, laying the groundwork to take the Eppolito and Caracappa case away from us to try them under RICO—and they were asking us to take a case on which they'd failed to meet the RICO standard. I couldn't imagine they didn't see the irony in all of this. But apparently they didn't."

Hynes agreed to Mauskopf's request; Brooklyn would take the case. There was no way two killers were going to walk. Both men were indicted for murder by Hynes's office; Polito chose to be tried by a jury, while Fortunato put his fate in the hands of a judge. In 2007 the judge found Fortunato guilty of murder—one day after a jury had acquitted Polito on the same charges.

But when Mauskopf called Hynes, Vecchione wondered if the Feds might see this case as the model for the mafia cops. Under this scenario the U.S. Attorney had little to lose by pursuing a RICO case against the cops. Even if they failed to make it stick, they knew that Hynes's office was there to cover their misjudgment. And if they succeeded, he had to admit, the penalties faced by the cops would be much more severe than anything possible under state law.

As far as he concerned the deal he'd made with Mark Feldman was still in effect: Even if the drug investigation going on in Vegas allowed the Feds to connect the dots and beat the RICO time problem, Brooklyn would still get the Hydell murder. That's where it all started, with Betty Hydell. And solving that particular case was Tommy's passion. As long as they got that one, Vecchione would be thrilled to see the Feds put the cops away for a couple of hundred years.

But somehow, he just didn't believe it was going to work out that nicely.

CHAPTER 10

On May 26, 2004, Burt Kaplan was sitting in a cell at the Metropolitan Detention Center in Brooklyn. His presence in Brooklyn was mostly his bad luck. Apparently he was being transferred out of the Allenwood Federal Correctional Complex in White Deer, Pennsylvania, for disciplinary reasons—he'd paid a prisoner $1,000 to assault another inmate—and the MDC was a convenient waystation. This was the opportunity the task force had been waiting for. Kaplan fell from heaven. Through Feldman, Bill Oldham had arranged for the One-Eyed Jew to be held there while he made his approach. Several months earlier Oldham quietly had taken an earlier shot at Kaplan, visiting him at Allenwood. Kaplan had made it clear at that time that he wasn't interested in making a deal. But Oldham persisted, hoping time would wear him down. So as soon as Kaplan had gotten settled at MDC, Oldham called Dades. "The old man's in Brooklyn and I'm gonna go see him," he said. "Want to go with me?"

It was a very nice invitation. And completely unexpected. By this time the rift between the Feds and the state had become obvious and Dades wasn't interested in playing sidekick to the Feds. "No, that's all right," Dades told him. "You go ahead."

Two days later Oldham called again. He'd been to see Kaplan, he said. Apparently the meeting had gone well, because this time Oldham told Dades he thought Kaplan was going to come on board. Dades didn't believe it. The guy had resisted several years of offers from heavy hitters, and now he was going to flip after a single visit from Bill Oldham? That didn't make sense. "You sure about that?" he asked.

"He wants some time to think about it," Oldham said. Kaplan's lawyer was going to call him with his answer.

That was a phone call that apparently never got made. So Oldham decided to try him again. Three's a charm. But this time he called Joe Ponzi. "What are you doing, Joe?" he asked.

He'd caught Ponzi in the midst of a hectic morning. "Bill, what kind of question is that? What am I doing? I got a hundred people here doing a gazillion things. I don't know whether to shit or go blind, that's what I'm doing. What do you have in mind?"

"You got time to take a ride?"

Ponzi laughed. "Take a ride where, Bill?"

"Prospect Park. It's nice outside, we'll take a walk." Oldham paused, waiting for a laugh that never came, and then added, "Wanna go see Burt?"

Now he had Ponzi's attention. "What?"

"I'm going over to MDC to see him. You can come with me."

Ponzi's heart started racing. He'd been spending

too much of his life running the division, piling up paperwork. Even in this investigation just about all of the work he'd done had been administrative. This was his chance to get a piece of the action. "When?"

"Be outside the building in five minutes."

Joe Ponzi and Bill Oldham are about as different as sugar and lemon. Ponzi is buttoned-down in dress and manner. Old-school all the way. In the many years that Vecchione had worked with him he couldn't remember a single time Ponzi had walked into his office when he wasn't wearing a tie and jacket or his hair was less than perfectly trimmed. The man just exuded professionalism. He spoke softly but firmly and always treated people with respect, even when he was talking to a real lowlife. And he had quietly compiled an enviable record of putting away bad guys.

On the short drive over to MDC Ponzi wondered if he was making a mistake. He wasn't properly prepared for this meeting. He liked to know what he wanted to know long before he walked into a room. He liked to know all the details before he asked his first question. He'd done his homework—he'd read Casso's 302s and all the reports about Kaplan he could find—but he wished he'd had some time to figure out the best way to deal with the old man.

But there was no way he could have turned down Oldham's offer. No way. From everything he'd read or been told about Kaplan he found him to be an absolutely fascinating figure. A dying kind. He wanted to see what the old man looked like; he wanted to hear the tone of his voice, the way he used the language. He wasn't even certain he'd have the chance to speak with him.

And in truth he wasn't really very hopeful that he

could do what Feldman and Oldham and who knew how many other people had failed to do: convince Kaplan to grab a future. He just didn't have enough ammunition. He and Vecchione had spent considerable time talking about what they could offer Kaplan, how they could make nothing sound like something. Obviously, they would give him immunity from any state prosecution, but that was like offering a drowning man a cold drink. They both knew that the only thing that might entice the old man was a reduction in his federal sentence, and the state couldn't make that promise. Ponzi hoped that Oldham's presence at this meeting might reassure Kaplan that the U.S. Attorney was willing to cut a deal.

Before they got to the imposing building on Twenty-ninth Street, near the Gowanus Bay, Oldham told Ponzi about his previous meetings with Kaplan, sounding positive but leaving Ponzi with the impression that the chemistry between him and Kaplan hadn't been good.

Ponzi, Oldham, and a special investigator from the Eastern District named Joe Campanella waited quietly for Kaplan in a small conference room. Oldham had arranged for the old man to be brought down. Ponzi had spent a sizeable chunk of his life in colorless rooms just like this one, waiting for another bad guy to show up and tell his story. Finally Kaplan arrived and stood in the doorway. He was smaller than Ponzi had imagined, about five-eight and thin. He was wearing an orange MDC jumpsuit and dark-rimmed glasses. He looked a lot more like a Jewish grandfather from Brooklyn who'd worked a lifetime in the garment district than a career criminal. Put a pair of glasses on Robert Duvall and you've got Burt Kaplan.

One thing surprised Ponzi: The One-Eyed Jew appeared to have two pretty good eyes. Whatever was wrong with his eye, it wasn't an obvious deformity.

Kaplan saw Oldham sitting at the table and shook his head, clearly unhappy to be there. "Mr. Oldham," he began, "I told you we can't be doing this. We tried this before and I can't be seen here like this, talking to you."

That was part of the prison code: Spend too much time talking to law enforcement and people begin to believe you're cooperating. That just made life a little more dangerous. Looking at Kaplan, Ponzi decided he was both surprised and truly angry. Obviously he hadn't agreed to this meeting. So much for Oldham's claim that he was ready to roll over.

"Please, Mr. Kaplan, come in." Oldham was equally polite. "Just give us a few minutes. I want to introduce you to a few people." Reluctantly, Kaplan sat down. After Oldham had made the introductions, he handed the meeting to Ponzi. "Joe, why don't you tell him?"

Joe Ponzi estimates that in his career he's conducted more than 2,500 polygraph tests and at least as many interrogations. He knew the drill. "Mr. Kaplan, the Brooklyn District Attorney's office has unearthed some evidence about Louis Eppolito and Steve Caracappa that's breathed some new life into that investigation . . ."

Ponzi was careful not to reveal too much. His rule about that was clear: You want to get information from the subject; you don't want to provide information.

". . . and the state is now working in conjunction with the Feds on this investigation concerning the allegations against these two police officers."

Kaplan put his palms on the table and leaned forward. "Mr. Oldham knows... what's your name again?" Joe Ponzi. "Mr. Ponzi," Kaplan repeated. "With all due respect, I've been down this road with Mr. Oldham before. The night I got arrested for the pot case"—when he said that Ponzi could see his whole face tighten into a snarl; obviously he was still furious about that conviction—"that night I got pitched by the FBI, the DEA, the DA, every chief and inspector from the police department; I had more business cards from law enforcement in my pocket than I ever seen in my life. Every one of them, they told me I could go home that night. All I had to do was tell them whatever it is they think they know about these two guys." Ponzi noticed that he was careful not to confirm that he actually did have information about the case. "I told them and I'll tell you now, no disrespect, I don't mean to hurt anybody's feelings. But I've done seven years and I can do the rest. If God is good I can do the rest of this. See, I live my life a certain way. That's the way I choose to live. And I could never put myself in a position where I would have people calling me a rat or saying that I turned my back. Nobody's gonna accuse me of going bad."

"Going bad," to Kaplan, meant cooperating with law enforcement. There it was again, Ponzi thought. The code.

"You know what?" Ponzi replied, leaning forward just slightly to show he was not intimidated or dissuaded, knowing the importance of his body language. "If that's the code you've chosen to live by, I could respect that, but I'm missing something here." He had Kaplan's attention. He stared right into his eyes. He spoke evenly, never raising his voice. "First of all, if my memory serves me correctly, the infamous Mr. Gaspipe

Casso flipped on you. That's first. Second of all, when he flipped he admitted that he'd put out a contract on you while he was on the lam." He paused, letting his words bounce around the room. "You, his so-called friend for life. You, who met him through Christy Tick. You, who's been around these guys your whole life and believe in whatever it is they believe in. He put a hit out on you.

"And then, then who are we talking about here? These two guys are cops. We're not talking about wiseguys." Ponzi was very careful not to tell Kaplan that the only thing he had to do was tell him about the two cops. That wasn't the way it worked. There is no such thing as conditional or limited cooperation; it's all you know or no deal. But he wanted to put as much emphasis as possible on Eppolito and Caracappa. "Mr. Kaplan," he continued, "this is different. We're talking about two guys who had shields and guns in their pocket and swore to an oath. These guys not only were supposed to uphold the law, but they had a responsibility to every other cop and they betrayed them . . ."

On occasion Bill Oldham tried to say something, but every time he opened his mouth Kaplan would either put up his hands to block him, meaning "I don't want to hear what you've got to say," or would simply look at him and scowl. Ponzi got the feeling—that's all it was, a feeling—that Kaplan was at least listening to what he had to say. That there was the beginning of the beginning of a rapport. That was the first step in the big dance.

In this meeting Kaplan revealed only a little about himself to Ponzi, telling him that he was "ninety percent legitimate businessman and ten percent gangster," but just as casually claiming, "I been around gangsters my whole life. I lived my life a certain way; you know what I mean. And when I picked up the paper and saw that this guy or that guy had gone bad, it made me physically sick."

For a first conversation Ponzi thought it was going well. Kaplan had made it clear he wasn't interested in talking, but he hadn't walked out of the room. That was something. After about twenty minutes of conversation Ponzi decided to take another shot at him. "Listen, Mr. Kaplan, I just want you to know I couldn't be more serious about this and the people back in my office couldn't be more interested and I'm not going away. No disrespect to you, but I don't want you to think I'm here now and then I'm going to ride off into the sunset. You know, you could very well find yourself at Rikers Island tomorrow, writted out of the federal system and into the state system."

For the first time, Kaplan reacted to Ponzi. He said evenly, leaving no room for any doubt that he was serious, "Young man, don't do that. Don't try to threaten me. I could overmedicate myself any time I want. Believe me, I will commit suicide before you put me in some cell at Rikers." His whole face was turning red with anger. "I told that guy"—he indicated Oldham— "that I want to go back where I was and play pinochle and bullshit with my guys and take my walks and do what I want to do. I don't want to be in this place anymore. And you just listen to me: I'm never going to allow anybody to drag me like an animal and throw me on fucking Rikers Island. You understand me."

It was a statement, not a question. Ponzi nodded, knowing that if he took one more step in that direction he'd be in the shithouse with Oldham. Kaplan had made it clear that he was resigned to spending the rest of his life in prison—on his own terms—and he wasn't about to be threatened. Ponzi never mentioned another word about changing his living conditions; instead he tried to dig into Kaplan's mind, to try to understand why he was so offended by the possibility of putting away two rogue cops. "You know, Mr. Kaplan, you look like you're in pretty good health. Wouldn't you like to spend the rest of your life at home with your family?"

Kaplan wouldn't respond to questions about his family during that meeting, perhaps believing that showing any sign of weakness might be taken to mean he would cooperate. Instead he continued to come back to the pot bust that had put him in prison. Almost ten years later he was still furious about that, insisting that he had been framed. And his attorney was still filing appeals. "I can't help being bitter," he said. "I was a pot dealer, but the bales of shit they rolled into the courthouse, that was not my stuff. And then they put this fucking perjurer on the stand. And I defy you to tell me the last time somebody got a sentence like I got on a pot case."

They went around the block, sometimes talking at each other rather than having a conversation. It was like two gears just slightly out of sync. Each time Kaplan began complaining about his drug conviction or the fact that "Gas" had fucked him every which way, Ponzi quietly tried to put him back on track. "Listen, you know this story has been out there ten years and I have reason now more than ever to believe that it's true. Let me be honest with you. You and I both know that you hold the key to this thing. I'm convinced for a variety of reasons that the story you can tell is going to be the definitive story."

No matter how Ponzi approached the subject, Kaplan just wouldn't bite. "I don't know what you're talking about," he said. "I wish I could help you, but I can't." Throughout the meeting, every time somebody walked past the room, the old man looked over his shoulder. Ponzi assumed Kaplan was worried somebody would figure out this wasn't a simple lawyer-client meeting and put out the word that he was cooperating.

Kaplan started getting really edgy, eventually getting up and pacing back and forth across the room. Finally, he said, "Look, I really gotta go. I wanna go. Again, no disrespect, you seem like a fine young gentleman, but I don't even want to be in this room. I told this guy already . . ." His anxiety was growing into anger. "I wish I could help you, but I can't."

"You know you can help us, Mr. Kaplan," Ponzi said right back. "You can help us and we can help you."

He was done. "I wish I could; I can't."

He began walking slowly toward the door. Ponzi was desperate, believing that if he let Kaplan walk out the door he might never get another shot at him. For the first time he raised his voice. "Listen to me," he said. "You're telling me these guys had nothing to do with any of this?"

He didn't even stop. "That's what I'm telling you."

"Then stop right there!" Ponzi practically shouted at him. "I want you to look me in the eye and tell me these two guys had nothing to do with the abduction and murder of Jimmy Hydell. Look me in the eye and tell me that and I'll never come back here. I give you my word, you'll never see me again."

Kaplan continued walking toward the door.

"You can't do it, can you?" Ponzi challenged him. "Go ahead, turn around, look me in the eye and tell me how wrong I am, tell me these guys got nothing to do with the murder of Eddie Lino. Tell me that Casso is a complete fucking pathological lunatic liar and I give you my word as a man you will never see me again."

Kaplan grasped the doorknob and turned it, pushing open the door. By now Ponzi was shouting desperately, "Mr. Kaplan! Mr. Kaplan! Look me in the fucking eye and you tell me that these two guys had nothing to do with the murder of Nicky Guido. I dare you to look at me, turn around and look at me and tell me that and I swear to God you'll never see me again."

Kaplan stopped. Slowly he turned around. His face was red with anger. Very deliberately, never taking his eyes off Ponzi, he walked back to the table and sat down.

Nicky Guido, the innocent kid; that was the key. Ponzi was stunned, absolutely stunned. He didn't know why Nicky Guido struck a nerve in Kaplan, but he did. Maybe because this was the one completely innocent person who was killed perhaps due to his actions. Whatever it was, something about Nicky Guido caused him to stop and come back into the room. Sitting down, he pointed a warning finger at Ponzi. "That's the problem with you guys. You fucking guys think you know everything."

Ponzi smiled. "Mr. Kaplan, I don't purport to know everything or anything. But I think you do. I think you do and I want to hear it from you. Why don't you tell me what I don't know?"

Kaplan just sat there silently, looking at the biggest step he'd take for the rest of his life. And all he had to overcome to take that step was everything he'd ever done or been or believed.

Ponzi knew when to shut up.

"I need some time to think about it," he said softly. He wanted to talk to his lawyer, he said, mull it over a little. Probably, Ponzi guessed, he wanted to see if he could live with the idea.

"How long?"

He shrugged. "I need sixty days."

"You can have thirty."

"I need forty-five days."

They argued back and forth for a few minutes, but both of them knew it was all show. Kaplan held the winning ticket; he could take as much time as he needed and nobody would dare push him. He had been careful not to mention either cop by name, but at the very end of this meeting he asked Ponzi a question. "What if there were more than two?"

Ponzi tried not to reveal his shock. "What does that mean?"

"What if wasn't just these two guys?"

More than two? More than Eppolito and Caracappa? Ponzi tried to press him. "I don't know what you're talking about."

Kaplan smiled knowingly. He'd tossed out the bait but wasn't prepared to reveal any more information. Rising, he stuck out his hand and said, "It was nice meeting you, Mr. Ponzi." He walked out of the room without looking back.

Ponzi, Oldham, and Campanella sat there for another few seconds. There was no deal, not even the outline of an agreement—Kaplan hadn't even asked what they could offer him—but he was interested. The moment he'd turned around and come back into the room Ponzi had begun thinking they had him—but he'd seen too many guys touch the possibility and get burned. He might get back to his cell, shake his head, and decide he just couldn't do it. It happened; it happened too often. Once, Ponzi remembered, somehow he'd managed to convince a stone-cold killer named Victor Breland to flip. Breland asked for a sheet of paper and began making a list of the murders he had some knowledge about. Ponzi left him alone—and when he returned to the room a few minutes later Breland stuck the paper in his mouth and swallowed it. "I can't do it," he said. "I changed my mind. I can't do it."

So when Ponzi got back to his office the most he dared tell Dades, Vecchione, and Feldman was that Kaplan showed some interest. "There's at least a possibility," he told them. He wasn't superstitious, but hey, you never know.

Each of the investigators on this case had been through this particular process too many times to feel confident Kaplan would flip. But the possibility . . . it was pretty damn exciting.

A month later, on July 30, Tommy Dades officially retired from the NYPD. Exactly twenty years to the day and out. He'd actually turned in his shield and completed his paperwork in early May, then spent his accrued vacation time, but July 30 was the official date. The enormity of his decision didn't really hit him until the papers kicked in, and then it hit him much harder than he had expected. "Being a cop was the best thing that ever happened to me," he says he finally understood. "It saved my life. Because most of the people I grew up with went the other way. Their lives got turned upside down; they started using drugs or ended up criminals. I was right there with them.

But the day I put on that uniform something good began happening for me. I put my life into it. And when I finally decided to quit I made a hasty decision. But when it ended, the way it ended, it made me feel like I was on the bottom of the barrel."

Dades began running a boxing gym on Staten Island for the Police Athletic League, teaching kids how to protect themselves. But he also got a brand-new badge when he began working for Joe Ponzi. As a new detective investigator, Dades was back on the cops case—at least temporarily.

While everyone was waiting, often impatiently, for Kaplan to make his decision, the investigation rumbled forward. The meetings were now being held almost exclusively in the U.S. Attorney's office and were run by Assistant U.S. Attorney Robert Henoch. Henoch was another one of those solid, no-nonsense prosecutors, a lieutenant colonel in the army reserves who had served in the Middle East. The meetings generally lasted about two hours and usually were attended by eight to ten investigators. The faces changed meeting to meeting. DEA agent Mark Manko was there most of the time. Joe Campanella was there, and Bobby I. An able young prosecutor from Vecchione's office, Josh Hanshaft, had been cross-designated to represent the state on the case and attended most of the meetings. After dropping out for a brief period Bill Oldham was back on the case. Ponzi would attend an occasional meeting. Feldman would drop in and spend a few minutes. This certainly wasn't a cohesive, spirited group held together by the pursuit of a noble cause. Rather there were continuing relationship problems, between both individuals and jurisdictions. And progress was achingly slow.

Henoch did his best to hold the team together. He would sit at the head of the table, his binder open in front of him. He was calm and organized, a list maker, proceeding logically and methodically, rarely showing any emotion. During each meeting the team would review whatever progress had been made and Henoch would hand out new assignments. Everybody would get an assignment—here's three things for you to do, here's three things for you to do. People who had expertise in a specific area would get whatever work there was to be done in that area. Much of that work consisted of searching for old records and files; if they could be found—and a lot of records disappear in a decade—then someone would pore over them, sifting for a nugget. The work wasn't glamorous, it wasn't made for TV; instead it was the essence of detective work. Corroborate this piece of information. Find out where that guy lived. Get the computer ID locator and pull up this record. See if you can find someone with a fifteen-year-old memory. There were a thousand paths to follow, most of them leading nowhere.

Out in Las Vegas Louie Eppolito was still hustling to make his big deal. He was working on several projects, including a script about the NYPD's Harbor Patrol Unit. Legendary Las Vegas casino owner Bob Stupak had been talked into hiring him to write a screenplay about his extraordinary life; he paid him $5,000 but canceled the deal after reading the first few pages. Renowned TV producer Dick Wolf supposedly had *Mafia Cop* under option for several years, although not much seemed to be happening with that project. Finally Eppolito argued with Wolf, demanding he return the rights if he wasn't going to develop the movie. Wolf agreed, and Eppolito told his friends that another company was getting ready to make the film. According to those same friends, Louie also claimed he'd done some work spicing up some dialogue for Pulitzer Prize–winning writer David Mamet, showing off a beautiful ring that Mamet supposedly had sent him in appreciation of his effort. If people listened to Louie, director David Lynch had called him several times, and his close friend Robert De Niro really wanted to develop *Mafia Cop* but wouldn't put up any money to option it.

Eppolito played the tough-guy role so well that it had become apparent he wasn't acting. That was Louie Eppolito: He just couldn't keep his mouth shut. He bragged to the FBI's cooperating witness, Steve Corso, that when he had been caught red-handed with confidential NYPD documents concerning wiseguy Rosario Gambino he beat "a federal case," after an FBI agent admitted the wrong man had been arrested. In actuality, not only had Eppolito never been arrested, the only charges brought against him in that case had been made in an NYPD administrative hearing.

The DEA set up a simple scam. Corso had proposed putting together a three-movie package and raising $6 million by selling shares to the public, estimating they could make as much as $250,000 just in filing fees. Louie was gung-ho for the deal, putting up three screenplays he'd written as his contribution in return for stock. Some of Eppolito's legit friends were considerably less enthusiastic. One of them, a stockbroker, suggested, "Louie, let me meet this guy. There's just something wrong about this. It doesn't sound right."

"No, no," Louie said. "Believe me, this is the chance for all of us. We're gonna have some money, we're finally gonna get to make some movies." Reality never got in the way of Louie Eppolito's fantasies. "We're gonna be the first real movie company in this town. We're gonna have complete control."

A low-budget movie producer friend who was going to be part of the deal pleaded with him, "C'mon, Louie, what'll it hurt? Why don't you just let us meet this guy? In five minutes we'll know if he's for real."

Eppolito refused and continued to meet with Corso, and Corso continued to tape every single word he said.

Meanwhile, in New York everybody was waiting for Burt Kaplan to make his decision. A month passed, then two months, and they were deep into the summer. Still no word from the old man. As more time passed Vecchione and Ponzi and Dades began to doubt Kaplan was going to flip. Whenever they got together or spoke on the phone they'd wonder what was going on in his mind. Obviously he was wrestling with the concept, which was a good sign, but thus far it didn't look like he was winning the match. They also spent a considerable amount of time speculating about his tantalizing suggestion that there was a third player in this scenario. They racked their brains trying to figure out who that might be. There was absolutely no hint of another dirty cop mentioned in Casso's 302s. Not a clue. It had to be a cop, but who? And how did he fit into the program? They tried to figure out who Louie was closest to, who Steve was closest to, who they trusted enough to bring into the inner sanctum. And did Gaspipe know about this mysterious player and protect him for some reason?

Whoever it was, they knew they weren't going to put a name on him until Kaplan handed it to them. *If* Kaplan decided to flip.

Occasionally Ponzi would wander across the street to the U.S. Attorney's office to find out what was going on. At that time Kaplan was being represented by a noted civil rights lawyer in Alabama, who would have to negotiate any deal that was made. "You hear from the lawyer?" Ponzi asked Feldman.

"Yeah, Burt's still thinking about it. He wants to talk to his family before he decides."

Ponzi and Mark Feldman had been close friends for two decades. But as the weeks passed he began to think that maybe the U.S. Attorney had already met with Kaplan and Hynes's office was being iced out. Until the day in August when Robert Henoch called. "You ready?"

"Ready for what?"

"We're flying down to West Virginia to see Burt. I just got the call. His lawyer's gonna be there."

It turned out Kaplan hadn't agreed to anything more than a second meeting; this was just a meet-and-greet, a feeling-out process, but based on his previous hard-line attitude both Vecchione and Ponzi were optimistic he was going to flip. Mark Feldman, Henoch, Ponzi, and Mark Manko from the DEA flew to Morgantown. Oldham was supposed to go with them but failed to show up at the airport; he explained later that he had some difficulty making the flight.

During Ponzi's more than three decades in the DA's office he'd seen numerous investigators travel on business to a lot of interesting and sometimes exotic places—and, he mused, he got to go to Morgantown, West Virginia. Kaplan was being held nearby in a federal prison in Glenville, West Virginia. They met with Kaplan and his attorney in a secure DEA facility. This time Kaplan was dressed modestly in trousers and a T-shirt rather than a prison jumpsuit.

The lawyer was tough, telling the investigators at the beginning of the meeting, "I want you guys to know, I don't represent cooperators."

Oh, that's just dandy, Ponzi thought when he heard that. *Now how the fuck is this going to work?* But the lawyer did his job, letting Kaplan make his own decisions and providing the legal advice he needed to do it.

The beginning was almost the end. Kaplan knew exactly what he wanted in return for his testimony. He wanted the government to admit officially that there had been some irregularities at his pot trial. That would cause the verdict to be overturned or at least provide him with the basis for a resentencing. And he was adamant about it.

Since the deal had to be made with the Feds, that decision was up to Mark Feldman—and he wasn't about to relent. He couldn't make that happen, he explained, but instead he offered, "You cooperate with us fully and we'll bring back the extent of your cooperation to the court, and we'll do everything in our power to get you a resentencing."

They sparred over the details for a long time, unable to reach a compromise. Ponzi sat quietly, afraid that the deal was going south. In negotiations like this one the grunts, the cops and the investigators, always want the government to give the informant whatever he needs so that they can hear what he has to say. Ponzi was thinking, *Just sign the fucking thing and let's go,* but he knew that neither side was ever going to do that. This was poker for life. Sometimes he could just look at a guy and make a pretty good guess whether or not he was bluffing to get a better deal. But Kaplan? Kaplan knew his value and made it clear, without any smugness or arrogance, that the government couldn't make the case without him. His confidence in that reality just leaked out of his pores—*You want two dirty cops? Then you've got to help me.* Would he walk away if he didn't get exactly what he wanted? Ponzi couldn't even make a decent guess. But he believed without any doubt that Kaplan was capable of doing exactly that. The old man was tough enough to live inside until he died. That was quite a choice he had to make.

And Mark Feldman? Mark Feldman played by the rules; he wouldn't even hint at anything more than he was legally entitled to offer.

Eventually they maneuvered around that roadblock, agreeing to see what compromise could be worked out. Kaplan had additional concerns. His reputation was at stake. If he agreed to cooperate and was moved to a location to be debriefed, his name would no longer show up on the Bureau of Prisons registry. The registry is a website often checked by inmates, and usually, when someone disappears from the site, there's a good chance he's "gone bad." That worried Kaplan. Not only would it destroy his reputation, if he ever had to go back into the general population, it could cause him potentially fatal problems. Nobody likes a rat, even when he's ratting out dirty cops.

Feldman and Henoch said that they might be able to manipulate that listing for a while, but clearly if he flipped, at some point people were going to know about it.

When all of the preliminary discussions were done Burt Kaplan finally began talking about the only subject that mattered. He told them he was going to whet their appetite, he was going to give them a taste of the information he could provide—while making sure they knew there was a lot more. A whole lot more. Kaplan was a *schmatte* salesman; selling was his art. This time though, rather than a truckload of Calvin Klein rip-offs, he was selling his memories. The price was negotiable, so like any great salesman he was trying to convince them he was selling gold.

Kaplan eased into his story. Initially he referred to Eppolito and Caracappa with broad generalizations or characterizations, being careful not to use their names. Eventually he added a wink to his dialogue—*You know I know their names, you know I know who they are.* And finally he began talking about them in very personal and specific terms.

He was looking directly at Ponzi the first time he said their names. Louie and Steve. A chill literally ran down Ponzi's spine. *Geez,* Ponzi thought, *we got them. We fucking got them!* But the impassive expression on his face never changed.

Kaplan gave them the Lino hit. He gave them Dilapi. And finally he told them about the day they'd grabbed Jimmy Hydell. It was a Saturday and he had called Eppolito that morning to tell him Gas was getting impatient. "C'mon, guys, what's going on with this?" he asked.

Eppolito had told him, "We're chasing the kid all over town. We've been out to Staten Island a few times already to search around his house." Later that day Eppolito had called to report, "We got him. We finally got him."

Ponzi didn't ask too many questions that first day, content to let the Feds hear as much as they needed

before negotiating their deal. But he was impressed by
the old man. Kaplan spoke with confidence and clar-
ity, and with enough resignation and sadness in his
voice to convince Ponzi that this really was a tough,
tough thing for him to do. He was betraying the ideals
of a lifetime.

It was much later that Kaplan finally identified the
mystery man, the third man. It turned out they had
known who it was all along. This whole thing had
started with Eppolito's cousin, Frank Santora. "It
wasn't the two of them alone," Kaplan said. "It was
the three of them. Santora was the connection to the
cops."

By the end of the day Kaplan had firmly established his bona fides. He'd sold himself. No one
doubted that his testimony could put Eppolito and
Caracappa away for the duration. But Ponzi noticed
one other thing: Kaplan appeared to like him. Often
after revealing a certain piece of information he'd
glance at Ponzi as if he was looking for approval. In
response Ponzi was always encouraging, nodding and
smiling, *That's good, go on, tell me a little more
about that*. Ponzi felt the two of them had established
a certain comfort level. That was a big part of the art
of interrogation: Become the man the subject needs
you to be.

Kaplan had made his pitch, but now they had to try
to close the deal. After that first meeting Kaplan's
lawyer was in fairly constant communication with
Feldman's office. Kaplan was adamant that the Feds
assist him in overturning his conviction or at least
paring down his twenty-seven-year sentence. The U.S.
Attorney, Roz Mauskopf, was equally adamant that
that was not going to happen. Her office was not going

to concede that anything improper or inappropriate had taken place. Instead, their offer was pretty straightforward: Cooperate with us, give us substantial information, and at some point we will attempt to get you a resentencing.

At the same time, Feldman was making the necessary arrangements to house Kaplan in the New York metropolitan area—just in case. They were also pushing Kaplan to find an attorney who lived in the area, someone who could be with him on a regular basis.

Vecchione, and to a somewhat lesser extent Dades, was confident Kaplan was going to take a deal. Ponzi wasn't sure; he was too experienced to confuse hope with reality. Almost a decade earlier Kaplan had turned down a much better offer, but that was before he'd spent nine years behind bars and was looking forward to basically nothing for the rest of his life. Times change. Kaplan's daughter Deborah was a respected civil court judge and she and her husband had just adopted a baby from Russia, his grandchild. And just maybe Kaplan had finally accepted the fact that the old rules no longer applied. Even Casso had rolled over like a puppy, going on national TV to confess, on *60 friggin' Minutes*!

There were other things in the equation that Kaplan had to consider; he didn't know for sure how much the government had on the cops, but it wasn't too much of a leap to imagine one of them begging for a deal—and putting him on the bull's-eye.

Whatever his reasons, Burt Kaplan flipped. As soon as Ponzi heard the news he called Mike Vecchione. "No kidding," Mike said, impressed. "That's great."

Tommy Dades was less excited. "We're out of it

now," he said. "Now Feldman doesn't need us for nothing."

Kaplan took the promise. In a secret appearance in a Brooklyn courtroom in late August he stood before Judge Jack Weinstein and pleaded guilty to kidnapping, money laundering, obstruction of justice, racketeering, and murder. Among the specific crimes he admitted to was facilitating the murder of Nicky Guido. At the same time he agreed to drop all of his legal motions appealing his marijuana conviction. Burt Kaplan was making the biggest bet of his life.

The government guaranteed absolutely nothing except that they would write letters to the judges considering his fate acknowledging the degree of his cooperation. When asked later what kind of deal he'd made, he shrugged and admitted, "Zero to life." He did admit that he received one additional benefit: "The government helped me get some teeth."

Kaplan was moved to New Jersey. His debriefing began in early October 2004 and lasted six months. Day after day, week after week, Burt Kaplan matter-of-factly described in incredible detail the greatest betrayal in the history of the New York City Police Department.

Kaplan met with representatives of the U.S. Attorney's office, the DEA, the FBI, and the Brooklyn DA's office in a large hotel suite located in the Morristown, New Jersey, area. He was housed in a local jail—and hated it. He was inside with a lot of young punks and low-level shitheads, definitely not the class of criminal with whom he had long associated. He was there under an assumed name and nobody knew who he was. After his debriefing had begun, the Feds arranged for him to be carried on the Bureau of Prisons website as "in transit" for almost three months, so the fact that he had flipped remained a secret.

He was allowed to dress casually for these meetings and there was always a supply of his favorite foods, bananas and nuts, on hand. It was a pretty loose atmosphere—where was he going? His keepers went with him on long walks, often with federal investigator Joe Campanella, which he savored. After Bobby I joined the debriefing team, he would go with him to the various locations Kaplan had described, usually places he had met the two cops, like a rest stop on the Long Island Expressway, a cemetery, or even Caracappa's apartment.

The people allowed to participate in Kaplan's debriefings changed through the months, but Rob Henoch ran the show. Initially the interrogation went slowly, because Henoch absolutely insisted that the questions asked Kaplan could not be leading, meaning they couldn't contain nuggets of information that he could simply regurgitate. Cops are notorious for asking questions laden with detail and whenever someone did that Henoch would explode.

The final question that had to be answered was, how was the quality of Kaplan's memory? Nobody yet knew how his age, his medical problems, and his nine years behind bars had affected his mind. If he ever got on the witness stand a good defense attorney was going to use every small mistake he made to attack his testimony. If he said the curtains were white and they turned out to be yellow, the jury would know about it. A good defense attorney would chip away at each detail until the jury doubted Kaplan remembered his own name. From the very beginning he complained that his memory was not good. He preferred a very structured question-and-answer format, but Henoch wouldn't permit that. He wanted every detail to come from Kaplan. He didn't want a defense attorney to be able to claim that Kaplan had been fed the right answers. In fact, after they'd establish a rhythm, when someone asked a leading question Kaplan would shake his head and warn, "He's going to give you a demerit for that one."

It turned out the old man's memory was extraordinary, better than anyone could have hoped. He remembered conversations and locations; he remembered the layout of Caracappa's mother's apartment, the color of his cat, and his wife's first name. He remembered Eppolito's girlfriend's name and the clothes people wore and the places they met. It was a depth of detail that no one could possibly know if they hadn't been there.

As the questioning continued it also became apparent that he was very fond of Caracappa—but despised Eppolito. Like most of the questioners, Joe Ponzi had initially believed that Eppolito was the leader and Caracappa was just going along with him. But as the days and weeks passed he began to realize that it probably was the other way around—the taciturn Caracappa had in fact called the shots, while letting his boisterous partner stay out in front. As far as Kaplan was concerned, Eppolito was a pig, a glutton, and a fool. The two cops used to visit him at his house, he said. When he knew one of them was coming over, he would turn out the porch lights. Ponzi liked that metaphor—most people turn *on* the lights when expecting guests, but for these guys Kaplan preferred the darkness.

Once, he said, he got into an argument with Eppolito and kicked him out of the house. Ponzi knew he didn't mean physically; Eppolito was a tough guy, nobody tossed him around. After that though, Kaplan refused to speak to the two cops. Until Caracappa showed up at his house to make amends—and brought Kaplan some cookies as an apology.

The tale Kaplan told was astonishing. While Ponzi had known at least some of the information, the extent of Eppolito and Caracappa's betrayal, their complete depravity, astonished him. At times he'd just put his head in his hands and wonder, *How the hell could these two skells go to work every day, look people in the face, and then screw them so completely? Could they have really hated the people they worked with that much?*

Over the next six months Burt Kaplan told the whole story, from his first conversation about the cops with Frank Santora in the Allenwood Prison Camp in 1982—"Frankie approached me and said his cousin was a detective and, if I wanted, his cousin could get me information and could help me if I had problems"— right through his last meeting with Louis Eppolito in Las Vegas more than a decade later, when he was on the run and loaned him $65,000—although Louie had asked for $75,000 for a down payment on a house. He told them about murders and kidnappings; he told them how Caracappa had alerted Casso to the presence of cooperating witnesses like Otto Heidel and painters union official James Bishop. He told them how Louie had found a secretly recorded audiocassette in Heidel's apartment after he had been murdered—he and Casso had listened to it together and heard both Casso and Vic Amuso's voice. On one of the tapes, Kaplan remembered, Heidel took a takeout order from Amuso, who wanted soup. Kaplan told them how Casso had tracked down the men who had attacked him and murdered them. He told them about the attempt to whack Sammy "the Bull" Gravano that Eppolito and Caracappa eventually admitted they couldn't pull off. He told them how Caracappa had tracked down Anthony Dilapi's location in California by writing to his parole officer—twice. He told them how Eppolito had gleefully recounted the cold-blooded killing of Eddie Lino just off the Belt Parkway. On and on, detail after detail, names, places, small crimes and murders; he told them about how much Casso paid for each job and the fact that Gaspipe had finally put the cops on his payroll at $4,000 a month. Once Kaplan began talking he spilled it all, everything he knew, everything, more than anyone would have dared hope.

Kaplan remembered details that Casso had neglected to include in his 302. Gaspipe's initial dealings with the cops apparently took place in 1985, Kaplan said, when Gaspipe asked him if he could launder two stolen $500,000 treasury bills. One of Kaplan's associates, a Hasidic banker named Joe Banda, used an Orthodox Jewish jeweler to successfully cash the first T-bill in Europe. Kaplan never knew the jeweler's name. When European law enforcement got a whiff of this jeweler's trail, Casso and Kaplan were afraid he would roll over and decided to kill him. At Kaplan's request, Santora asked the cops if they wanted the contract. Were the two detectives willing to commit murder to cover a money laundering scheme? Santora told Kaplan that they would do the job for $30,000.

Several days later Santora told him that the cops had used a police car to pull the jeweler to the side of the road, informed him that he was a suspect in a hit-and-run, and told him that he had to appear in a lineup.

The unsuspecting jeweler went along with them and was handed over to Santora, who shot him and buried him. Kaplan didn't know exactly where they killed him or where his body was buried. Only years later, after Santora's killing, did he find out that Santora had kept some of the cops' payment for himself.

According to Kaplan, Eppolito and Caracappa liked the work. They even refused payment from Casso for getting him the names and mug shots of the people who had tried to kill him. That was a favor, they told him, evidence of the quality of the material they could provide.

Ponzi, and later Vecchione, speculated that Casso must have believed he'd hit the wiseguy jackpot when he realized what he had: two NYPD detectives at the top of the information food chain offering to work for him. In the whole history of organized crime there had never been anybody like these two guys. It was like having family members on the job.

It was one-stop shopping. When Gas complained that he couldn't find Jimmy Hydell he paid the cops $35,000 to kidnap and deliver him. While some of Kaplan's confession simply corroborated evidence that Tommy Dades and the other investigators had already gathered, he added a considerable amount of detail. For example, Santora told Kaplan that after the cops had handed over Hydell, he'd put him in the trunk and driven to the Toys "R" Us parking lot. The whole way Hydell was banging on the inside of the trunk. Finally Santora got so irritated that he stopped the car, opened the trunk, and punched Hydell several times, until he finally shut up.

It was from Kaplan that everyone finally learned

what had happened to Jimmy Hydell in the basement of mobster James Gallo's house. It was brutal. And it lasted a long time. Kaplan had heard it directly from Casso. Although Jimmy Hydell wasn't a made guy, his uncle was a significant member of the Gambino family. Betty Hydell had almost no relationship with this particular brother-in-law. But Casso, a member of the Lucchese family, knew that he couldn't whack the nephew of a Gambino without permission. So rather than risk possible retribution from the uncle, or other Gambinos, family boss John Gotti for instance, he invited a faction of Gambinos to the basement to hear right from Jimmy Hydell's mouth that he was part of the hit team and that Mickey Boy Paradiso, a Gambino capo, had given out the contract. Only after the Gambinos gave their permission to kill Hydell did Casso proceed.

And then he began shooting Hydell, over and over, but he shot him in parts of the body that would produce incredible pain but wouldn't be fatal.

Casso told Kaplan that Hydell had said to him, "I know you're going to kill me, Anthony. I want you to promise me one thing: I want you to throw my body out in the street so my mother can get the insurance money."

Casso had agreed, but it never happened. Hydell's body disappeared and Kaplan didn't know what had happened to it. And definitely he did not ask.

If Kaplan didn't know the answer to a question he didn't make it up or speculate. As Ponzi knew, some people try to impress their questioners by having an answer for every question they're asked. Not Kaplan. He knew only what Casso told him. That's it. Once, someone wondered why Kaplan hadn't asked Casso a particular question. Kaplan practically looked right through the person who asked that question, telling him, "You don't ask this guy questions. He's not that kind of guy. That could only get you hurt. Gas would tell you what he wanted to tell you. Most of the time you didn't want to know, 'cause it was safer that way."

Often at the end of a long day with Kaplan, Ponzi would call Vecchione or Tommy Dades. In a general way he would tell Vecchione about Kaplan's testimony, explaining that much of it corroborated Casso's 302 almost word for word. Vecchione didn't ask too many questions. Usually he'd just chuckle, mostly in disbelief. What a deal Casso had passed up.

Tommy Dades didn't want to know what was going on. Nothing. With the growing distrust between the state and the Feds, he believed that the fewer details he knew about the investigation the better it was for him. "I'm happy it's going well" was the most he would tell Ponzi. "I don't need to know."

Rarely in Joe Ponzi's career had he spent so much time with a single witness. Most of his previous encounters had lasted only a day or two, three at most, just long enough to do a polygraph or flip a guy. But the debriefing of Burt Kaplan went on for months, and over that time he began to develop a relationship with the old man. Ponzi had always been very careful never to become friendly with one of these guys; this was his job, and that meant never allowing any of it to become personal. But as the days passed he did develop a rapport with Kaplan. "We developed a strange kind of bond," Ponzi explained. "I think he knew that I was a straight shooter and he liked that. I think he recognized me as someone who got it. I never like to characterize relationships with people like that as 'I liked him,' but I'd be hard-pressed to tell you I didn't.

"Burt Kaplan was a smart guy. I thought that he had an understanding of who he was. In fact, once he said about himself, 'I'm a criminal. I'm being honest here, I'm a criminal.' He accepted the fact that he'd picked this life, and he wasn't the slightest bit apologetic about any of it. I thought he understood people and knew how the game was played. I don't think he felt terribly bad about any of this; I think he liked that life but felt that if Santora had lived things would have turned out differently.

"I thought he respected me if not liked me."

Kaplan sometimes referred to Ponzi as "Chief," and usually when Joe came into the debriefing room Kaplan would greet him with some sort of friendly comment. "Nice suit," he would tease him. "It's refreshing to see a guy dressed like a businessman." Other times he'd appraise the quality of Ponzi's suit, making it clear he was not impressed. Once, after Ponzi had missed a few sessions and then shown up and begun peppering him with questions machine-gun style, he said, laughing, "Whoa, look who's here. I guess they brought in the big guns today."

Several different times Kaplan looked right at Henoch and told him pointedly, "You know, the only reason I'm here is because of that guy." Meaning Ponzi.

Henoch didn't respond particularly well to that comment. From the first day, he maintained absolute control of Kaplan. It was obvious that if the Feds thought they could make a RICO charge stick—which was looking more and more likely—Henoch would be prosecuting the case, and piece by piece he was very deliberately building his prosecution.

As early as possible in the process Ponzi began bringing Bobby Intartaglia to the meetings. That was an obvious choice. Bobby I went a long way back with Kaplan. After the attempt on Casso, detectives had discovered that the car he was driving was registered to Kaplan's clothing business, Progressive Distributors. Bobby I conducted an extensive surveillance of Kaplan's warehouse on Staten Island. He'd snapped thousands of photographs.

Kaplan and Bobby I got along very well. They knew a lot of the same people, they spoke the same language, they'd even gotten started in their careers at about the same time. Kaplan was comfortable with Bobby I's easy manner. Intartaglia also formed a nice relationship with Kaplan's wife and would bring her with him for visits. Eventually, when Ponzi began cutting back on the number of meetings he attended—the debriefing was proceeding very well and he was busy running a hundred-person bureau—Bobby I took his seat at the table.

After Ponzi successfully flipped Kaplan, any leverage the state might have had disappeared. The Feds stormed the barricades, and Henoch began pushing Brooklyn out of the equation. At one point Vecchione officially cross-designated Josh Hanshaft to represent the office. That meant he was going to be Joe Hynes's man on the prosecution team. But any illusion Hanshaft had that Henoch was going to welcome him disappeared the first time he went down to South Jersey to meet Kaplan. He drove down with Bobby I. When they got there, rather than putting Hanshaft to work, Henoch wouldn't let either of them in the room with Kaplan. He made them wait outside in the hallway for a couple of hours. Bobby I was furious, complaining loudly, "We're supposed to be working together. What are we doing here?"

When Ponzi got to the office and saw Hanshaft and Bobby I sitting outside like schoolboys he went inside to talk to Henoch to find out what was going on. During a sometimes heated conversation Henoch said flatly, "I'm not going to allow my witness to talk to—"

"*My* witness?" Ponzi was incredulous. He rarely loses his temper, but this time he was tiptoeing on the edge. "What do you mean, 'my witness'? I'm the one who turned this guy. 'My witness'? Are you kidding me?"

Henoch backed off and brought Hanshaft into the debriefing room to meet Kaplan. But Henoch was never forthright with Hanshaft; he never voluntarily shared information about the case or made him feel like he was part of the prosecution team. When Hanshaft finally confronted him, insisting, "Tell me what you want me to read so I can assist you," Henoch simply tossed a book of press clippings to him. Hanshaft believed from his first day on the case that Henoch had no interest in keeping him around—and perhaps was already figuring out how the state was going to be tossed off the case.

When Vecchione learned about Ponzi's confrontation with Henoch he went to see Joe Hynes. "It's not over yet," he told him, "but it looks like we're getting the boot here."

There was nothing Hynes could do about it at that point. "Just keep me posted," the DA said. "Let's just see how it plays out."

Hanshaft finally approached Henoch, telling him, "Rob, I don't need to know about everything if you're not comfortable with that. I understand your concern about information getting out. But I'm here. I'm not going to sit at these meetings with my thumb up my ass. You need to involve me more. Partition the case; just give me a piece of it."

Henoch gave him the Eddie Lino murder. For Burt Kaplan, Eddie Lino was just another job for his cops. It was typical of the work they did for Gaspipe. As Kaplan explained, so calmly he might have been talking about a truckload of designer suits, "Casso wanted to kill Lino because he'd approved of the original plot against him. He asked me to ask the cops if they wanted to take the contract." The agreed price for the job was $75,000. Kaplan was in the New York Eye and Ear Hospital, recovering from cataract surgery, when Eppolito shook him awake. "We got him," he said, slapping down a newspaper on the food tray. He told him the story in detail, including the fact that Caracappa had been the shooter.

Kaplan said he had asked Eppolito, "So how come Steve shot him instead of you?"

Eppolito replied, "Steve was always the better shot."

Hanshaft set out to make himself an expert on the murder of wiseguy Eddie Lino.

And Kaplan just kept talking.

CHAPTER 11

"Isn't it true, Mr. Kaplan, that in exchange for your testimony against my client the government has agreed to reduce your twenty-seven-year prison sentence?"

"No. There's no such agreement."

"And isn't it true your daughter recently adopted your first grandchild? A child you'll never be able to hold while you're in prison?"

"That doesn't have anything to do with it."

"And didn't the government spend six months with you reviewing the testimony you're giving here today?"

"Nobody reviewed anything. They asked me questions and I answered them."

"So let me ask you this, Mr. Kaplan. Wouldn't you say just about anything to get out of prison?"

"Objection!"

Mike Vecchione could just imagine how the defense attorneys would attack Kaplan's credibility. He'd been there several times in his own career. But sometimes you've got to use some grit to clean up the mess.

In 1993 he'd put a killer on the witness stand as his primary witness in a case in which an off-duty police officer, Robert Cabeza, had used his shield to get behind a bulletproof safety partition in a liquor store and then killed the store owner. His accomplice flipped to try to get a better deal. When this accomplice testified, Cabeza's lawyer portrayed him as a lying murderer, willing to say anything to cut a deal for himself. *Ladies and gentlemen of the jury, he's a convicted murderer; are you telling me he wouldn't lie?*

The best way to avoid that, maybe the only way, is to get as much corroborating evidence as possible. A prosecutor has to prove to a sometimes skeptical jury that his witness is telling the truth, and he does that by providing supporting evidence.

Kaplan had been better than a road map. He'd been their GPS, not only providing the directions, but giving them a multitude of worthwhile stops along the way. The trial strategy was obvious: Kaplan would testify first, describing in detail the scope of Eppolito and Caracappa's betrayal. He would be followed on the witness stand by a series of other witnesses who would corroborate his testimony and add their own independent experiences. The job of the task force was to find those witnesses, as well as whatever physical evidence was available. If Kaplan said Eppolito drove a Cadillac, they needed to know the mileage. If Kaplan said Caracappa had a black cat, they needed to find out that cat's name.

Some witnesses who would appear were obvious: Tommy Dades, for instance. After Kaplan testified that Casso had asked him to see if the cops could get Nicky Guido's address, Dades would tell the jury how he discovered that Caracappa had run a computer search of all the Nicky Guidos in Brooklyn on November 11, 1986, and mistakenly supplied Kaplan with the address of an innocent young man—six weeks before that man was murdered. Then the jury would see the printout; maybe they'd even get to hold it and feel the link to the dead man.

Betty Hydell certainly would testify. Juries relate to mothers, particularly a mother who can identify the people who abducted her son. After Kaplan informed the jury that Casso hired the cops to locate and pick up Jimmy Hydell, Betty would take the stand—maybe she'd even point dramatically at Eppolito and Caracappa—and identify them as the detectives she had seen outside her house the day her son disappeared.

Tommy Galpine, Kaplan's gofer, who was serving a sixteen-year sentence for the same marijuana deal in which Kaplan was sentenced to twenty-seven years, would almost certainly flip once he learned that the old man had made a deal. Galpine could both support Kaplan's allegations as well as testify about his own dealings with the crooked cops. Somebody had to go talk with him.

Certainly the task force would try to find the eyewitness to the murder of Eddie Lino, a man who could confirm much of what Kaplan claimed he had been told by Eppolito. Several former wiseguys living happily in the Witness Protection Program would be approached to see what and how much of Kaplan's testimony they might be able to support. Henoch's list of potential witnesses was a long one, and as the investigation progressed it would get substantially longer.

In addition to the computer printout a substantial amount of documentary evidence would be introduced to support Kaplan's claims. Eppolito's financial records would show that he had received a lot of money from an unknown source at about the time Kaplan testified he'd loaned him $65,000 of the $75,000 Eppolito had requested. Hospital records would prove Kaplan was recovering from cataract surgery when Lino was killed. Real estate records would prove Steve Caracappa's mother lived on Staten Island, right where Kaplan said he had gone to meet him. Motor vehicle records would show that the car Casso was driving when attacked was registered to Kaplan's company. By the time the case was ready to be tried the task force would have turned a mountain of paperwork into steel links between Kaplan, Casso, and the two cops.

And there was at least one more lead that needed to be pursued. It probably was going to be another dead end—at best it was a long shot—but it was one of those intriguing possibilities that a good detective needs to close down. The garage on Nostrand Avenue. The place where Jimmy Hydell had been transferred from Santora's car to Casso's car. Tommy Dades had spent several months trying to find it. He didn't know why he felt it was so important. Chances that a bystander had seen something worthwhile, remembered it, and could be located were south of nonexistent. But Dades just had a cop's itch about this place. So when he went back to work on the case after joining Hynes's office, he made finding it his primary objective.

What seemed like such an easy transition from the NYPD to the DA's office turned out to be a lot more difficult than Dades had anticipated. As a first-grade detective he'd enjoyed a great degree of independence; as long as he produced, he pretty much structured his own days and nights. As the new guy in Hynes's office he had very different responsibilities. Maybe it was just the culmination of too much happening too soon, maybe he should have taken some time away from the job, but it didn't click for him in the detective investigator's office. He struggled there, but rather than complaining to Ponzi or Vecchione, after four months he resigned. Both Ponzi and Vecchione tried to talk him out of it, tried to reason with him, but he'd made up his mind. He walked out the door and didn't look back.

For the first time in his adult life Tommy Dades wasn't on the job. A lot of his identity had been tied into that shield and without it he was drifting. Nothing in his life that mattered seemed tied down. He retreated into his PAL gym, spending long hours there every day, teaching kids how to defend themselves. *Keep your guard up, deflect the punches. That way the other guy can't hurt you.*

If only the rest of his life was that basic.

One afternoon several weeks after resigning Dades decided to try one last time to make peace with his father. He left a message, pretty much neutral in tone, a simple "I never heard from you again" kind of thing. In response he received a nasty phone message telling him never to call again, not to write. I'm not interested in hearing from you, his father wrote, I don't want anything to do with you. If I had any other phone numbers for you, I'd call and tell you that to your face.

Tommy called again, this time letting loose some of the anger he felt. On his father's answering machine he left this bitter message: Here's every phone number you possibly can call to get in touch with me, but I don't think you've got the balls to say that to my face. If you decide that you want to take a trip and say it in person, I suggest you make sure it's a one-way ticket, because believe me, you'll never make it back to Minnesota.

His father left one more message. It was pretty much to the point. You're a loser, he said. You don't know what happened between me and your mother. You don't know the truth. If you had any pride, you'd lose my phone number.

Tommy responded with a final blast. When he hung up the phone that time, knowing it was the last time, he actually felt a little better.

At the beginning of September Mike Vecchione began the first of what eventually would be four trials of Brooklyn Democratic leader Clarence Norman. Although far less glamorous than the Mafia cops case, it had far more important implications. In a recent primary election Norman had run his own candidate against Joe Hynes. And with Norman pulling the strings to bring out regular Democratic support, that candidate had had a real chance to win. In heavily Democratic Brooklyn winning the primary guarantees victory in the general election. Norman had made it clear that if his guy won, he intended to walk into court and basically spit in Vecchione's face and tell him to get the fuck off the case.

He had the power to do just that, if his candidate won. Norman's candidate lost. Hynes was set for another term. When Norman walked into the courtroom he barely looked at Vecchione.

It still wasn't an easy case. The state intended to bring four different charges against Norman in four trials. Unfortunately, the Court of Appeals had agreed to hear a challenge to the strongest charge, so while waiting for a decision from that court Vecchione had to bring a secondary charge against Norman.

He was also worried about the jury. Juries can be fixed; he knew that to be absolutely true because it had happened to him in a wiseguy murder trial. The vote for conviction had been eleven to one, and years later he learned that one vote had been bought. There was no possible way he could have won the case. In this situation he was well aware that Clarence Norman was among the most powerful black men in New York politics—and nobody knew how far he might go to stay out of prison.

The charges against him consisted of three felony counts of accepting illegal campaign contributions and a misdemeanor count of concealing contributions from his own campaign treasurer. His defense attorney called it a case of poor bookkeeping—and maybe it really wasn't a strong enough case to bring down the Democratic party leader.

But by the time Vecchione finished his summation to the jury it was no longer about a few thousand dollars in illegal campaign contributions, but rather about upholding the American democratic process. It was about ethics and integrity and the misuse of political power. And it took the jury one day to find Norman guilty of all charges. The conviction automatically caused him to be expelled him from the New York State Assembly, where he had been the number two man, and caused him to be disbarred as a lawyer and give up his leadership of the county Democratic Party. Sentencing was delayed until after the second trial, which was scheduled to begin the following January. Vecchione was already at work preparing for that one.

While Tommy Dades was wrestling his personal demons and Vecchione was prosecuting Clarence Norman, the investigation they had started more than a year ago in a windowless room in the Brooklyn DA's office had become a major investigation involving literally hundreds of investigators from at least five federal and state law enforcement agencies spread across the nation. Dades's casual phone conversation with Betty Hydell had grown into a multimillion-dollar effort to put two dirty cops away for the remainder of their lives. Plus. The cold case had become scalding hot.

As the investigation proceeded late into 2004, so did the legal maneuvering. Joe Ponzi had remained close friends with Mark Feldman and the prosecutor kept him in the loop. A lot of the time, Ponzi believed, Mark was using him to unofficially pass along information he felt Mike Vecchione should know. On a professional basis both Dades and Ponzi often got frustrated by their friend Feldman during this investigation, but their personal relationship remained strong. Both of them had tried hard to work out some sort of accord between him and Mike Vecchione, but that just wasn't going to happen.

One winter afternoon Ponzi was sitting in Vecchione's office, bringing him up to date. Then he mentioned casually that DEA agent Mark Manko had appeared before the grand jury and testified about Kaplan's statements.

Vecchione looked up. "What are you talking about?"

"Don't you know?" Ponzi seemed surprised.

"No, I don't know. Are you telling me they started the grand jury presentation?" Ponzi nodded. Vecchione paused to let that news sink in. "What about our deal to get Hydell? What about us going in with Kaplan, what happened to all that?" He shook his head in disbelief. "Tommy was right. We're getting fucked over here. This is complete bullshit."

Very basically, a legal case begins when a prosecutor presents evidence to a grand jury, then gives that grand jury a charge under the law that fits the evidence. The prosecutor explains exactly what the statute says. If the grand jury believes it has seen sufficient evidence to suggest that a crime may have been committed under that particular statute, it issues a true bill. A true bill means an indictment has been returned and the accused person or persons has been charged with a crime under the specific statute. Then the indictment, the formal accusation charging a defendant or defendants with a crime, is drawn up. The grand jury meets in secret, the proceedings remain private, and there is never any type of public record of what happened in the grand jury room.

So Vecchione knew absolutely nothing about these proceedings until Ponzi alerted him. He assumed the fact that Feldman or Henoch had gone to a grand jury meant they believed they had sufficient evidence to make their RICO charge stick. But even if that was true, Feldman had agreed to take the Hydell case out of it, to let Vecchione try Jimmy Hydell's murder. It certainly didn't look like that was going to happen.

Vecchione was livid. It wasn't just ego, it was the extraordinary sense that he had been conned. He picked up the phone and called Feldman. "I can't believe you're doing this," he said. "We had a deal, Mark. We agreed that we would take Hydell, you would take the RICO if you could make it."

Feldman started to hedge. "That's not really the way

I remember it," he said. "I think I said that if there was a RICO we would take it. Well, there's a RICO."

"Yeah, you did say that," Vecchione agreed. "But you said we would have the murder, you would have the RICO. I went out on a limb and told my boss that we had a deal. You think I'm going to make something like that up?"

Now Feldman backed off completely. "No, but I think maybe you misheard me," he said evenly. "I don't think I ever said that."

Vecchione was incredulous. "C'mon, what are you, kidding me? That's exactly what you said." He was practically screaming into the phone. "I don't understand; how can you deny it? We went through it several times. There were other people there who heard every word. I guarantee you that's not the way Joe Ponzi remembers it."

Mark Feldman was adamant. "I'm just telling you, Mike, that's not the way I remember it. I'd like to speak to Joe and find out how he remembers it. But until—"

"Well go ahead. He's sitting right here." Vecchione put Ponzi on the speaker. "Ask him."

Being in the middle between two people he liked and respected was an unpleasant position for Ponzi. "That's not what you said, Mark. You did say that we were going to go first with Hydell and then you would get the RICO."

After a long, thoughtful pause, Feldman said, "Well, maybe there's something we can do. Maybe there's a compromise here. Give me a little time to get back to you."

Vecchione was burning when he hung up the phone. As he remembers, "For them to tell us that they didn't say exactly what they said to me was such an act of cowardice and betrayal that I couldn't find the words to explain it."

The fact that he'd been anticipating this confrontation for quite some time didn't make it any easier to accept. But there wasn't much he could do about it. That was one thing he knew for sure. Very quietly, in the past several weeks he'd tried to find a different route to Kaplan. He'd asked a couple of young lawyers in the office to find out if it was legally possible to get the old man out of federal custody. Specifically, he wondered if there was some sort of writ he could file in federal court to compel the Bureau of Prisons to hand over Kaplan so he could put him in front of a grand jury. He had spoken to attorneys in the office about that idea and they all pretty much had the same response: *Are you nuts?*

"How about this?" he'd suggested. "We'll tell the judge Kaplan's a witness in a murder case and that the Feds won't let us have him. That they're obstructing governmental administration."

"You really want to start a war?"

"Yeah, I do," Vecchione had replied. He knew if he ended up in court it probably would get ugly, but if there was even a slight chance the state would prevail it would be worth taking the shot. "We're getting screwed here." But there was no pot of gold at the end of this particular legal rainbow. Kaplan was the sole property of the federal government, to do with whatever they pleased. And handing him over to the state of New York apparently wasn't on their agenda.

Feldman called a day later. This time his tone was more conciliatory. "We'd like to come over and talk to you about this. I think we can probably satisfy everybody's concerns."

Vecchione wasn't optimistic. "Yeah, well, we'll see." The news that Feldman had gone back on the agreement had spread rapidly throughout the office. A lot of people working there knew Mark Feldman and liked him and respected him. A few of them, like Ponzi, had worked with him when he was in the DA's office. He'd been a stand-up guy. A relentless prosecutor who didn't back down. This just wasn't the kind of thing he did. It didn't make sense.

Nobody really knew what was going on in the U.S. Attorney's office. Some people speculated that Feldman had been so certain the state wouldn't make the case that he hadn't bothered to clear his agreement with his boss, Roz Mauskopf, or even the head of the Criminal Division. Now he was stuck having to tell the United States Attorney for the Eastern District that the biggest case that office had prosecuted in several decades was going to the state first because he'd made a commitment to let them try it first. And that couldn't happen.

They met in a conference room. In addition to Rob Henoch, Feldman brought his deputy Greg Andres with him. Feldman probably didn't know the history, but that was not a wise decision. As far as Vecchione was concerned, Andres was a typically arrogant poker-up-his-ass know-it-all Fed. His animosity toward Andres went back to a wiseguy case in which Tommy Dades and Mike Galletta had put away Bonanno boss Joe Messina, only to have Andres credit the FBI for work it hadn't done.

Ponzi and Josh Hanshaft were with Vecchione. It wasn't exactly an old Western showdown at ten paces, more like a new Eastern District confrontation, briefcases across a mahogany table. Feldman laid it out. "Look, Mike," he said, "we really believe this is what's best for the case." When Mike started to respond Feldman said, "Just hear me out first. We've got a good RICO case here. If you take the Hydell murder case out of the big picture, take it out of the RICO and put it in the state case, that leaves a big hole in the story. We want to tell the story from beginning to end, so we need to use everything. If you take out Hydell, you remove a big piece of the case. It just doesn't make sense to do it that way."

Andres continued, "If you put Kaplan in the grand jury, you're gonna expose him to cross-examination—"

"Who said we have to go first?" Mike interrupted. The Feds were afraid that if Vecchione put Kaplan on the witness stand before they got a chance to try their case, the cops' defense attorneys would be able to use his testimony to attack his credibility. If he made even a slight error—maybe the wall was painted green, not red—or contradicted himself it could have a damaging effect on the RICO case. The defense could kill him on his cross-examination. So the Feds wanted Kaplan clean when he testified against the cops. Vecchione understood that; that's why he countered by suggesting the Hydell trial follow the RICO case. "You guys are going to trial faster than I am. Let us put the guy into the grand jury and get an indictment, then you use him to try your guys."

"C'mon, Mike," Andres said in a tone that sounded awfully condescending to Vecchione. "We can't expose him to the grand jury."

Among the many legal advantages the federal government enjoys is that hearsay evidence is permitted in cases brought to a grand jury. For example, rather than Kaplan having to personally appear in front of the grand jury, an agent who took his testimony could repeat it to the jurors. Under New York State law the actual witness—in this case Kaplan—must testify before the grand jury.

Vecchione shook his head in disbelief. "What do you think, I'm a newcomer? You think I'm going to put this guy in the grand jury and not prepare him thoroughly enough to get what I need without being inconsistent? Let me tell you something; I don't know Kaplan, I've never said one word to the guy, but I can guarantee you that by the time I put him in the grand jury I'll know every word he's gonna say. What's the big deal? I can do this."

"It doesn't make sense," Henoch insisted. "If we take out Hydell we ruin the continuity of the story. If you put Kaplan in the grand jury I'll have to turn those minutes over to the defense."

For Vecchione, this was a lot more than legal strategy; it was an attack on his professionalism. "Believe me, I can put Kaplan into the grand jury without screwing up your case."

Andres responded, "We would never take a chance on that happening."

Vecchione glared at him, trying to maintain control. Part of him, the emotional part, was urging him to reach right across that table and just grab the arrogant son of a bitch. We would never take a chance on that happening? Who the hell did he think he was? "You don't even know me. I've tried more cases than you can count. I'm not the new kid on the block. So don't give me that bullshit about you guys being better than us because I know I'm better than all of you."

Feldman did his best to calm everybody down. "Now look, let's just look at what's best for the case . . ."

Vecchione listened as Feldman laid it out as dispassionately as he was able. And gradually he had to admit that what he was saying had a lot of merit. Maybe he didn't like it, it wasn't part of any deal, but he had to be honest with himself. For the greater good of the case, it made sense. No matter how angry he was he never forgot that the goal was putting two skells away forever.

As angry as Joe Ponzi was with the Feds, he agreed with Feldman. "Everything flows from Hydell, Mike. That's where the whole sequence of events starts. If you rip that out you lose the whole continuum. Then you just got a lot of pieces."

Vecchione might have kept fighting but he knew that no matter how strongly he believed he could convict the cops for the murder of Jimmy Hydell, he wasn't holding any cards. He wasn't even holding the box the cards came in. This was the reality: The Feds could do absolutely anything they wanted to do and there was nothing he could do to stop them. Kaplan was the case and Feldman had Kaplan. Without Kaplan it was desperation time. *C'mon, Judge,* any good defense attorney would say, *they're coming at my guy with this cheesy old case and an old lady? You gotta be kidding me; twenty years later and that's all they got?*

Vecchione had made his best argument and Feldman hadn't bought it. End of story.

But Mike also was forced to admit that Feldman made sense. Ponzi had strongly felt that way for some time and had been trying to make Vecchione see it. Putting these guys away for Jimmy Hydell might make some people feel better, but it wouldn't begin to tell the whole story of their corruption. And that was a story that needed to be told in its entirety. Too many people had suffered because of these guys, and their families deserved to have a piece of this prosecution. Maybe even more importantly, the punishment for the one murder—even if it meant that Eppolito and Caracappa would spend the rest of their lives in prison— most definitely did not fit the magnitude of their crimes. As far as Vecchione was concerned, if burning in hell for all eternity was a sentence, Eppolito and Caracappa would deserve it. But as that is not yet part of the penal code, the penalties available under RICO were considerably greater than for a state murder conviction. Mike finally accepted the fact that it made sense for the Feds to take the whole case.

It was time to begin the salvage operation. So Vecchione began looking for ways to find the compromise Feldman had offered.

Given the reality of the situation, what he wanted, what he needed, was to make sure that the state got every last bit of the credit that it had earned for making this case. "Okay," Vecchione said. "I'll present it to Hynes and get his okay. But if I'm going to go to my boss, here's what I need in return. I want our people to be in on the arrest. I want to hold the press conference announcing the arrests right here in our office. I want the DA to make the announcement that we broke the case, brought it to this point, and we've arrested, along with the Feds, Eppolito and Caracappa. Then he'll turn it over to Mauskopf and she can continue the press conference. And then I want to cross-designate Josh to work with you."

Feldman nodded. "That sounds good," he said. "I don't see a problem." He said it with real conviction, sounding one step short of absolute sureness. "I know it's difficult for you, but believe me, it's best for the case."

They shook hands. "I have to go talk to the DA first because he's still expecting us to do this case," Vecchione told him. Although he didn't say it, he still believed there was at least a fair chance he was going to get the case back. No matter how he looked at it, he believed the Feds were going to have a very tough time making a RICO stick. The Feds were confident the continuing drug enterprise would extend the statute of limitations, but Vecchione just didn't see it that way. The cops had committed most of their crimes for Casso and Kaplan in conjunction with the Lucchese crime family. The statute of limitations on the individual crimes they had committed had run out years earlier. The only thing that left was RICO. And Vecchione just didn't see how drug deals made by Eppolito in Vegas to pay his bills could be construed as being in the furtherance or the benefit of the Lucchese crime family. Most of the people the cops had worked with were gone. This was going to be a stretch that would make Spider-Man proud. Without the determination that the drug deal benefitted the Luccheses there was no basis for a RICO. And if there was no RICO, well, guess who got the case back to prosecute?

Ponzi and Vecchione went up to Hynes's office. Ponzi laid it out for Hynes: "Boss," he told him, "I think it would be a terrible disservice to yank the Hydell murder case or any independent act out of the guts of this story. This story is best served intact. This thing needs to stay together. Just look at this, this is the best of both worlds. We get the credit for making the case but we don't have to worry about trying it." As long as the office got the lion's share of the credit, which they had earned, Ponzi was very satisfied with the deal.

Vecchione agreed. He had to bury his ego to do so, but he did see the wisdom in keeping the whole case together. "You know how much I want to do this, how hard we've all worked on it. But Feldman makes a lot of sense; it's probably the best thing for the case." Vecchione laid out the agreement for him. "The quid pro quo is that we'll be part of the arrest team, they'll cross-designate Josh Hanshaft as the assistant, and the U.S. Attorney will come over here for the press conference. You'll announce the arrest and talk about our role. Then you'll say something like for the good of the case we're turning it over to Roz Mauskopf. And then she'll say whatever she wants to say."

Hynes gave a lot of authority to his people and respected their judgment. "Okay," Hynes said, "if you guys think this is the best way to do it, then let's do it."

In a phone conversation later that afternoon Vecchione and Feldman reviewed the details and agreed on the deal. Contrary to the cliché, Mark Feldman had successfully made a federal case out of it.

Personally, Vecchione was devastated. Like any effective trial lawyer, he has an ego. He knows how good he is in the courtroom. This was his case, and he was going to win it; he was going to convict two dirty cops. As far as he was concerned, handing it over to Feldman was a big personal setback. He hated that feeling, hated it. But he also believed that handing it over was the right decision for the case, and that had to come before his personal desires.

Tommy Dades almost laughed out loud when Vecchione told him about the decision. He wasn't surprised. "Didn't I tell you right from the beginning that they were gonna fuck us? So they fucked us. What do you expect?" But he was a team player, even when he was no longer officially on the team. From the very beginning of the case he had been keeping Betty Hydell informed of the progress, step by step. After all those years she had finally begun to feel hopeful that somebody was going to pay for her son's murder. And now Tommy had to tell her that no one was going to be charged with the murder of her son. "Look at it this way, Betty. This is best suited for the federal system. They're gonna charge them with everything, so chances that they're gonna get convicted are much better. And it isn't just the twenty-five-to-life we can give them, it's mandatory life. And we're gonna tell the whole story; believe me, nobody's gonna forget about Jimmy."

Betty Hydell and Tommy had become close friends over the past few years. He'd given his word and then made it stick. When he told her this was the best thing for the case, like just about everyone else with a stake in it, she reluctantly accepted it.

Meanwhile, Dades's replacement on the task force, Pat Lanigan, was making some real progress toward finding the garage where Hydell had been handed over. Patty Lanigan was another one of the seasoned old pros. Like Ponzi, he had come from a cop family: His grandfather had joined the force in 1920 and had been one of the founding members of New York's Emergency Service Squad. Lanigan had put in his twenty with the NYPD, spending some of that time working with the legendary Jack Maple creating the computerized response team concept, then becoming one of the original members of the newly formed Cold Case Squad. In fact, he was the first member of that squad to use DNA to break a case, using it to amplify nearly invisible traces of the victim's blood soaked into the feathers of a down jacket owned by the accused killer.

Like a lot of other cops, he'd retired after having a real tough time working at the World Trade Center on 9/11 and in the weeks that followed. After spending more than a year sitting home watching a contractor rebuild part of his home, he'd gotten a job in Ponzi's office in December 2005, pretty much filling Tommy Dades's spot.

Lanigan and Dades had met only once, while digging for a body on a golf course. That was a Bobby I case. Supposedly the strung-out son of a wiseguy drug dealer had been killed and buried behind the seventh hole on the Dyker Beach Golf Course in Brooklyn. Lanigan and Dades's partner Mike Galletta had been at the police academy together, so while the backhoe was ripping up turf, introductions were made. It was a nice day in the sun, although it turned out that there was nothing in the holes but dirt.

By the time Lanigan joined the task force it was meeting every day. Henoch partnered him with an FBI agent and gave them various assignments: Serve this subpoena. Get an address for that guy. See if you can find these files. It was typical grunt work, laying the groundwork for the big battle.

Meanwhile, Kaplan's stories about his relationship with Eppolito's cousin, Frank Santora, had aroused a lot of new interest in the long-dead wiseguy. All the old files on him had been pulled. With the addition of

Kaplan's explanations, a lot of things no one previously had paid much attention to suddenly became important. It turned out Santora had been in the middle of a lot of the action. Very early in Kaplan's debriefing he'd explained how his relationship with Eppolito and Caracappa had blossomed: When Casso had decided that Jeweler #1—the Orthodox Jew whose name Kaplan never knew—couldn't be trusted to keep his mouth shut and had to be whacked, Kaplan asked Santora if the cops could do the job. This was their litmus test, to see how far they would go. Santora reported back to Kaplan that his cousin and his partner had found the guy, pulled him over on the New York State Thruway, and delivered him to Santora at a garage, where Santora had executed him and buried him.

That garage again. Santora had also been at a garage where Jimmy Hydell had been transferred from the backseat of the gray Plymouth, which resembled an unmarked police car, into the trunk. That's why Dades had been trying to locate it.

And then one morning, while talking about something else, Kaplan mentioned casually that Santora had "a relationship" with some guy who owned either a tow truck company, a garage, or both; he wasn't positive about those particular details and he didn't know the guy's name. Santora had told him that "Louie kept a car in that garage" or "someplace right nearby." He didn't know where the garage was though; he'd never been there. He thought it was somewhere in the vicinity of Bedford Avenue, but he wasn't really sure.

That location had always made sense to Tommy

Dades; it was only a couple of blocks away from the Sixty-third Precinct—where Eppolito had been assigned.

It was Bobby I who figured it out. Among the items found on Frankie Santora's body after his murder was his address book. A copy of that book had been sitting in his file since 1987. Page by page, A to Z, Bobby I was working his way through it. And way in the back he found Valiant Towing.

Valiant Towing was owned by someone whose name hadn't popped up anywhere else: Peter Franzone. Franzone turned out to be a hardworking guy, a sixth-grade dropout, a tow-truck driver who had eventually bought the business. Eventually he'd bought an auto-body shop on Nostrand Avenue between Avenues H and I. Strung out in a line in an alley directly behind that repair shop were several one-car garages that Franzone rented out. Garages. Henoch assigned Patty Lanigan and his partner to find Pete Franzone.

Meeting secretly, the grand jury had voted to indict former detectives Louis Eppolito and Steve Caracappa for violations of the RICO Act. The U.S. Attorney drew up the indictment. "The Enterprise," it began. "1. La Cosa Nostra (LCN) was a nationwide criminal enterprise also known as 'the mafia' and 'the mob' that operated in the Eastern District of New York . . . through entities known as 'families.'"

Seven paragraphs down it got to "The Defendants." "At all times relevant to this Indictment, the defendants STEPHEN CARACAPPA and LOUIS EPPOLITO were LCN associates. Specifically they were associated with the Lucchese organized crime family of LCN and, at times, they provided sensitive law enforcement information to the Lucchese Family that was utilized by various New York City–based LCN families . . ."

The core of this indictment was sixteen criminal acts committed for the benefit of the Lucchese crime family. To be found guilty of the RICO charge it had to be proven that Eppolito and Caracappa "would commit at least two acts of racketeering in the conduct of the affairs of the enterprise." It was act two that caught Tommy Dades's attention: Clause D read, "On or about and between September 14, 1986 and October 31, 1986, both dates being approximate and inclusive, within the Eastern District of New York and elsewhere, the defendants STEPHEN CARACAPPA and LOUIS EPPOLITO, together with others, with intent to cause the death of James Hydell, caused his death, in violation of New York Penal Law Sections 125.25 (1) and 21.00."

There it was, right in front, the murder of Jimmy Hydell. The rest of the indictment included a litany of crimes that Feldman and Henoch felt certain they could prove, including eight murders, two attempted murders, murder conspiracy, and several acts of providing confidential information to the Lucchese crime family.

The inclusion of Hydell's murder satisfied Dades, but the clauses that most interested Vecchione were numbers fifteen and sixteen. These were the charges that held the RICO together. Number fifteen concerned "Unlawful Monetary Transactions," the proceeds of "narcotics trafficking" that took place "between December 1, 1994 and December 31, 1995," and sixteen, which occurred "between December 2, 2004 and the date of this filing," also concerned laundering the proceeds from Eppolito's drug deals in Las Vegas. Without those charges, on those dates, the statute of limitations would have prevented the U.S. Attorney from successfully charging the cops under RICO.

Now it was up to the Feds to prove their case. As Vecchione had predicted, that turned out to be a lot more difficult than they'd believed.

CHAPTER 12

The indictments were written but remained sealed as Roz Mauskopf's office began making plans to arrest Eppolito and Caracappa in Las Vegas. Vecchione wondered if the two cops had even the slightest idea that their history was about to become their future. Even as the case slipped away from him, he felt great satisfaction, and some pride, knowing these two skells weren't going to get away with their crimes. He wished he could be there for the arrest just to see the look on their smug faces.

While the actual arrest would be routine, the moment the cops were taken into custody search warrants had to be executed and witnesses had to be approached. That required considerable coordination. The original arrest date was postponed because the investigation out in Las Vegas was still in progress, and a second date was scheduled. That second date was also postponed. Supposedly a third date was picked, mid-March 2005. At seven A.M. on a Friday morning several weeks before the arrests were scheduled, Tommy Dades's daughter woke him up. The kids were getting ready to go to school. "The TV people are outside," she said. "They want to talk to you."

Dades opened the door in his underwear, his hair sticking straight up. A camera team was standing on his front step. A producer introduced herself, then explained, "We're from *60 Minutes*. Do you think we could ask you a few questions?"

Tommy was surprised to see them. He'd had a phone call from a *60 Minutes* producer a couple of nights earlier. Maybe it was the same person; he didn't remember. She hadn't gone into any detail about the case so Dades assumed they were simply checking out rumors. He'd told the producer that night that he wasn't talking to anybody about anything at any time. But here they were, standing on his porch. It was a cold morning so he let the two women into his house. He told them politely that he wasn't talking to anybody, he just wanted to be left alone. Then he called Feldman, who was furious when he heard about it. If the media knew about the case, there was a real chance Eppolito and Caracappa would also know about it. Just get them out of there, he told Dades. Don't talk to them.

Tommy explained the situation to them. One of them asked, "How about after the indictment?"

"Call me after that and we can talk about it. But I'm not even telling you there is an indictment." In fact, these producers knew a lot more about the progress of the case at that moment than Dades did. They knew all about Burt Kaplan, and they knew about other witnesses, much more than they should have known. Eventually they left Tommy's house without ever turning on their cameras. But once again the arrest date was postponed.

There were a lot of people who wanted to know who had leaked that information to the media. Feldman was irate; now that he really had a case he was seriously concerned that *60 Minutes* was going to tip off the cops in Vegas, ruining the ongoing investigation. In the U.S. Attorney's office it was widely believed that someone in Joe Hynes's office had leaked the story out of anger. Feldman called Vecchione and asked him some pointed questions, making it clear he believed the leak had come from Brooklyn. "Mark," Vecchione told him, "I don't have the slightest idea how *60 Minutes* found out, but I can tell you it didn't come from here."

Feldman obviously didn't believe him, pointing out that *48 Hours* had recently done a piece about Vecchione's investigation into a corrupt divorce judge.

Vecchione tried to maintain his composure. "Are you saying that I was somehow involved in leaking this to *60 Minutes*? Mark, you couldn't be more wrong. Tell me how that makes sense. We're already going to get the credit after the arrest is made; what else do we need? You think I want to screw up the prosecution? Is that what you think?"

That conversation ended badly. The source of the leak was never firmly identified, but Vecchione later learned that a DEA agent very loosely connected to the case was talking regularly with a reporter at the *New York Post*. He found it out when that reporter told him one day, "Boy, did I make a big mistake; I meant to call [the DEA agent] and I called the wrong number. I called Mark Feldman and left a message for him, thinking it was the other guy. Feldman called me back and we really got into it."

Eventually Feldman told Ponzi that he knew this

DEA agent was talking to the newspapers. And months later Vecchione read a story in a national magazine that extensively quoted this same DEA agent, further convincing him that this agent was the source of all their headaches. And that did surprise him, because throughout the entire investigation he never met this agent or saw him at any of the many task force meetings.

But at that moment it didn't matter where the information came from; the damage was done. Whatever little trust remained between the U.S. Attorney and the Brooklyn DA's office was just about gone.

A few days later Pat Lanigan and his partner finally got a look at the garage on Nostrand Avenue. They drove past it several times, as always just trying to get the feel of the place. It was a pretty run-of-the-mill repair shop, although it was impossible to see what was going on around back, where the row of garages was located. Peter Franzone had sold the whole operation years earlier. Lanigan had identified the new owner and through him had tracked down Franzone. It was time to go talk to him.

Franzone was working as a maintenance man for the Housing Authority in Sheepshead Bay, Brooklyn. Lanigan and his partner went to his apartment on Avenue I first. When his wife answered the door, Lanigan identified himself and his partner, "Special Agent [name withheld] of the FBI," and explained that they wanted to speak with her husband. Just like on TV. "Don't worry, he's not in any kind of trouble," Lanigan said reassuringly.

"Just wait right here," she told them. They were standing in the hallway. "Right here. Don't move. Don't go anywhere." She started to walk away but turned. "Don't move, okay?" They didn't move. And Peter Franzone wasn't home. So they drove to Sheepshead Bay.

Pete Franzone was short, about five feet four inches tall, and somewhat swarthy. But mostly he was nervous. As Lanigan recalled, "There's good nervous and bad nervous. He was bad nervous." Franzone agreed to return with the investigators to their office to answer some questions. At first the questions were very general: *Did you own the garage? What was the time frame in which you owned it? Did you rent the garages out?* Gradually they got a little more specific: *Did you know any police officers? Did you have any police cars on the lot? Did any police officers leave cars in a garage?*

Franzone said he didn't know any police officers. He didn't rent to any police officers. No police officers left cars there. Lanigan nodded and smiled and didn't believe one word. He knew Franzone was lying, he just didn't know why.

When Lanigan asked to see the bill of sale of the garage Franzone agreed to provide a copy. He said it would take him a day to find it though. "That's fine," Lanigan told him, "I'll come by tomorrow and pick it up."

While Lanigan was in the field, U.S. Attorney Roz Mauskopf was on the phone with Joe Hynes. Apparently writer Jerry Capeci, the respected organized crime expert, and *Daily News* reporter John Marzulli had called her office asking questions about the case. It was clear they had an inside source. It was just as clear that like Feldman, Mauskopf believed the source was someone inside the Brooklyn DA's office. "Now that the media knows about this we're going to have to push this ahead," she said. The arrests were going to be a week early. She told Hynes precisely when Eppolito and Caracappa were going to be arrested, and then added, "And of course you'll come over here for the press conference."

"Wait a second," Hynes said. "Vecchione and Feldman have a deal. I thought we'd agreed that you're supposed to come over here for the press conference."

"No, no," she said firmly. "We're going to do it here."

Vecchione exploded in anger when Hynes told him about the phone call. Minutes later Ponzi was in Vecchione's office and they were talking to Feldman on the speakerphone. "We had a deal, Mark," Vecchione said. "We agreed you guys would try the case and we would do the press conference, and that the DA would announce it along with Mauskopf in our office, then turn it over to you guys."

Feldman's voice was clear and firm. "I never said that to you."

Vecchione took a calming breath, then said quietly, "Mark, you're a liar. Ponzi heard every word of it."

Ponzi agreed. "That was the deal, Mark. We were going to do this here, you guys would try it."

Feldman persisted, "Well, I don't remember it that way and I don't have the authority to commit the U.S. Attorney to come to your building for a press conference."

Vecchione said evenly, "You really fucked me. You've made me look like a fool."

"That wasn't my intention."

Vecchione ignored him. "I went to my boss, I told him what the deal was. And now you're giving me this bullshit. You don't have the authority to do what you did? I have nothing to talk to you about." And then he slammed down the phone.

He just looked at Ponzi and shook his head.

Slightly after six P.M. on Wednesday night, March 9, 2005, Louis Eppolito and Steve Caracappa walked into the upscale restaurant Piero's Italian Cuisine and New England Fish Market. The restaurant is on Convention Center Drive in Las Vegas, just off the famed Strip, the place where dreams live. It's the perfect kind of Vegas place; Jerry Lewis often celebrates his birthday there and the owner was once married to actress Diahann Carroll for several weeks. As the two retired detectives entered they probably didn't even notice the four men walking only a few feet behind them. As Eppolito and Caracappa approached the maître d', the world collapsed on them. Five men, including FBI agents, DEA agents, and Bobby Intartaglia from Joe Ponzi's investigative bureau, rushed out of the bar and pushed them against the oak-paneled wall, shouting that they were under arrest. As they had been taught, the agents took absolute control of the room with overwhelming force. According to witnesses, the agents drew submachine guns. When they frisked Eppolito they discovered a loaded, chambered .45-caliber semiautomatic handgun in his waistband. Within four minutes Eppolito and Caracappa were whisked out of the restaurant and taken to a Vegas jail to be held without bail.

Neither of the cops said a word as they were hustled out of the restaurant. An agent called Tommy Dades the next morning to give him the details and mentioned casually that Eppolito had fallen asleep in his cell. Tommy smiled when he heard that. That's another piece of cop knowledge. It meant that Eppolito had no fight left in him. Dades knew from a lot of experience that when you accuse an innocent guy of an atrocious crime and put him in a cell, he doesn't stop screaming. The only thing that slows him down is a straitjacket. But guilty men don't react that way. When the guy is guilty, he's relaxed; he's busy thinking about how he's going to get out of this jam, and he goes to sleep.

Almost simultaneously, police arrested Eppolito's twenty-four-year-old son Anthony Eppolito at his father's home on charges of distributing methamphetamine. When he was arrested Anthony Eppolito was in possession of about an ounce of the crystal meth, which law enforcement believed he was intending to sell.

Once Eppolito had collected rare snakes, but in his Vegas home detectives discovered an arsenal large enough to equip a rebellion. Among the 131 guns they found were five assault rifles, fifty semiautomatic pistols and submachine guns, and a gold Luger pistol. They also found supposedly incriminating e-mails between Eppolito and Caracappa as well as several NYPD files.

Joe Ponzi was surprised when he heard about one of those files in particular. It contained all the original paperwork from a murder case that he had worked, a 1986 murder that Eppolito had solved. What was Eppolito doing with that particular file, he wondered. That wasn't a cold case; the convicted killer, Barry Gibbs, was still serving his twenty-years-to-life sentence. Ponzi remembered the case well; Gibbs had been convicted of killing a purported prostitute named Virginia Robertson. Her body had been discovered by the Belt Parkway. There had been one witness, an ex-marine with a drug problem who claimed he had seen Gibbs dispose of the body from three hundred feet away, and while Gibbs didn't fit the witness's description, Eppolito had arrested him because he lived near the victim and had been known to have sex and do drugs with her. That witness had picked Gibbs out of the lineup, and according to Detective Eppolito he'd said, "That's him; I'm a hundred percent sure. I'll never forget his face as long as I live." And while the eyewitness was the key to the conviction, a jailhouse snitch in prison with Gibbs on Rikers Island had told Ponzi that Gibbs had admitted the crime to him. Apparently that confession included some details that hadn't been reported in the newspaper. At the time Ponzi had believed the snitch's story had the ring of truth to it. This witness had also testified at Gibbs's trial, although the jury claimed it had dismissed his story. So while Gibbs had screamed pretty loudly that he was innocent, eventually he was sentenced to nineteen years in prison.

So why was Louie holding that file? Ponzi was curious, but he'd spent enough time trying to figure out the motives for the crimes of Louis Eppolito.

The day after the arrests were made the U.S. Attorney issued a press release announcing the indictment. "The indictment alleges that beginning in the early 1980s, the defendants, while serving as New York City Police Department detectives also secretly worked as associates for organized crime . . .". Roz Mauskopf acknowledged the assistance of the NYPD and investigators from Hynes's office at the bottom of a long list. Hynes was then quoted as crediting "Mike Vecchione, Chief of the Rackets Division, [who] led an outstanding team, and I want to especially praise retired NYPD Detective Thomas Dades and Investigator William Oldham of the U.S. Attorney's Office for their tireless efforts in reopening this dormant investigation, along with Detective Robert Intartaglia and retired NYPD detective Doug Le Vien for their work in bringing this case to where we are today . . ."

That same morning Patty Lanigan drove out to Sheepshead Bay to pick up the bill of sale from Peter Franzone. The arrest of Eppolito and Caracappa the night before was all over the news. He wondered if Franzone knew about it. The moment he saw the guy he knew the answer. "He was white," Lanigan remembers, "just pale white. And even more nervous than he'd been the day before."

As Franzone handed him the receipt Lanigan explained, "I'm going to tell you something. This is nothing personal. I'm an investigator for the DA's office, but the gentleman who was with me yesterday is an FBI agent. You know what happens when you lie to an FBI agent?" He decided it was time to take his shot. "Listen to me, we know what happened there. We're giving you an out. If you don't take it, they're going to lock you up. You really should be truthful as far as what happened back in the day."

Peter Franzone's life had been turned inside-out in a day. He never saw it coming. Lanigan was bluffing; nobody except Franzone knew what had happened at that garage—but Franzone couldn't know that. His options were basically nonexistent. Lanigan called his partner and told him they were going back out to see Franzone later that afternoon. "He's ready," he said.

A couple of hours later Franzone climbed into the backseat of their car. Lanigan and his partner turned and looked at him. "Look, Mr. Franzone," Lanigan said, "you really should be honest with us. What you told us yesterday doesn't fit."

Franzone's mouth quivered. He shook his head slightly. "Don't you see," he said, almost pleading, "I'm afraid." He began crying. "I'm afraid."

Lanigan glanced at his partner. Pay dirt. "Just calm down, Mr. Franzone," the FBI agent said. "You don't need to be afraid anymore."

"They had a car," he began. "I rented a garage to them in there. He paid me in cash."

The story came out in disconnected pieces. Twenty years of walls were tumbling down. As every cop knows, when a guy finally breaks down you just let him keep talking, you let him blurt it out, you keep your mouth shut and you listen, even if none of it makes sense. You ask the questions later. "I saw the newspapers," he continued. "I knew as soon as you came to me. I've been holding it in all these years . . ."

After about twenty minutes Franzone was exhausted. The investigators explained the procedure. They wanted him to talk with Henoch. When they got out of the car that afternoon they knew they had the garage, they knew they had Franzone. But in fact, they had no idea what they really had.

In Las Vegas, Robert Henoch appeared in court to argue that Louis Eppolito and Steve Caracappa should be held without bail. The cops were represented by noted criminal lawyer David Chesnoff, who told reporters that the government had based the whole case on "organized crime figures who are trying to save their lives . . . The government is relying on the word of rats." Judge Lawrence Leavitt didn't buy that argument, saying, "Let there be no doubt. These defendants pose a danger to the community," and rejecting their request for bail.

Amazingly, one of the people claiming credit for the arrest was Anthony "Gaspipe" Casso. Vecchione took a deep and somewhat sad breath as he read a letter that Gaspipe had written to the *New York Post* complaining that he was being overlooked. "Like always," Casso had written, "the feds have downplayed my cooperation, while knowing well it would undoubtedly bring to light the government's wrongdoings . . ."

Casso also admitted in this letter that he had been contacted by investigators from Hynes's office who asked for his full cooperation, telling him his "information is right on the money and [Hynes] would like to seek his full cooperation on the matter." The state offered him immunity, he wrote, but he couldn't cooperate because the Feds refused to agree to that deal.

So close, Vecchione thought as he read the letter and thought about his many conversations with Casso's attorney, D. B. Lewis. *So damn close.*

U.S. Attorney Roslynn R. Mauskopf's press conference took place in the Eastern District offices on Friday, March 11. Joe Hynes had finally decided he wasn't going to participate and sent Vecchione and Ponzi to represent the office. The press conference was just about ready to begin by the time they got to Mauskopf's office. Vecchione was shocked when he walked in and saw Charlie Campisi, head of the Internal Affairs Bureau, sitting there. But he was even more surprised when the press conference began and Mauskopf immediately offered congratulations to the IAD for their efforts in the case. "It was amazing,"

Vecchione recalls. "They did absolutely nothing. The first thing they did in the case was show up that day. Their only connection to the case was to tell me they couldn't find the files we needed a year earlier.

"I heard later that the U.S. Attorney wanted Police Commissioner Ray Kelly to be there, but there wasn't a way in hell that Kelly was going to stand on that podium and be embarrassed by having to announce this horrible case against the department. So the fall guy became Campisi. It wasn't Campisi's fault that he was there. To me he looked terribly uncomfortable, and Mauskopf compounded that by giving him credit that hadn't been earned. I wanted to ask him what he was doing there, you don't have anything to do with this case. But I didn't say anything because I didn't want to embarrass the District Attorney or myself.

"Then she thanked the U.S. Attorney's office in Nevada, who did very little. Then she thanked the FBI, which wasn't even in the case for much of the first year. And finally she thanked the DEA, Charles Hynes, and me."

Even Ponzi, who tries hard to be conciliatory, was amazed that so little credit was given to the people in Hynes's office who made the case. One of the primary reasons he had supported Feldman's decision to try the case was the knowledge that his office would at least receive credit for their work.

As Vecchione sat there listening to Mauskopf spin her fantasy of law enforcement cooperation he tried hard to focus on the fact that two really bad guys were finally getting the justice they'd earned. That was what really mattered, he knew that, but he hated seeing the people who had built the foundation for the case a decade after the Feds gave up on it, and helped

build it into the headlines, being screwed. The credit
shouldn't matter, he knew that, but it did. When Mauskopf handed him the microphone to say a few words
he could barely disguise his disgust. This was a business of trust, of ethics, and these people had looked
him in the face and lied to him.

So after thanking Mauskopf, which was tough for
him to do, Vecchione said that the case had been
made by Detective Tommy Dades, Joe Ponzi, and Bill
Oldham. Mauskopf hadn't even acknowledged Oldham. Vecchione believed that was because Feldman
and Oldham had problems with each other during the
investigation.

Coincidentally, Hynes's office had previously
scheduled a press conference that same day to announce indictments in a completely different case, a
case involving workman's compensation fraud. So
when the Mafia cops press conference ended reporters
hustled over to Hynes's office. And it was there that
Hynes talked about the investigation and acknowledged the work done by his people.

Dades didn't bother watching Mauskopf's press
conference or reading about it. The fact that the cops
had finally been arrested—and it had been New York
cops who had caught them—made him very proud.
He loved the fact that they were cleaning up their
own dirty laundry. And nothing that the Feds did at
that point would have surprised him. Vecchione
could hear the echo of Tommy's voice floating in the
air: *"I'm telling you, Mike, you watch, they're gonna
fuck us."*

Peter Franzone, accompanied by his attorney, voluntarily appeared in the U.S. Attorney's office. At
first, his answers to Lanigan's questions were vague.

The line of individual garages he owned was near a train station and people who commuted to Manhattan would leave their cars there. He had met Frank Santora when he'd come around Franzone's body shop to get his cars repaired and they'd become friends. On occasion Santora had even joined him on towing jobs. As far as Franzone knew, Santora was a salesman, although admittedly he never told him exactly what it was that he sold. Eventually Santora introduced Franzone to his cousin Louie, a detective assigned to the local precinct. Louie left his vehicle there, parked in one of those garages in the back. What kind of vehicle? Lanigan asked. Like a detective's car, Franzone said. He'd take it out and use it, then bring it back.

That was weird, Lanigan thought. Police officers don't make a lot of money. Why would a detective have a personal car that looked like an unmarked police car and park it in a private garage near the precinct, when he could have parked it at the precinct for free, and then make monthly payments in cash? Cops generally don't throw money away like that. Obviously Eppolito was hiding something. Maybe more than just the car.

Franzone was a tough interview. He didn't give up too much, but Lanigan kept after him. They met several times that week, and each time, Lanigan walked away with a little more information and a lot more questions. The guy was definitely hiding something, but what was so big that after twenty years he still was afraid to talk about it?

During one interview Franzone had mentioned that he owned some property in Pennsylvania. That was interesting. This property you got in Pennsylvania, Lanigan asked him, did Santora ever go there?

Franzone was noncommittal, wishy-washy. "I don't know. He might've."

"How can you not know? The guy went there or he didn't go there." Franzone said he just didn't know. Did Louie ever go there? Did Caracappa ever go out there? Franzone didn't know. That was an interesting thing not to know.

The fact that Franzone did not want to talk about that property intrigued the investigators. They knew that at least two bodies that Kaplan had associated with Santora—the jewelry dealer from the Treasury bonds, who had still not been identified, and Jimmy Hydell—had not been found. A field in Pennsylvania is a pretty good place if you don't want a body to be found. Finally Lanigan took a shot. At one of these meetings he suddenly asked Franzone, "So where's the body buried?" He didn't know that there really was a body. He wasn't even referring to a specific body. Just, "So where's the body buried?"

Franzone claimed he didn't know about a body. Any bodies.

Lanigan persisted. Every time they sat down he'd find a way to ask him, "What about the body?" The more Franzone insisted he didn't know what the investigators were talking about, the more the investigators began to believe there really was a body—and that it probably was buried on that land in Pennsylvania.

This was not the only lead that Lanigan and his partner were pursuing, but they kept at this one, believing there was an answer to their question. As had happened between Kaplan and Oldham, eventually Franzone decided he didn't want to deal with Lanigan. One morning Lanigan got a call from the U.S.

Attorney. The message was simple: "Franzone's giving us a body."

A body. After all this time they were finally going to be able to link a body to the two cops. They met in Franzone's lawyer's office in Manhattan, and when Lanigan got there he was informed he wasn't welcome in the meeting.

He gritted his teeth and didn't say a word. His FBI partner went into the meeting and heard Peter Franzone's story. One afternoon in 1985 or 1986, Franzone wasn't exactly certain, Louie Eppolito had driven to the shop. A few minutes later Santora and two other men walked up. Franzone hadn't seen either of them before. One of the men was obviously an Orthodox Jew; he was wearing a yarmulke and had a beard. The other one was wearing a dark trench coat with its collar turned up to hide his face. All four of them went around back into one of the parking garages and pulled down the metal door.

Maybe a half hour later Santora and the guy wearing the trench coat emerged. Santora asked Franzone to come on in the back; he wanted to show him something. Franzone walked into the garage—and he could hardly breathe. The Orthodox Jew was dead, lying on the ground. At that moment he realized Santora wasn't actually a salesman. "Santora told me I hadda help bury the body because I was an accessory. And then he told me if I ever go and tell anybody, he was going to kill me and my fucking family."

Franzone had kept the secret for two decades. For more than twenty years he'd lived in fear. There wasn't a day that passed that he wasn't terrified he was going to be killed. When Santora was killed he went to the wake, he admitted, just to make sure everybody knew he would keep the secret, that he would never tell anybody. Even if he had found the guts to tell someone, he said, who was going to believe him? And if he did talk, Detective Eppolito had the power to have him arrested, for just about anything, and have someone kill me in jail.

Franzone had helped dig a deep hole beneath the cement floor. As he dug he had to be wondering if they would let him out of that garage alive. When he'd finished, Santora reached for his hand and helped him climb out of the hole. Then together they rolled the body into it. Franzone couldn't believe he was caught in the middle of a murder, helping bury a still-warm body. But he was thrilled to be breathing and would do whatever was necessary not to make Santora angry. They poured lime over the body, mixed some new cement, and encased the body in it. Franzone never found out who he'd buried or why he'd been killed. He didn't want to know; he just wanted to forget it.

Santora never mentioned the job again or paid him for the work, but when Franzone's son was born he did give him a plastic garbage bag full of brand-new baby clothes—so new the price tags were still attached. Franzone graciously accepted the gift, then threw out the clothes because he feared they were stolen and he wanted nothing to do with Santora.

He was positive that the lookout was Louie Eppolito, he said, but he couldn't identify the man in the trench coat until sometime later, when he met Steve Caracappa at Santora's daughter's sweet sixteen party.

Like just about every person who flips, once Franzone gave up his most sacred secret he didn't stop talking. Tommy had seen the same thing happen countless times; once an informer finally makes the decision to talk he opens his brain and everything in it pours out. A good detective let it happen and made sure to be suitably impressed: For at least a few minutes the person talking was the center of the universe. He was important; everybody cared about him.

Franzone was typical. Obviously he was relieved to finally be able to tell someone about the horror he'd been living with. He went through the whole story, shovel load by shovel load. The people listening to him had to act as if this was the most interesting story they had ever heard, and in this case it just might have been.

So when Franzone then started talking about a second murder, without being asked, without even pausing, everybody in the room sat up straight. This was some big secret this guy had been keeping. The second murder had taken place a few months later; this was another murder the investigators knew almost nothing about. Santora had shown up at the place on Nostrand Avenue with Eppolito and several other men. Minutes later, just like before, the horror movie came true again. Santora called Franzone inside. The men were struggling to wrap the body of one of the men who'd walked in with them in a tarp and needed help. Franzone helped lift the body into the trunk of the car. Santora drove away, leaving Franzone living with that fear that never went away.

Lanigan listened patiently as his partner told him Franzone's story. He was a cop; out of habit he never showed his excitement—he never wanted to give away that edge—but he was thrilled. The first body was obviously Jeweler #1. Jimmy Hydell's body would have been perfect—it would have tied the whole prosecution together—but Casso had never told Kaplan what he'd done with the bullet-riddled corpse. But Kaplan had credited another body to the cops, a body that according to Franzone was still in the ground where it had been buried almost two decades earlier. Finding that body would prove Kaplan was telling the truth.

Lanigan knew how close they had come to missing it. If Franzone had remained silent, if he'd kept his secret, the body never would have been found. At best, there might have been an excavation in Pennsylvania, but nobody even suspected the garage. It was just Tommy's itch that kept them searching for it. And without a body the case against the two cops would have been a lot tougher, a whole lot tougher.

Pete's garage, the auto body shop with a line of rental parking garages directly behind it, was not far from the neighborhood in which Lanigan had grown up. He knew the streets very well. And now he knew where the body was buried.

The current owner of the site was less than cooperative, so the investigators had to get a search warrant. A recovery team was put together to dig up the body of Jeweler #1. It was a crime scene, a very old crime scene, but it still had to be treated as if the murder had been committed the day before. Whatever they found there was going to be used as evidence and had to be documented. Because of his familiarity with the area, Lanigan was assigned to coordinate the dig. He knew several members of the evidence-recovery team, having worked with them once before to dig up a body off Bedford Avenue and Tenth. The team included crime scene investigators, a forensic photographer to document the chain of evidence, an entomologist who would verify that the body had been in the ground for decades by studying insect activity, a heavy-machinery driver to operate the backhoe, and a coroner from the City Medical Examiner's office, as well as Lanigan's partner and several other investigators.

The entire dig team met the evening before they were scheduled to put shovels in the ground. Lanigan took them to the garage and showed them where to dig. According to Franzone, the body was under the cement in the fourth garage from the rear of the body shop. Lanigan looked at the spot, just stared at the cold cement floor, and tried to imagine what had happened there nineteen years earlier. Finally, they were going to wake up the ghosts.

After visiting the staging area where they would meet at five thirty A.M. the following morning, they all went back to the Eastern District office to review exactly what was going to happen. Then they all went home. Lanigan was hoping to get to bed early; it was going to be a long day.

His cell phone rang on the way home. It was Joe Ponzi informing him that the Brooklyn DA's office had been severed from the investigation.

Mike Vecchione had been in a conference room when Mark Feldman reached him. "I'm calling on behalf of the U.S. Attorney," he said coldly. The message was pretty straightforward: You guys are out. Feldman explained that they believed Hynes's office was the source of the leaks to the media and that those leaks had endangered the entire case. "From this day forward you're off the case."

Vecchione was beyond dumbfounded. He said evenly, "Obviously, you've made up your mind. You didn't call to discuss it, you just make this pronouncement? It's my opinion you never wanted to go along with the deal anyway."

Josh Hanshaft was walking out of the Brooklyn DA's office, on his way over to the U.S. Attorney's office, when a detective called him over. "We hear you're out," he said.

Hanshaft misunderstood. "You guys are out? For what? For a day, a week, permanently?"

"All of us," they told him. "You're not even allowed to go back there."

Hanshaft didn't understand what was going on. He went back upstairs to wait for someone from Mauskopf's office to provide an explanation. That was just a common courtesy. Something like, "Sorry it didn't work out, Josh, it didn't have anything to do with you, we'll work together someday." But that call never came. A day later Vecchione told him officially that they were all off the case. All of them.

It was several days later, while walking through the lobby of the Brooklyn DA's office building, that Hanshaft saw Rob Henoch on the phone. Henoch didn't even put down the phone to say a few words to Hanshaft. Instead he simply shook his hand and smiled. Hanshaft walked away.

What surprised Hanshaft was a story that appeared in *Newsday* after he had been booted. *Newsday* reported that Josh had been escorted out of the building with his belongings by federal agents. That story was completely inaccurate; Hanshaft had never returned to that building. There was nothing in that office that he needed or wanted. But he got the irony; there was only one place that story could have been leaked from— and it wasn't Joe Hynes's office.

Joe Ponzi had been at an event with District Attorney Hynes when Feldman reached him. "This is one of the most difficult decisions I've ever had to make," Feldman said. "But you guys are out."

At first, Ponzi remembers, he couldn't even process what Feldman was telling him. Then he said, "You've got to be fucking kidding me." Then it began to sink in: For the first time in his career he was being booted off a case. He didn't know if he was more insulted or angry. But he was very angry. He'd spent years working closely with the U.S. Attorney, he had been trusted in many cases with extremely sensitive information, and suddenly he couldn't be trusted? He saw it as a direct attack on his integrity and that hurt. "All of a sudden a wall dropped down," he remembers, "and I was an outsider looking in. It was a horrible feeling."

Ponzi made a plea to keep Lanigan on the case. He offered to let them work out of the U.S. Attorney's office: "They'll stay over there," he said. "The only person they'll communicate with in this office is me, and I don't have to brief anybody about what's going on. If that's the kind of Chinese wall you want, I can build it for you. But let my guys stay; they can help you."

Feldman had made up his mind. He didn't believe Ponzi could make that happen, he said, although he was nice enough to add that he was sorry it had reached this point. Joe Ponzi and Mark Feldman had been friends since the day Ponzi began working in that office in 1977. Now Ponzi decided that he would never talk to Mark Feldman again.

It hurt the case. Eventually Henoch would admit to Ponzi, "Losing your guys was a huge blow to us." But what made it even more painful for Ponzi was what happened several months after he had been "excised," as he tactfully describes it, from the case. This case was one of those rare times he'd actually established a relationship with a source, and he remained sorry that he had never gotten the opportunity to tell Burt Kaplan why he'd suddenly disappeared. So one afternoon he asked a player still in the mix, "When you see him, say hello for me and tell him I hope he's well."

That person responded, "I'm sorry, Joe, I can't do that. Kaplan is really pissed off at you. He blames you for a lot of things."

Ponzi couldn't believe it. After Brooklyn had been booted from the case several articles had appeared revealing private information about Kaplan, including a piece written by Jerry Capeci and a long and inaccurate article in *Vanity Fair*. Ponzi was proud of the fact that he had spoken to absolutely no one about Kaplan or the case. Publishers and movie companies were waving contracts at him, offering him a lot of money to come on board—which was perfectly legal—and he had refused every offer. So information about Kaplan could not possibly have come from him—or, for that matter, anyone from the state. Suddenly Ponzi realized that someone had suggested to Kaplan that either he or the DA's office was the source of those leaks. Ponzi couldn't believe Kaplan was blaming him. But once again, there was nothing he could do but swallow his unhappiness.

The most bitter investigator was probably Bobby I. Since joining the task force he'd been among its most active members. He'd established a strong relationship with Burt Kaplan and his wife. Intartaglia is one of those people who talks about himself in the third person; as he said to Ponzi, "How can he throw Bobby I off the case? It doesn't make sense."

Ponzi tried to explain. "Listen, he didn't take Bobby

I off the case. He threw the entire Brooklyn DA's office off the case and we happen to be part of that institution. So we went with it."

Tommy Dades wasn't surprised by Feldman's decision. He had warned Vecchione that he had been expecting "to get booted like a football" for a long time, but in his case the insults went a lot further. Tommy was in the gym one afternoon when he got a call from Betty Hydell, who was very upset. Betty and her daughter Lizzie had been asked to come into Mauskopf's office. When they got there, she said, they were treated more like prisoners than victims. Tommy was very familiar with the Feds' arrogant attitude, that we're-smarter-than-everybody-else demeanor. Apparently they had spoken to Betty and Lizzie in a very insulting manner. While she was being interviewed by a prosecutor from Mauskopf's office, an FBI agent, and a top DEA official, Betty told him, "They said some very bad things about you."

"What are you talking about?" Dades asked.

He found it difficult to believe what he heard. "[Dades] put words in your mouth. He suggested to you what to say, didn't he?" the prosecutor had said to Betty and Lizzie.

Basically, they were accusing Tommy of making up the whole story, for whatever reasons, then feeding it to Betty, who went along with it to avenge her son. That was the kind of bullshit Dades expected to hear from the defense, but from federal prosecutors? Were they out of their minds?

Then they warned both Betty and Lizzie not to speak to Tommy Dades again.

Betty had replied, "We'll talk to him anytime we want." With that, Betty and Lizzie told them to go

fuck themselves and walked out. The Feds had successfully alienated a key witness.

Tommy managed to smooth things over with Betty
and Lizzy Hydell. Some of those people just don't know
what they're doing, he said. Then he reminded them
that making the case against Eppolito and Caracappa
was too important to walk away from. "You got to talk
to them," he said. "Just ignore them as best you can."

The first thing Tommy did was call Mark Feldman
to tell him what was going on. He knew Feldman very
well, and he knew Feldman had nothing to do with this.
"No matter how you feel," Tommy said, "if you want to
have beers with me or throw me out the window, it
don't matter, but you never talk bad about another law
enforcement officer in front of witnesses. That's
bullshit. How stupid were these guys? How could they
say those things without knowing my relationship with
Betty? They totally underestimated our friendship.
Betty and Lizzie trust me; they don't trust you people at
all. You just underestimated them."

Feldman was apologetic and agreed to try to find
out what had happened.

But Tommy didn't wait for Feldman to handle the
situation. Instead, he called the DEA agent and
warned he was going to "come over there and yank
you out of that fucking office. How can you say that
crap about me? I brought you into the case!"

The agent had no real answer. Tommy hung up,
believing it would be impossible for the U.S. Attorney
to be any more disrespectful to him and Vecchione
and Ponzi and Bobby I, the whole New York City Police Department and the Brooklyn's DA's office, than
they had already been. He didn't want anything to do
with them ever again; he just wanted to be left alone.

Several weeks later everyone in Hynes's office associated with the case was served with a subpoena to turn over to the U.S. Attorney all the paperwork they had on hand, including notebooks, address books, files, anything and everything that concerned the case. As Tommy remembers, "These were the same people that I had been having weekly meetings with and they subpoenaed me under the threat of prosecution if I didn't hand over everything that I had pertaining to this case. They were threatening to prosecute me!"

Vecchione was equally furious. "Basically, they treated us like we were criminals, that we were possessing materials we had no right to. I remember having to go upstairs to the office where all our detective investigators had packed up all their stuff, all their notebooks, reports, everything, to make sure it was all going to be sent over to the U.S. Attorney's office. We sent over a mountain of material. And all of us felt like shit; these were some of the best detectives in New York and they were being told they couldn't be trusted. It was unnecessary and shameful."

Dades had been wrong about one thing. Mauskopf's office had found a way to be more disrespectful.

CHAPTER 13

The cold case that had been forgotten for more than a decade had become the lead news story in America. To many people it seemed more like a movie plot than a true story: Two of the NYPD's most honored gold-shield detectives had actually spent much of their careers moonlighting as hit men for the Mafia, often using their shields to set up victims, and in their bloody trail they'd left at least eight bodies. Probably more.

Cops as *The Sopranos*. The media loved it. The overweight Eppolito even looked a little like a badly aging James Gandolfini. *The United States of America vs. Louis Eppolito and Stephen Caracappa* was shaping up to be one of those super-trials so beloved by the cable networks and tabloids. This was going to be the World Series of jurisprudence, and so it attracted an array of legal heavyweights.

Presiding over the trial was eighty-three-year-old Senior Judge Jack Weinstein, who had come off the streets of Brooklyn to become one of the most respected jurists in the nation. Lawyers have been telling this joke about Weinstein in the federal courthouse for more than two decades: God has been seeing a psychiatrist lately—because He thinks He's Jack Weinstein.

During his almost thirty years on the federal bench Weinstein has ruled on everything from school desegregation cases to Agent Orange litigation. He'd sat on several high-profile organized crime cases, but this one, he would eventually say, "is probably the most heinous series of crimes ever tried in this courthouse." He was the perfect choice: too old to care about getting his picture in *People,* yet sharp enough to guarantee a fair and orderly trial. And coincidentally, Weinstein and Kaplan had met several times in the courtroom. In 1967, Weinstein's first year on the federal bench, he had sentenced Burt Kaplan to five years' probation in a fraud case. In 1972 Weinstein put Kaplan in prison for four years when he was caught with a truckload of stolen goods—although the judge gave Kaplan an extra two months before he had to report to prison so he could work through Christmas to help support his family.

Robert Henoch was going to be assisted in the prosecution by Mitra Hormozi and Dan Wenner. It wasn't a glitzy team, but they would be very well prepared and they would lay out their case in an extremely professional manner.

In contrast, the cops were going to be defended by celebrity lawyers Bruce Cutler and Ed Hayes, both of whom often appeared on TV as expert commentators and even cohosted their own show on Court TV.

Bruce Cutler was an odd choice for Louis Eppolito to make. He was another Brooklyn guy, having graduated from Brooklyn Law School to go to work in the Brooklyn DA's office. But he had become famous as John Gotti's lawyer, the mob mouthpiece who had successfully helped "the Dapper Don" beat three raps, and often and loudly told people that John Gotti was an honorable man. It didn't seem to make a lot of sense for Eppolito, who would be trying to prove he had nothing to do with organized crime, to pick an attorney known specifically for his work defending the onetime boss of the Gambino crime family.

Mike Vecchione found himself smiling when he learned that Eppolito had hired Cutler. "Bruce and I went back a long way. We had worked together in the Brooklyn DA's office when we were both young attorneys and had become very friendly. He's an excellent defense lawyer and loves high-profile cases. When I heard Eppolito had hired him I remembered one story he told me. In the 1930s Abe Reles was the most feared hit man belonging to Murder Inc., the organization of killers who did the work for organized crime. When Reles was caught, to save his life he became a government informant. One of the people he implicated for murder was mob boss Albert Anastasia. To protect him before Anastasia's trial he was kept under guard at the Half Moon Hotel in Coney Island. Although there were six cops guarding him every minute, one morning he supposedly took a dive out the window to his death, becoming known as 'the canary who could sing, but not fly.' And Bruce told me that one of those cops guarding Reles was his father, police officer Murray Cutler.

"So when Eppolito hired Bruce I thought, *Boy, that's appropriate.*"

Vecchione knew and respected Eddie Hayes too,

although their relationship was professional. Hayes was just as flamboyant as Cutler; a member of the International Best-Dressed List Hall of Fame, he was well known as the inspiration for the central character in Tom Wolfe's novel *The Bonfire of the Vanities*. Tom Hanks had played him in the movie. Coincidentally, like Louis Eppolito, he'd actually had a bit part in Martin Scorsese's *Goodfellas*. But Hayes had established himself as one of New York's top lawyers, representing an eclectic mix of clients ranging from Robert De Niro to Andy Warhol's estate. While he had tried criminal cases, that wasn't the area in which he'd built his reputation. There were reasons for that, as he told *New York* magazine: "First, most high-profile criminal trials you lose. Second, the money's terrible. Third, that's not the role I wanted in society."

Celebrity lawyers like Cutler and Hayes are very expensive; they normally charge a lot more than either Eppolito or Caracappa could have afforded on their NYPD pensions. But Vecchione assumed both of them had taken the case for little money and a lot of publicity. "That's not at all unusual; lawyers do it all the time, even well-known lawyers like Cutler and Hayes. I did it myself when I was in private practice. I defended a female police officer who'd been fired for posing naked in a men's magazine. I didn't think it was fair—the pictures had been taken before she became a police officer—so I took her case for free. The publicity was my payment. I didn't know what Cutler and Hayes were being paid for defending Eppolito and Caracappa, but I did know they were going to receive an enormous amount of very valuable publicity."

The biggest problem that Cutler and Hayes were going to face in this case was the case. Kaplan's testimony and the supporting evidence would make it very tough, maybe even impossible, to convince a jury that their clients had nothing to do with these killings. So Vecchione guessed they probably wouldn't focus on that. Rather than tearing down the mountain, they would try to undermine the foundation. They would attack the RICO charge. That's what he would have done. He was also concerned that Cutler and Hayes's dramatic courtroom theatrics and emotional appeals would overwhelm Henoch's methodical presentation and perhaps sway one juror. And one juror was all they needed.

Cutler's public-relations offensive began in late April, the day Eppolito and Caracappa were arraigned in Brooklyn. As reported by the *Daily News,* Eppolito's daughter, Andrea, "a voluptuous, raven-haired beauty—turning heads in a tan suit with a plunging neckline . . . launched an emotional appeal for her father.

" 'My father loved being a cop. He was so proud of all the things he did while working for the city. He protected women. He protected children. He worked with the elderly.' "

Cutler claimed that Andrea had asked his permission to tell the media how much she loved her father. He said, "She flew out here to be near her father—and brought his heart medication. Family support means the world to Lou."

The first suggestion that Vecchione was right about the Feds' ability to bring RICO charges against the cops came during their bail hearing in July 2005. Judge Weinstein questioned the validity of the RICO charge, calling it "weak" and "relatively stale," and wondered aloud if the statute of limitations might have run out years earlier. He told them that they were going to have a serious problem with the statute of limitations if they continued to insist that it be tried that way. Weinstein was outwardly skeptical that selling meth in Las Vegas was a perpetuation of their criminal activity for the Lucchese crime family.

In opposing bail, Henoch argued, "The defendants remain the same violent men they were in the 1980s and 1990s," and played portions of taped conversations made in Vegas in which Eppolito "made it clear he associates with people who are willing to murder at his request."

Weinstein rejected that argument, writing ominously, "The weight of the evidence adduced thus far is not strong." Deciding that Eppolito and Caracappa posed no danger to society, he granted $5,000,000 bail. To secure payment, the two cops and several members of their families put up their homes and other property. Among those relatives volunteering his home was Eppolito's brother-in-law, retired detective Al Guarneri, to whom Jimmy Hydell had reached out, apparently for protection, the day he disappeared.

After hearing the judge's comments and being released on bail—which included confinement to their relatives' homes—the boisterous Eppolito happily showed reporters his brand-new ankle bracelet. The Mafia cops walked out of Jack Weinstein's courtroom with hope.

Weinstein's warning had the prosecution worried. Essentially he was telling them that he didn't buy their continuing conspiracy claim and that they better do something quick to change it if they wanted to survive in his courtroom. If he threw out the RICO they were going to have to turn over the case to the state. Without that conspiracy all they had were some minor drug charges, crimes they could just barely connect to Caracappa.

Tommy Dades still didn't believe the RICO would collapse, telling columnist Denis Hamill, "The feds are very, very conservative out in Vegas and they had several opportunities to review the application for a RICO . . . for them to approve it means they didn't think the case was weak or 'time-blocked.'

"But if it becomes a state case again the feds would hand over Kaplan as a witness, and along with Betty Hydell and several other witnesses, these guys who disgraced the badge are dead."

A month later Henoch was back in Weinstein's courtroom to add a ninth murder to the indictment, the 1986 killing of Jeweler #1, who finally had been identified as Israel Greenwald. As Dades and Lanigan had learned, the dig in Pete's garage had been successful. Under several feet of concrete the evidence recovery team had unearthed the skeletal remains of a man—precisely where Peter Franzone said the body had been buried. Adding this killing to the indictment would allow Henoch to put Franzone on the stand, and Franzone was the only witness who had actually seen Eppolito and Caracappa at a murder scene and could identify them. Once again, the two cops pleaded not guilty.

During this hearing Weinstein made it even more clear that he wouldn't accept the RICO charge; he just didn't believe the drug case was connected to the Luccheses. He told Henoch, "I'm puzzled by the prosecution . . . You've come up with the same problem you came up with before. If [the murders are] a separate conspiracy from the drug case, you're out."

In mid-September Mauskopf's office finally

changed its obviously defective RICO charge. At a hearing during which they charged the cops with a tenth murder—the victim was not identified but was presumed to be the unidentified man that Franzone had helped roll into a tarp and lift into the trunk of Frankie Santora's car—they "retooled" the indictment. Rather than claiming that Eppolito and Caracappa's crimes were committed for the furtherance of the Lucchese organized crime family, the government came up with a novel solution. As all that RICO requires for a conspiracy charge are two or more people, the updated indictment stated that Eppolito and Caracappa ran their own "racketeering enterprise," and their crimes were for their own benefit. According to the rewritten indictment, the Eppolito-Caracappa conspiracy lasted twenty-three years and included ten murders and seventeen other crimes in New York and Las Vegas, committed for the purpose of making money for its members and associates. According to the government of the United States, instead of working *for* the Luccheses, they worked *with* them.

Judge Weinstein did not seem impressed. After lecturing the prosecutors about the weakness of their indictment, he suggested they charge Eppolito and Caracappa with ten counts of murder in aid of racketeering rather than claiming they committed the ten murders and all their other crimes as part of a criminal enterprise that might be barred by the statute of limitations. Weinstein then postponed the trial until February 2006.

Vecchione knew Henoch couldn't do that. He just didn't have enough evidence to make ten counts of murder-for-hire stick. When he first heard Weinstein's comments he thought, *It's all over. We're getting it back*. As he says, "The federal government had other statutes they could use against the cops if they wanted to; they could do what Weinstein suggested, for example, or they could charge them with conspiracy in the furtherance of murder. It's my belief that the Feds insisted on the RICO because they had to vindicate taking the case away from us.

"There is a state parallel to conspiracy; it's called murder. But if the Feds were going to charge them with conspiracy there would have been no valid reason to take the case away from us."

Seeing the government confusion, Cutler sensed victory. He told reporters that he and Hayes were filing a motion to dismiss the charges. "It's the same can of soup," he said. "Just a different label. Now they've created a fantasy crime group."

After pleading not guilty to the tenth murder, Eppolito agreed. "I'm glad [Cutler] smells what the government is shoveling," he said. "It's disgusting what they're doing to me."

While the legal maneuvering continued in preparation for the trial, investigators were searching for additional evidence against the cops. In late spring, Kaplan's "kid," Tommy Galpine, had seen the light and taken a deal. Prosecutors agreed to make their best effort to get his sixteen-year sentence reduced if he cooperated completely. Galpine had been with Kaplan for every crime along the way. He could corroborate most of Kaplan's testimony, as well as add his own encounters with the two cops. Galpine described his job as doing whatever Kaplan told him to do: "I'm a doer, not a talker."

But he proved to be a very valuable talker. He told prosecutors that he had delivered to Frankie Santora a

Plymouth Fury tricked out to look exactly like an un-marked police car—presumably the car parked at Pete's garage that might have been used to pick up Jimmy Hydell or stop Eddie Lino. According to Galpine, the car looked so real that when he was driving it through Brooklyn some kid had come running up to him screaming, "I need help!" Galpine told him, "Call the cops," and drove off.

Galpine could also testify that he had flown to the Caribbean to deliver $10,000 to Eppolito. The problem was that he had only spent two hours sitting at the airport waiting for a return flight, so he wasn't even sure which island he was on. Galpine would be a valuable witness for the Feds. He had supported Kaplan throughout his life in crime, he had actually handed the cops cash from Kaplan, and now he was going to support him in his new life as a "rat."

Mobster Al D'Arco, who had told Tommy Dades in a phone call months earlier that he really didn't know anything about the mob cops, remembered that Casso had told him he had proof that Bruno Facciola was an informant and wanted him to whack Facciola. D'Arco admitted he'd shot Facciola in both eyes, stabbed him, shot him in the head, then stuck a frozen canary in his mouth. D'Arco never learned the names of Casso's informants but knew they were "bulls," mob slang for detectives.

Among several surprising discoveries made by investigators was the fact that Peter Franzone was not the only person who had been living in fear of former detective Louis Eppolito. Barry Gibbs, for example, was completing the seventeenth year of his nineteen-year sentence for the murder of Virginia Robertson when investigators found the original NYPD case files in Eppolito's Vegas home. In the past, several people had believed Gibbs's claim that he had been framed, among them Peter Neufeld and Barry Scheck, founders of the Innocence Project, but there was nothing they could do to prove it because the NYPD had been unable to locate the case folder.

After the file had finally been found in Eppolito's house, two DEA agents located the original eyewitness—but this time that witness told a very different story. This time he admitted that Eppolito had frightened him into identifying Gibbs. He had "bribed and intimidated" him, he said, threatening to go after the witness and his family if he refused to pick Gibbs out of the police lineup and testify against him in court. That statement made sense to Tommy Dades, who remembered the tape of Eppolito bragging to Corso that he had threatened to kill his contractor—and the man's whole family.

The witness told the investigators that Eppolito had told him who to pick out of the lineup and that he had lied on the witness stand, knowing his testimony would convict an innocent man, but said, "I don't want this cop after me. My family was on the line here. If I had to do it again, I'd do it again." And if he hadn't identified Gibbs, he said flatly, he'd be dead.

Court papers filed by his attorney quote this witness as saying he "believed and continues to believe that Barry Gibbs is not the person he saw disposing of the body."

In late September Barry Gibbs walked out of prison a free man and a bitter man, telling reporters, "I was a legitimate guy. And I lost everything. What happened to me can happen to any one of you people and any one of your families."

What nobody could figure out was why Eppolito had kept the folder all these years, except to make absolutely sure it could never be looked at again. There was some speculation that he was covering up for the real killer, a mob associate who could be linked to Robertson. But Bruce Cutler defended his client, claiming Eppolito had the file because he was writing screenplays about cases he'd worked. He didn't address the fact that Eppolito apparently had been holding the file for two decades.

Joe Ponzi didn't know what to think about the whole story. While the DA's office was deciding what to do about Gibbs, the jailhouse snitch called Ponzi. "He was really upset," Ponzi explains. "He said, 'How can they let that guy out of jail? You know he's guilty.' I told him to cool down and let the whole thing play out. And then I reminded him, 'Nobody's calling you a liar.' "

Ponzi had also spoken to the eyewitness who had recanted his testimony. And after that conversation he didn't know what to believe—except that the witness was as unreliable now as he probably had been in 1988. "I don't know if it's from drug abuse or the school of hard knocks, but he was highly suggestive. There's still a part of me that doesn't believe completely that Gibbs was railroaded and framed.

"What I know for sure is that the verdict was predicated on the one witness's account and that guy had either become unreliable or was unreliable back then. You just never know how much people change; that's one of the real problems with cold cases. I believe the DA's position was that Gibbs had served almost his entire sentence, so if he erred, it was on the compassionate side."

"The Mafia cops case," as the newspaper had begun referring to it, was getting the full American media treatment. Several participants in the case had signed book contracts. At least three movies about the case were announced. Even Eppolito's autobiography, the now ironically named *Mafia Cop,* was optioned by a movie studio. *New York* magazine, *Vanity Fair,* and *Playboy* all ran cover stories about the case. Somewhat nostalgically *New York* decided "the Mafia Cops' case could be the last of the red-hot organized-crime trials: equal parts titillating and chilling." The *Vanity Fair* story erroneously reported that during the 1980s Kaplan had been a confidential informant for the FBI, a charge that, if true, could have destroyed his credibility, and with it the whole case. The FBI denied the story and it went no further than a few headlines. Vecchione assumed that information had come from the DEA agent quoted extensively throughout the whole story.

It seemed like there was a new revelation every day. Reading these stories, Tommy Dades felt vindicated. The case was leaking inside information like cheesecloth and the state had absolutely nothing to do with it. No one in Hynes's office had even known that Jeweler #1 was a man named Israel Greenwald, for example, until they read it in the papers. In *all* the papers. The U.S. Attorney had used previous leaks as an excuse to sever the state from the case, but the leaking continued long after Hynes's office had been shut out.

It seemed like everybody was trying to get a piece of the action—especially Anthony Casso. Casso was sitting in his cell out in Supermax, the Feds' impregnable prison in Florence, Colorado, with infamous criminals like Ted "the Unabomber" Kaczynski, Mafioso Greg Scarpa Jr., Oklahoma City federal building bomber Terry Nichols, traitorous FBI agent Robert Hanssen, and shoe bomber Richard Reid, watching the only real hope he had left disappear. A year earlier Mike Vecchione had offered him the opportunity to become the five-hundred-pound gorilla, an offer he'd rejected, so instead he had become the invisible man.

Casso was desperate, doing everything possible to inject himself into the trial. Supposedly he'd tried to negotiate a deal with Feldman in which he would tell him where he could find Jimmy Hydell's body in return for a twenty-year cap on his sentence, an offer the U.S. Attorney found easy to refuse. The government already had a body that could be linked to the cops; they didn't need another one.

In July Casso wrote to Mark Feldman claiming that Al D'Arco, who was listed as a prosecution witness, was lying. According to Gaspipe, D'Arco had absolutely no knowledge about the two detectives. His letter also claimed that one unidentified victim, who supposedly was whacked because Eppolito and Caracappa told Casso he was a rat, was actually not an informer.

Feldman paid absolutely no attention to the letter. Presumably, he felt it was so obviously absurd that he didn't even bother passing it along to the defense.

But Casso wasn't through; he was just waiting for the right opportunity. And the only thing he had was time.

With the massive publicity about the trial, Judge Weinstein realized there was insufficient seating in the recently opened new federal courthouse to accommodate the large number of reporters and spectators expected to attend, so he moved the trial back to the old courthouse, to a fourth-floor courtroom that provided seating for more than twice as many people. Fittingly for this cold case, it was out with the new, in with the old.

Ironically, one of the few people in law enforcement not paying close attention to this case was the man who had started it. After leaving Hynes's office Tommy Dades was spending much of his time at his PAL gym on Staten Island, trying to find the center to his life. He was suffering through some rough days. In a relatively short period of time he had lost his mother, his home at the police department and the DA's office, and then his home and his family. He had been rejected by his father and finally had received that humiliating letter from Feldman's office demanding he return everything he had in his possession relating to the case. He probably had been more hurt than insulted by that letter. "All I was trying to do was the right thing and I was left with nothing. As far as I knew they were still intending to call me as a witness in the case, but that didn't have a lot of meaning to me. I was just trying to get through the day and sometimes that was tough. Some of it was my own fault, I knew that, but it was hard to understand how you could give so much to the system and get back so little."

Joe Ponzi, meanwhile, had somehow managed to patch up his relationship with Feldman and Henoch—and had actually become involved in the case again. As he explained, "It took me about two months to get past the venom I had in my heart and soul. I had said some things to Henoch for which I was very sorry; he had said some things to me for which he was just as sorry and we got past that. Mark Feldman? I owe too much to him, I owe my career to him, so there's probably nothing he can do that would make me hate him. My anger with him was always professional, never personal."

Even with the rift between the Feds and the state, the U.S. Attorney continued to need the cooperation of Hynes's office, and Ponzi served as the go-between. In preparation for the trial, Henoch made a steady stream of requests for materials that had not been covered by the subpoena, among them old wiretap transcripts, case folders, and access to the many people in the office who had done extremely valuable work on the case, people like Bobby I, Patty Lanigan, and George Terra. The wounds weren't healed—that would take a long time—but at least a temporary salve was put over them. The resentments were never allowed to get in the way of the mutual objective.

So Joe Ponzi began speaking fairly regularly to the prosecutors. He wasn't officially back on the case, but Henoch began confiding in him, telling him what was going on and even asking for suggestions about how certain sticky problems might be handled.

Ponzi, in turn, was keeping Mike Vecchione informed about the Feds' progress. For Vecchione, it was sort of like watching his son go off to college; he'd done everything possible to get to this time, now all he could do was stand on the sidelines and root— and be prepared to step in if his help was needed.

That was still very possible. If Weinstein ruled that the U.S. Attorney was time-barred from making the RICO stick, the state would have to step in immediately. Vecchione and Ponzi wanted to be prepared for that eventuality, so they spent time deciding which crimes they would prosecute if the case came back to Brooklyn.

Vecchione, meanwhile, was already deeply immersed in another high-profile and extremely bizarre investigation. Not long after being thrown off the Mafia cops case, Josh Hanshaft got a call from the new owner of a funeral parlor complaining she had been defrauded out of $300,000. It seemed that the previous owner had accepted prepayment for funerals and kept the money, and bereaved families were showing up with deceased relatives demanding the funeral for which they'd previously paid. Hanshaft listened carefully; it sounded to him like a relatively simple case of fraud—until she added, "Oh, by the way, the old owners, they were doing something with the corpses, they were taking bones out of the bodies."

Excuse me? As Hanshaft reported to Vecchione, "The best I can determine is that these people are stealing body parts."

Just when Vecchione thought he had seen the worst of human scum, the next case had come along, and maybe these people were even a little worse. Although these cops were going to be tough to beat—what could be worse than killer cops?—by the time Eppolito and Caracappa got sentenced Vecchione was investigating people who stole diseased tissue and organs from bodies and allowed them to be used in more than a thousand transplantation procedures.

It was a modern horror story: Funeral directors were selling body parts and when necessary for showings they were actually replacing them with PVC tubing. So Vecchione's division was working on that case while Eppolito and Caracappa waited for their trial.

Throughout the summer into the fall Weinstein ruled on numerous prosecution and defense motions as each side angled for the slightest advantage, and everyone waited for the only ruling that really mattered: Would the judge allow Henoch's RICO to stand? "A ticking time bomb," Weinstein had called it, and obviously he was having difficulty accepting the prosecution's creative solution.

Jack Weinstein finally answered that question in early December when he announced, "The case has to be tried and will be tried." It was clear from his remarks that he wasn't entirely convinced the jury-rigged RICO charge was valid, and certainly he wasn't very happy about it, but the case against the cops was too important to throw out of his courtroom on a legal technicality. It was "vital" this trial take place, he said, "particularly in a case which raises such serious doubts about the police department and its relationship to the public."

Besides, if he was wrong, if the RICO wouldn't stand up, there would be ample opportunity later in the case for the defense to make that argument.

Mike Vecchione was neither surprised nor terribly disappointed when he heard about Weinstein's tepid acceptance of the indictment. He'd done his job; without their work there would have been no case and Louis Eppolito and Steve Caracappa would have gotten away with murders. The disappointment he'd felt at not getting his chance to convict those two skells had mostly dissipated, and so long as they got the punishment they deserved, he would be very pleased.

Besides, he had the parts of a thousand bodies to worry about.

The trial was finally scheduled to begin in March 2006, a full year after the two cops had been arrested. In January, Eppolito and his wife, Frances, were indicted for failing to report income from several sources, including his work as a screenwriter. The most damning evidence came from Louis himself, who had bragged about hiding income to the undercover accountant. Just to apply a little more pressure, IRS agents arrested Frances Eppolito outside her Las Vegas home.

In early February the Feds attempted to add several other crimes to the indictment, mostly minor stuff compared to the original charges. Both men were accused of literally putting on masks and robbing neighborhood delis to pick up some quick cash, Caracappa supposedly used cocaine when he was working in narcotics, and Eppolito offered a bribe to a doctor in an attempt to receive a tax-free disability pension.

It was also in February that Tommy Dades read in the newspaper one morning a prosecution announcement that neither he nor Bill Oldham would be called as witnesses in the trial. He wasn't the slightest bit surprised; if anything, he was relieved. Weeks earlier defense lawyers had subpoenaed both his and Bill Oldham's NYPD personnel records in a quest to discover any and all "disciplinary actions which concern their credibility." Tommy knew what that meant; when he got on the stand they were going to question him about his affair. They were going to bring up the whole Internal Affairs investigation. It wasn't his credibility they were going to try to destroy, it was his reputation. And the publicity just might have been the final blow for Ro, might have been the end of his marriage.

Mauskopf's announcement gave no reason for the decision, but it was obvious. Both Dades and Oldham had signed book deals; Dades had also made a movie deal. The U.S. Attorney was concerned that Cutler and Hayes would try to convince jurors that the two investigators had made up this crazy story so they could profit from it. Ed Hayes said exactly that: "The question is whether the government witnesses told Dades and Oldham what happened, or Dades and Oldham told the government informer what to say so they could sell the story."

The fact that this was complete bullshit wouldn't stop the defense lawyers from making the argument. *Isn't it true, Detective Dades, that if my client isn't convicted that movie will never be made?* Who knows how much damage that suggestion might do to the prosecution's case? The defense needed only one juror.

Jury selection began on March 6. One week later, on March 13, Prosecutor Mitra Hormozi gave the opening statement. These two men "weren't traditional mobsters," she told the jury. "They were better. They were two men who could get away with murder. Why? Because they were New York City detectives . . . The defendants went into business together and the business was crime."

She skillfully outlined the case against Eppolito and Caracappa. She began with the murder of Jeweler #1, Israel Greenwald, describing how Santora told Patty Lanigan's terrified witness, Peter Franzone, "Start digging or I'll kill your family. Start digging or I'll kill you. Franzone felt he was digging his own grave."

Then she told the jury about the murder of Jimmy Hydell, Tommy Dades's case, the one that got this whole thing started. The cops were paid $30,000 to deliver him to Anthony Casso, who tortured him before killing him.

Next she talked about "the most tragic victim," Nicky Guido, another killing Dades had successfully linked to the cops. To emphasize the brutality of that murder, she showed the jury never-before-seen photographs of Guido's bloody, bullet-riddled body slumped over the steering wheel of his new red Nissan Maxima.

In his opening statement, Bruce Cutler attacked the witnesses who were expected to testify against his client, witnesses he called "the lowest form of life. They call each other tough guys, goodfellas, until you take away their gun . . . and the jail door slams behind them. Then they wet their pants and call their mommy, the government." Playing as much to the packed spectator section, which was jammed with reporters, as the jury, he told them that the people who were going to testify against his client were men who "kill, kill, steal, make money, beat up, steal, kill, kill, make money" and were responsible for "at least ten murders, maybe twenty, five arsons, six tons of marijuana at least, kidnapping, extortion, union fixing . . . the swill, bottom of the barrel, the sewer."

Ed Hayes was equally tough, describing the prosecution's witnesses as "pigs," "animals," and "disgusting."

The prosecution really began making its case against the cops the next day, when the mobster Joe Ponzi had flipped, Burt Kaplan, took the stand. "I paid them," he said flatly. And then, with about as much emotion as if he were describing the new line of women's clothing he was selling, the balding and be-spectacled witness described his long criminal association with the two detectives. "They brought me information about wiretaps, phone tapes, informants, ongoing investigations, and imminent arrests. I passed it to Anthony Casso. If he got some information that had to do with him, if there were informants, he would have them killed."

Kaplan admitted that he had conspired with Eppolito and Caracappa to commit three murders: "Jimmy Hydell, Eddie Lino, and the jeweler. I don't know the jeweler's name."

Kaplan held back nothing. He confessed to a long list of crimes, he admitted he was a "degenerate gambler" who had lost more than $3 million in his lifetime, and he described himself as a "rat," as a guy who had "gone bad." "I know what I am," he said sadly. "I'm being honest. I'm a criminal."

"He was the ideal witness," Vecchione says. "In all the mob trials I've done I tell my witnesses, 'Don't hide anything. Don't shade anything. Tell it exactly the way it was.' I always tell them, 'I don't care what you did. That's what makes you believable. You are the worst of the worst; tell that to the jury. Don't try to look like a good guy, because you're not. That's why you're in the position to know what you know.' Kaplan admitted every bit of it. He didn't hold back on anything. He identified himself as a rat. He understood who and what he was. There was no reason for the jury not to believe him."

Tommy Dades had absolutely no desire to attend the trial, but Joe Ponzi wanted to be there. He had known Detective Louis Eppolito for more than three decades, and he certainly wanted to see Burt Kaplan testify. And so he was sitting in the courtroom when Kaplan explained why he had decided to cooperate. "My wife and my daughter had been asking me to cooperate from the first day I was arrested. I didn't do it . . . I was in jail nine straight years and I was on the lam two and a half years before that. In that period of time I seen an awful lot of guys that I thought were stand-up guys go bad, turn and become informants. As I told Steve the night I left to go on the lam. I asked him if he could guarantee me that Louie would stand up . . ."

Watching Kaplan on the stand, it was hard for Ponzi not to think back to their first meeting. Kaplan had insisted he would never "go bad." Ponzi had often wondered what it was that caused the old man to change his mind. What makes a hard case like Burt Kaplan flip? Until this moment it was the one question for which he had no answer.

". . . and Steve said, 'Yeah, I could do that.'" But when Kaplan learned that there was strong evidence against the two cops, he said, "I didn't think they would stand up and I was tired of going to jail by myself. I figured I would be at the defense table right now, and Steve and Louie would be sitting up here."

There it is, Ponzi thought. *He couldn't trust the cops.*

Kaplan admitted he hoped to have time cut from his sentence so one day he could hold his grandson. "I wanted someday to be able to spend some time with him, but I can't honestly say I did this for my family. I did it, in all honesty, because I felt that I was going to be made the scapegoat in this case."

From time to time Ponzi would look at the defense table. "Eppolito and Caracappa rarely moved," he says. "I could see that Louie had lost some weight, but Caracappa was still 'the Stick,' thin and taut. Truthfully, I wasn't entirely comfortable sitting there. I never wanted those two guys to think it had become personal with me, because it was never personal. I knew what they had done and I knew they needed to be punished for it. But it was never personal with me.

"Eppolito never even glanced in my direction; I never made eye contact with him. But on the second or third day of the trial I looked at the defense table and Caracappa was glaring at us. It was an angry, fixed glare. I thought that was bizarre; I thought, *Fuck you, buddy, you did what you did. Now who do you think you are, looking at me like I betrayed you?*"

At one point during a break in the trial Caracappa was talking to a private investigator working for the defense while looking directly over the man's shoulder at Ponzi. Caracappa covered his mouth with his hand as he spoke to the PI. Ponzi felt certain he was saying, "That's Larry Ponzi's kid."

Bobby I, who was sitting next to him, disagreed. "No, he's talking about me."

But he wasn't; Ponzi knew that.

At night Ponzi would discuss the trial with his father. But as the trial proceeded Larry Ponzi began to realize how wrong he'd been about the two cops. "He knew Louie was a little out of his mind," Joe explains. "But doing mob hits? No. He thought that Louie had Steve bamboozled and that he was overbearing and overwhelming and he sucked him in and maybe that's what happened with Caracappa. But as the trial went on he became convinced he totally misread their relationship." Larry Ponzi's observation was shared by a lot of people: Rather than Eppolito running the show, it was the quiet, icy cool Caracappa who had made the decisions.

"I always liked Steve," Kaplan told the court. Burt Kaplan was on the stand for three days, for more than fourteen hours. Henoch skillfully led him through a litany of crimes he'd committed with Eppolito and Caracappa, from the day in prison Frank Santoro told him about them until he went on the lam years later. In response to Henoch's questions he explained how the cops had provided confidential information; he described the kidnapping of Jimmy Hydell, who had begged Casso to dump his body in the street so his mother could collect the insurance; he remembered how Eppolito had shown up one night in his hospital room to describe the Eddie Lino hit; he told the absolutely transfixed courtroom about the murder of Jeweler #1, eventually linking the two cops to a dozen different murders. He told the jury how Casso paid them for a murder or for the information they provided; he talked about meetings at rest areas near exit 52 on the Long Island Expressway and in a Staten Island cemetery. Joe Ponzi had spent a lot of days in courtrooms, but rarely had he seen so strong a witness. It was a bravura performance. Kaplan provided detail after detail after detail. Watching him, Ponzi couldn't help feeling just a little proud.

At one point Kaplan talked about his disdain for all the other wiseguys who had "gone bad," who had become informers. Now he was one of them, at different times describing himself as "a rat," "an informant," and "a stool pigeon." But the closest he came to admitting he had any regrets about his past was telling Henoch, "As I look at my life in retrospect, I did a lot of unsettling things."

There was only one slight hiccup in his testimony. When responding to questions about the Nicky Guido murder, Kaplan claimed that the cops had demanded $4,000 for providing Casso with information about Guido. Casso refused. "Gee," he said, according to

Kaplan, "I just gave them a $5,000 bonus for that thing with Jimmy. Tell them they're getting pretty greedy." According to Kaplan, Casso eventually got the address of Nicky Guido—the wrong Nicky Guido—from someone at the local power company.

Dades laughed when Ponzi told him about Kaplan's testimony. "If you look at the timeline it hits you right in the face. Casso gets the names of the shooters from Hydell. At that time there were only eight Nicky Guidos in New York State. We know that because George Terra had run a group search. But only one of them lives in downtown Brooklyn. Right after Jimmy disappears Caracappa punches up this Nicky Guido on the computer. Six weeks from the day Caracappa runs Nicky Guido, the kid is killed. What's the coincidence of that happening?

"A couple of years later, in 1989, the day it was announced that Feldman had indicted the real Nicky Guido for shooting Casso, Caracappa runs another computer scan for the name. That's the day he found out they'd killed the wrong person.

"But the best way to introduce this in the trial was through my testimony, and there was no way that Feldman or Henoch wanted me to testify. Joe Ponzi and I were barely mentioned in the trial. They shut us out totally. So I don't believe they got Nicky Guido's name from the power company, the phone company, or anywhere else except Steve Caracappa."

At various stages in Mike Vecchione's career he had defended clients he believed to be guilty. Once, he'd saved the job of a cop who had been caught shaking down drug dealers, then selling the drugs he'd confiscated out of his squad car. On another occasion he'd successfully defended a hold-up man whose partner had killed a cabbie. That was the job of the defense attorney; give your client the best defense possible within the law. So he knew all the back alleys familiar to defense lawyers. But he didn't have the slightest idea how Cutler or Hayes could attack Kaplan's testimony. Burt Kaplan had been superb on the stand. A witness's demeanor is as important as his testimony; if a jury doesn't like him they might not believe him. But Kaplan had just the right touch of resignation in his testimony. And his knowledge of the smallest details, his ability to describe things that would be impossible to know if you weren't there, had been phenomenal.

Cutler's strategy was not to attack the details of Kaplan's testimony, but rather to try to destroy his whole credibility. It was your basic throw-everything-against-the-wall-and-see-what-sticks cross-examination. He rambled from subject to subject, touching just about everything from Brooklyn high school football to whether it was possible to see Bucknell University from the guard towers at Lewisburg federal penitentiary. He accused Kaplan of saying whatever the government felt was necessary in exchange for a get-out-of-jail-free card. Kaplan responded by admitting, "Whatever happens, happens. I said at the pretrial hearing, 'The government's doing this to get me to talk about two dirty cops.'"

Cutler read a long list of wiseguys whom Kaplan had implicated in crimes to buttress the claim that he would say anything about anybody for his freedom. To that Kaplan pointed out, "These weren't doctors or lawyers—these were gangsters."

Finally, in his testimony Kaplan had claimed he had met with the two cops face-to-face, often three or more times a month, for more than three years. He also admitted that for several periods during that time he had been under both audio and video law enforcement surveillance—at least some of that time by Bobby I. Cutler wondered aloud why there wasn't a single surveillance photograph or a single audiotape of Kaplan with Eppolito or Caracappa. Not one.

Kaplan responded that he'd been very careful when arranging those meetings. He used public telephones to call them; when they spoke they used the code name Marco; and they met only at night and in isolated places like a Staten Island cemetery or Kaplan's home.

No photographs. No tapes. It wasn't much of a defense, but after two days of cross-examination it was just about the only dent that Cutler was able to make in Kaplan's testimony.

Henoch proceeded to lay out his case with all the excitement and glamour of a mason constructing a brick wall. Day after day, witness after witness, he stood at a podium reading questions out of his notebook, rarely raising his voice. But slowly and carefully that wall grew higher and more solid.

Henoch wanted to introduce the physical evidence—the computer printout—that connected Caracappa to the murder of Nicky Guido while the gruesome crime scene photographs were still very much in the minds of the jurors. But rather than Detective Tommy Dades, he called a veteran detective from the NYPD Criminal Records Division. Detective Steven Rodriguez testified that Caracappa had used the NYPD computers for personal reasons. In 1985, for example, he'd run a criminal history check on his fiancée. It was a year later that he pulled the record of Nicky Guido—who was shot and killed six weeks later.

In his cross-examination, Ed Hayes asked Rodriguez, "If a middle-aged man was about to get married and he wants to do a check on his future wife, would that shock you?"

"Yes," Rodriguez replied, "yes, it would."

Hayes then argued that his client was too smart to run a computer scan that would have connected him to a homicide, noting, "You would have to be a falling-down moron not to know that these checks were kept in perpetuity by the police department."

Henoch objected to that comment, and Weinstein had it stricken from the court record.

The crooked accountant, Steve Corso, was the next witness. Corso was crucial; it was his testimony about the Vegas drug deal that would enable Henoch to make the RICO. Corso admitted that he had started wearing a wire for the FBI only after he had been arrested for stealing more than $5 million from his New York tax clients to support his gambling habit. And then Henoch began playing tapes on which Eppolito was heard telling Corso that his son, Tony, would provide designer drugs to Hollywood producers coming to town.

In addition to involving his son, Eppolito also used his attractive daughter. During his cross-examination Corso was asked if he had been interested in dating Eppolito's daughter. Yes, the accountant admitted, he was. "Eppolito told me if the deal went through and I got the movie money for him, he would suggest to her that she date me."

There was more. Supposedly Eppolito had been taped telling Corso that his daughter was "a classy woman" because she would never have oral sex on a first date. Fortunately Judge Weinstein refused to allow that tape to be played in his courtroom, explaining, "We're keeping the daughter out."

Outside the courtroom, Eppolito's daughter was his most vocal defender, calling him "[a] perfect scapegoat." Also outside the courtroom, Eppolito's gay son, Louis Eppolito Jr., openly discussed his dysfunctional relationship with his father. In a very strange way, their relationship almost paralleled Dades's experience with his own father. Eppolito's first son told reporters that the two men hadn't spoken in almost a decade; Louis Eppolito Jr. said, describing what his father had told him the last time they spoke, "If I was in front of him he would have punched me so hard in the face, I would have been picking my teeth up off the floor." Supposedly he was angry because his son refused to pick up an autographed copy of *Mafia Cop*.

The son and his life partner had attended almost every court proceeding and finally his father broke the silence between them, telling him, "The papers are wrong . . . It's all lies, everything's a lie."

Finally it was Betty Hydell's chance to testify. Literally two decades after her son was murdered she was getting the chance to face his kidnappers in a courtroom. Tommy spoke with her before she testified, telling her what to expect, trying to get her to relax. But she'd waited too long for this day. She was trembling as she answered the prosecutor's questions, probably as much from anger as nervousness. In almost the same words she had used to tell Tommy Dades about the day her son disappeared, she told jurors how the two detectives—"One was the big one, one was the little one"—had mistakenly tailed her younger son, Frankie, who was using his brother's car. Betty had followed them in her own car, she said, and confronted them. The driver pulled out a badge and showed it to her. But Betty did her own detective work. "I checked with motor vehicles and the plates didn't belong to that car. I just assumed they were undercover cops."

Everyone in the courtroom was anticipating the dramatic moment when the victim's mother pointed at Eppolito and Caracappa and said, "That's them. They are the people I saw that day." But it never happened.

"She made the point," Ponzi said. "The jurors got it. They didn't want to give the defense a chance to point out that twenty years had passed since she'd seen them, and after that day she'd seen Louis Eppolito on TV, she'd read his book and seen the pictures, maybe she was a little confused. The jurors knew who she was talking about when she said the fat one and the skinny one. They knew."

A string of other witnesses followed. As Louis Eppolito's wife sat impassively, his *goumada,* his Mafia mistress of six years, testified that Eppolito had met with Burt Kaplan in her Brooklyn apartment. Frank Santora's daughter testified that she had seen Kaplan, Eppolito, and Caracappa at her father's house. Burt Kaplan waived his attorney-client privilege to allow his former lawyer, Judd Burstein, to testify that Kaplan had called him one day in 1994 and told him that the *New York Post* was reporting Anthony Casso used two New York City cops to order killings. "This is a big problem for me," Burstein quoted Kaplan as saying. "I was the go-between."

In reinforcing Burt Kaplan's testimony, Tommy Galpine described the many tasks he did for him. In addition to moving furniture for Kaplan's daughter and taking her car for servicing, he put drops in Kaplan's eyes after his eye surgery, supplied the car to Eppolito and Caracappa that was used to kidnap Jimmy Hydell, copied NYPD files that Eppolito had given to Kaplan, and delivered money to Eppolito in the Caribbean. During his cross-examination Cutler pointed out that Kaplan had put Galpine "on the road to perdition." To which Galpine responded, "I had a choice and I made a bad one. I never thought I'd be sitting here, but here I am."

Peter Franzone admitted he was an illiterate sixth-grade dropout and then testified, just as he had told Lanigan, "I saw [Greenwald's body] leaning against the wall and Frankie told me that I got to help bury the body because I'm an accessory and if I didn't help him he would kill me and my effin' family." Franzone identified both Eppolito and Caracappa as participants in the two murders Santora committed in the garage.

By that time the prosecution got ready to rest its case—after twelve days, thirty-four witnesses, and an array of evidence ranging from the rusted watch found at the Lino murder scene to photographs from Burt Kaplan's daughter's wedding. It was an impressive prosecution, and when it was done it seemed like only a miracle could save the Mafia cops. And then the letter from Anthony Casso arrived.

He wasn't trying to throw a monkey wrench into the proceedings—he was tossing the whole tool cabinet. "This really was his last shot," Vecchione explains. "I think he finally understood what he'd lost when he refused to talk to us. He had been holding out for nothing, for nothing; the immunity he wanted in the Hydell killing wouldn't have made the slightest difference. His problem was that he had nothing left to sell.

"But the fact that he had nothing of value to offer didn't stop him from trying. If the prosecution didn't want his testimony, I guess he figured he would try the defense. So in early March he'd written to Feldman, swearing, 'I, Anthony Casso, hereby confess to have personally participated, as part of a three man team that shot and killed Eddie Lino in Brooklyn's Gravesend section. Detectives Eppolito and Caracappa are falsely being accused of this crime.

" 'Furthermore: As the former underboss and official acting boss of the Lucchese crime family, I can honestly prove to the honorable Jack Weinstein that Detectives Eppolito and Caracappa have never supplied confidential information to the Luccheses and in no way participated in the abduction of James Hydell.' He just kept going, writing, 'It was Kaplan and his partners . . . who robbed and killed Israel Greenwald, not the detectives.' Casso also claimed that he could prove Betty Hydell was lying when she testified she had seen Eppolito and Caracappa at her house. It was all crap."

The defense immediately asked Judge Weinstein to declare a mistrial, claiming Feldman had withheld exculpatory evidence. They also announced they were considering calling Casso as a defense witness. That made sense. They had nothing else.

During an hourlong telephone conversation with the defense attorneys, Casso said, "Let me tell you something, Kaplan is saying on the stand what I want him to say on the stand. I was supposed to be part of this . . . I told Kaplan if we bring this case to the government, we'll both get our freedom." According to

Casso, his wife and Kaplan's wife had carried messages between the two of them, setting up the plan to frame the two cops, forcing the government to offer them a reduction of their sentence in exchange for their testimony.

Ed Hayes called the conversation "a completely exculpatory account of what happened."

It was actually a reasonably clever plan. Clever, but not true. And easily disproved. Judge Weinstein ruled that the defense was entitled to call Casso as a witness, but reminded them, "He may have other things to say that he won't tell you on the phone . . . [He may try to] curry favor with the government—the only people who can help him."

The defense decided that Gaspipe should stay right where he was, and with that, Casso's last hope to influence this trial ended. And then the judge denied the motion for a mistrial.

Eppolito's entire defense lasted just over twelve minutes. Rather than calling any witnesses, Bruce Cutler simply read eleven citations Eppolito had received during his career, including the citation honoring Eppolito as the November 1974 cop of the month and a certificate honoring him for preventing an attack on students from a Coney Island Yeshiva and for "The Maintenance of the Jewish holiday of Purim." In addition, he read a portion of the dust jacket of *Mafia Cop*. That was it; Cutler didn't attack the evidence, he didn't call any witnesses, he just stood up and read for twelve minutes. Tommy Dades says, "This was one of the most unusual defense strategies I'd ever seen. I've been involved in trials where the defense didn't even try to do much, figuring the jury would understand that the prosecution hadn't proved anything. But this—I didn't get it, to be honest. It was like saying to the jury, 'My guy is so guilty we're not even going to bother.'"

Caracappa's defense wasn't much better. Hayes wasn't even in the courtroom. Instead he had flown to Los Angeles to meet with federal prosecutors about an entirely different case. Judge Weinstein was furious when he discovered Hayes's absence. He found him at the ritzy Hotel Bel-Air and they spoke on a speakerphone. Hayes explained he was going to be busy for the next several hours. Judge Weinstein had a different idea. "Mr. Hayes, you just tell the United States Attorney that your meeting is at an end. You're supposed to be here in court."

Although there was some speculation that Caracappa might testify in his own defense, he decided not to risk it. As Vecchione had learned many trials ago, that is something jurors notice and consider. "They want the defendant to look right at them and tell them that he isn't guilty. Jurors put themselves in the handcuffs of the defendant sitting there listening to this evidence and they think, *Boy, if I was accused of a crime that I didn't commit, there's no way you could keep me off the stand*. So when a defendant doesn't testify there's a belief that they were afraid, that they couldn't answer the prosecutor's question, so they're probably guilty. In this case they had two defendants who were afraid to testify."

Hayes's associate Rae Koshetz called two witnesses. One of them, Caracappa's ex-partner, testified that Caracappa had spent sixteen hours guarding the man who killed Rabbi Meir Kahane the night before Eddie Lino was killed and therefore he must have been too tired to chase and kill anyone. The second witness testified that the Caribbean island of Antigua was not known as a place to launder money.

Neither witness was able to refute a single charge. So the defense rested its case without actually putting up a defense. All that was left for them was the name-calling.

Prosecutor Dan Wenner began the three-hour closing argument for the government, describing the case as "one of the bloodiest, most violent betrayals of the badge this city has ever seen . . . These corrupt men . . . did nothing less than arm the homicidal maniac Anthony Casso with the ammo and means to leave an avalanche of death in his wake."

Wenner went through the details of each murder, artfully weaving together all of the threads the prosecution had presented into a thick noose. As he reminded the jurors, "Think how dangerous it is to frame a cop . . . Cops have time cards. Burt Kaplan testified about things that happened on certain days. How would he know that the cops weren't somewhere else on those days?"

Eddie Hayes began the defense summation. He did raise several legitimate questions, the most striking being the fact that Franzone hadn't mentioned that Greenwald was buried with a plastic bag covering his head, a black scarf knotted around his neck, and his hands bound—details Franzone certainly would have noticed if he actually had participated in the burial.

But it was his associate Rae Koshetz who made the only argument that could actually save the cops: The statute of limitations had expired. The last murder for which they were being prosecuted had occurred in 1990, meaning to make a conspiracy charge stick the U.S. Attorney had to prove at least one criminal act took place after March 2000. "Casso's allegations against Eppolito and Caracappa were dead as a door-nail by the dawn of the new millennium," she said. But to solve that problem the government had set up the drug bust and the money-laundering counts. "It's like wearing a straw hat with a winter coat," she told the jury. "It doesn't fit."

In his summation for Louis Eppolito, Cutler did little more than attack, attack, and then attack some more. According to Cutler, the government's witnesses were "cretins, subhumans, and gnomes." The diminutive Franzone was the gnome: "One of a race of dwarflike figures. He is a gnome, a cretin, a lowlife, a thief, a bum, a grave-digging killer who got away with it." Steven Corso was "a sophisticated, unctuous, polished lowlife thief." Burt Kaplan "lived a double life, a triple life, or even a quadruple life." Cutler even managed to attack the United States government, somehow linking the prosecution of two hero cops to the war in the Middle East.

The jury deliberated for only ten hours over two days. They asked for only three things: Early in the process they wanted to review the portion of Kaplan's testimony in which he explained why Casso had asked for his help in tracking down the men who had shot him. Later they asked about the audiotapes Otto Heidel had secretly recorded that Eppolito had stolen from the dead man's apartment. And finally they wanted cream for their coffee.

Almost everyone assumed the deliberations would last several days. There were seventy different counts to be debated and a tremendous amount of evidence to be examined. Beyond guilt or innocence on each count was the question of whether so many different crimes committed over nineteen years could really be considered parts of a single conspiracy. And after all that, the jurors had to decide if the statute of limitations had expired.

So when the rumor started spreading after lunch on the second day that the jury had reached a verdict, almost no one believed it. It was too quick; there was too much testimony to consider. But if it was true, Vecchione figured, doing the equations of the courtroom, it had to be guilty all the way. There was no possible way the jury could have debated each of the seventy counts and found for the defendants.

Joe Ponzi called Henoch when he heard the rumor. "I'm hearing there might be a verdict," he said.

Henoch didn't think so. "I'm not getting any vibe one way or the other. The judge isn't even going to be back from lunch until two forty-five. I don't think so." Ponzi returned to work.

When Judge Weinstein returned, about a half hour early, the marshals informed him that the jury had reached a verdict. Weinstein didn't wait for the media; he brought the jury back into the courtroom.

CHAPTER 14

June Lowe, Weinstein's courtroom deputy, faced the jury, read the first count, and asked, "Proved or not proved?"

The courtroom was absolutely silent. "Proved," the foreman replied.

She read the second count. "Proved or not proved?"

"Proved."

The third count, the fourth. Proved. Proved. They had murdered Israel Greenwald. Murdered Eddie Lino. Kidnapped Jimmy Hydell. They had provided confidential information to the Lucchese family. Every single count, seventy counts, proved.

It took eighteen minutes to complete the process and poll the jury. As the verdict was being read Eppolito and Caracappa sat stoically, silently, Caracappa shaking his head slightly in denial. In the front row Eppolito's daughter, clutching a rosary, began crying. A row behind her Elizabeth Hydell was smiling, nodding. A spectator in the rear of the courtroom was laughing with joy.

As the verdict was being read someone shouted into Ponzi's office, "Joe! Turn on the TV! It's on New York One. They're convicted." Ponzi watched for a few seconds. *Yes!* he thought. *Yes!* He immediately called Tommy Dades, who was in his apartment. "They were convicted on all counts," he said, "turn on New York One."

Dades turned on the TV—and called Betty Hydell. They watched it together. Betty was ecstatic. "Thank God," she said. "Thank God." She thanked Dades over and over, "If it wasn't for you . . ."

"Look at that," Dades said as the news spread from channel to channel, "just look at that." For the first time in so many months, he just sat back and relaxed. Something in his life was going right. Finally.

Mike Vecchione was in Chicago, having lunch with several of his students from Brooklyn Law School. They were there for a moot court competition. A New York radio reporter was with them. Her office called to give her the news. Vecchione took one minute to enjoy the feeling, then went back to work with his students.

In the courtroom Weinstein thanked the jury and released them. After they'd left the courtroom he revoked Eppolito and Caracappa's $5 million bail. Federal marshals stripped the two former New York City detectives of their belts, ties, and jewelry, emptied all their pockets, and began to lead them away. Caracappa hugged Ed Hayes and gave him a Mafia-like kiss on the cheek. Hayes got emotional, his eyes watering, and Caracappa comforted him, whispering, "Everything'll be all right."

As Eppolito was escorted out of the courtroom his daughter shouted, "It's not over, Dad!"

Outside the courtroom the defense lawyers announced they intended to appeal the verdict. Cutler said, "It's an appearance of justice, but it's not justice."

Eppolito's daughter angrily told reporters, "People have called this the worst case of corruption New York has ever seen. But it was not on my father's part and not on Stephen Caracappa's part. It was on the part of the United States government."

Roz Mauskopf made her first appearance of the trial a few minutes later, reading a prepared statement: "They didn't deliver us from evil. They themselves were evil personified. They did it as cops, and they did it as Mafia cops." They turned the "shield of good" into a "sword of evil," she concluded.

Later that afternoon Ponzi and Bobby I went over to the U.S. Attorney's office to join the celebration. Later they joined a large group of people who had a stake in the case at a restaurant on Court Street. Inside the restaurant Mauskopf made a point of acknowledging the effort made by the state. Only later did Ponzi realize that they'd forgotten to invite Patty Lanigan to join them.

That night several of the jurors spoke with reporters. "All the prosecution did was give us details, details, details," explained one of them, "and the defense didn't address it." Apparently there had been very little doubt about their guilt, and much of their time in the jury room had been spent debating the validity of the conspiracy charge, the RICO—or, as Judge Weinstein continued to refer to it, the "ticking time bomb." Eventually they decided the prosecution had given them all the dots, and they simply connected them. The juror added that both men had many opportunities to walk away from the mob life but made the wrong decision. "I'm sorry," the juror said, "but they have no morals."

Tommy Dades wondered if the jurors had really considered the defense claim that the statute of limitations had expired. "You never really know what happens once people get inside that jury room, why people reach the decisions they do. But I think in this case the evidence was just so overwhelming that these guys had committed so many terrible crimes and had absolutely no remorse about it that the jury figured, 'Screw 'em. These guys are dirty. These guys betrayed the city. Whatever happened in Vegas happened. And I'm not going to let these two murderers walk out of the courtroom on a technicality.' "

Eppolito and Caracappa were held temporarily in the Metropolitan Detention Center, the place where Ponzi had first met Burt Kaplan. Eppolito remained defiant, telling the media, "It was a perfect frame. It was a very well-thought-out plan. There's no more perfect frame than this. I didn't kill anybody." He claimed that Casso and Kaplan had ensnared him because of his well-known family ties to the mob—as well as his own problems with Internal Affairs during his career. "I was the most perfect scapegoat in history."

Caracappa seemed much more reflective. Near the end of the trial he'd had a long conversation with Felipe Luciano, who many years earlier had been a founder of the militant Puerto Rican group the Young Lords but later had become a respected reporter. Their paths had crossed for the first time just as Caracappa was beginning his career. "It was a different time," Caracappa told Luciano. "I remember my first collar. Second night on the job. One of those Tactical Police

Force guys was ahead of me and he walked me through the processing in court. Showed me how to do it. I was a rookie cop. And I remember just looking at him, even the way he stood. They had those long coats then. He'd put his hands back, so the coat was pulled back, and you could see the cuffs hanging a certain way, not like the rest of us, and his gun. They had a style. It was my introduction, my beginning. First collar. Second night on the job. And starting out, it all held so much promise."

They all had their memories, the good guys and the bad guys. Watching the cops go down, Mike Vecchione couldn't help but think back to his first major trial, to the moment when he had to make that decision about who he wanted to be. "It was a murder case; a wiseguy was the defendant. My first major case. So winning it meant as much to me as anything in my whole life. Late one night I was sitting in my office going through all the documentation. I had piles of reports, hundreds of pages. My door was closed. And then I found an interview that my main witness had done with Nassau County detectives. And in this interview he said something that was completely contradictory to what he'd said in the grand jury. *Oh my God,* I thought.

"As soon as I saw it I knew it was going to cause me a lot of trouble. Without this piece of paper my life is a lot easier. With this piece of paper I've got to work a lot harder and I still might lose the case.

"It would have been absolutely nothing for me to take that report and tear it up or just throw it away. No one would have known the difference. Not one person. I would be lying if I said the prospect of getting caught didn't enter my mind. It did. But I also knew it was the wrong thing to do. I could hear my father's voice in my head, and my mother, telling me that sometimes doing the right thing doesn't necessarily help you at that moment, but as long as you do it you know you never have to lie, you never have to cover up. One lie leads to another and another and another and then the whole house of cards falls down. Call it whatever you want, but for me that is my ethical substance.

"That case was tried three times. This was the case I found out later was fixed the first time. But cases never get better with age. And eventually the defendant was acquitted."

Vecchione knew, Dades knew, Ponzi, Lanigan, all of them; they all had been there, they all remembered that first time when they had to decide what kind of cop they wanted to be. Vecchione had walked away from temptation. But at some point while this trial was in progress, every cop, every man and woman in law enforcement, must have stopped and wondered what had happened to Eppolito and Caracappa. When was the first time they didn't walk away?

Dades had another suggestion. "These guys weren't cops who became criminals. They were criminals with badges. From the very beginning they were criminals who slipped through the system."

Joe Ponzi asked himself that question over and over, without ever coming up with a satisfying answer. "I knew Louie. I thought he was a good detective, maybe a little wild, but this? I just couldn't believe that he had gone into the police department with the intent to do this. There were times when I found myself starting to rationalize his actions. I don't know what could have possessed him to do this. Did he really have such contempt for other cops that he felt like, 'Fuck them, they deserve it'? I thought maybe he'd gotten screwed in the Rosario Gambino investigation. Maybe he didn't do anything and in his mind they did this to him based on his family and his upbringing. I was trying to rationalize an excuse. Later on people told me, 'Take it to the bank. He gave that document to Rosario Gambino and he didn't get framed or set up.'

"There is a side of me that thinks maybe they were both drowning in some level of financial debt and that's what motivated them. Obviously I don't excuse them for one day of it, but it's just so hard for me to believe that someone could go into the police department with the mind-set that he's going to become a cop and use the badge the way Louie did. It's just so hard for me to accept that."

The cops had been convicted, but there was still a lot of legal bookkeeping to be done. Eppolito and Caracappa were held in separate cells at MDC while Judge Weinstein was considering their appeal. At the end of the trial Eppolito had hugged Bruce Cutler, and Caracappa had hugged Ed Hayes, but the love didn't last.

Almost as soon as the cell door slammed behind the now infamous Mafia cops, they claimed they had not been adequately represented and fired Cutler and Hayes. Maybe they did believe that, but it is also accepted strategy. Blaming the lawyers at least guarantees a hearing. And on rare occasions it even results in the verdict being overturned.

But these guys seemed serious about it. In a hearing in early May, Eppolito's new lawyer, Joe Bondy, claimed in his motion for an acquittal or new trial that "Defense counsel spent the majority of Mr. Eppolito's closing argument speaking about himself, including he lost fourteen pounds during the trial, loved Brooklyn as a borough of bridges and tunnels and was an admirer of the great Indian Chief Crazy Horse . . . After uttering these broad-ranging irregularities, counsel then neglected to argue . . . the lack of evidence of the [RICO] offense."

In his own affidavit Eppolito claimed that Cutler had basically ignored him throughout the trial. He wanted to testify, he wrote, but Cutler refused to put him on the stand. "The last refusal represented the culmination of a relationship that was increasingly hostile and adverse."

Caracappa's new lawyer, Daniel Nobel, was less harsh, saying he was surprised by "the glaring lack of legal sufficiency" demonstrated by Hayes.

Judge Weinstein rejected the motion, but his comments while doing it left Eppolito and Caracappa with hope—and may well have caused some shivers in the U.S. Attorney's office. Focusing on the conspiracy charge that held the entire case together, Weinstein said, "It was not a strong case . . . The government was warned about this from day one and there is a sound basis for appeal. There was enough evidence, barely enough, to put it to the jury . . . But I concede a more learned jurist may disagree, and it wouldn't upset me at all to be reversed."

Sentencing was scheduled for the fifth of June. A week before that Daniel Nobel filed additional papers, and this time he didn't hold back on Ed Hayes. Nobel wrote that the two private investigators hired by Hayes would testify that he "made no serious effort to prepare for the trial and remained unfocused . . . The only effort by Mr. Hayes to present a theory of defense . . .

was a totally confusing and completely disjointed effort to blame the prosecution on an undefined conspiracy emanating from Washington, DC."

Eppolito's new lawyer criticized Cutler for "repeated failures to investigate relevant areas, inability to communicate with his client and a complete lack of trial preparation."

Whatever affection or even civility had existed between the cops and their lawyers was gone. "I was so personally offended," Cutler responded. "One day you're begged to come in and the next day you're knocked by the client, who to me is delusional in a certain respect. He's certainly ungrateful and shameless . . . They started off blaming the government and the prosecutors. Who's left? Us. I am rankled and angry."

"He's desperate," Hayes said of Caracappa. "Who else can he attack? I am surprised, however, since I didn't think he was like that."

On June 5 Judge Weinstein permitted the relatives of several of the victims to speak. Jeweler #1's now-grown daughter, Michal Greenwald, was especially poignant, glaring at the disgraced cops and telling them, "We loved our daddy, and having him disappear into thin air with no explanation was something I would not wish upon my worst enemy. Do you know what it feels like to visit a friend who recently lost a loved one and to be envious of them because they have a grave?"

And finally, finally, Betty Hydell had her chance to speak. "I was closer to you that day than I am right now and you deny it. I just wish you'd stay in jail the rest of your life, without family or friend, and you die in jail alone."

Eventually Louie Eppolito stood up in the courtroom and faced the families of his victims who had come to see justice done. With typical arrogance Eppolito smugly insisted he was innocent, that he had been framed, and invited these people to visit him in his cell so he could prove that to them. Then he began talking about his pride in his accomplishments as a New York City police officer.

And as he did, a man sitting in the spectator section interrupted, yelling, "Mr. Eppolito! Do you remember me?"

Eppolito looked, maybe he shook his head slightly. "No," he said.

Barry Gibbs, whom Eppolito had arrested for the prostitute murder, was getting what little satisfaction was available to him. "I'm the guy you put away for nineteen years. I'm Barry Gibbs. You don't remember me? You don't remember what you did to me? To my family?" Guards quickly hustled Gibbs out of the courtroom.

Judge Weinstein told Louis Eppolito and Stephen Caracappa that he intended to sentence them to life in prison without the possibility of parole, a one-million-dollar fine, and a seizure of assets, for what was, he said, "probably the most heinous series of crimes ever tried in this courthouse. There has been no doubt, and there is no doubt, that the murders and other crimes were proven without a reasonable doubt."

He delayed imposing the sentence until he ruled on the motions for dismissal made by their new lawyers on the basis of the "ticking time bomb." That seemed like it would be simply another legal formality. In most criminal cases the verdict is never the end, but rather the beginning of the next phase, the sometimes endless series of legal maneuverings and appeals that—as Casso had proved—could continue for years. Time is the one thing that prisoners have in abundance, and they often use it to attack their convictions. In this case though, one of the most respected judges in the business had weighed the factors and made his decision. It was highly unlikely that anyone was going to overturn Judge Jack Weinstein.

Except Judge Weinstein. On July 1, 2006, an extraordinary case got even more bizarre. As it turned out, according to Judge Weinstein, Mike Vecchione had it right from the very beginning.

Tommy Dades was working in the kitchen of his Staten Island house when Ponzi called him with the news. "You're not going to believe this," Ponzi said.

"What are you talking about?"

"Weinstein just threw out the RICO. You believe that? After the family impact statements were read and they went the whole nine yards that he overthrew the conviction because of the statute of limitations?"

Weinstein's ticking time bomb had exploded. Having spent his lifetime learning and respecting the law, Judge Jack Weinstein finally could not convince himself that the federal government's RICO charge was valid. He couldn't accept the prosecution's contention that a continuing connection existed between eight murders and other mayhem, and one ounce of methamphetamine sold in Las Vegas a decade later. It must have been an enormously difficult decision; he had no doubt about the guilt of the accused, and he understood the risks of his decision, but he valued the law far above the consequences of his decision. As far as Judge Weinstein was concerned, "Once Anthony Casso and Burton Kaplan had both been arrested, once the two defendants had both retired from the police force and reestablished themselves on the opposite side of the country, the conspiracy that began in New York in the 1980s had come to a definite close."

It wasn't about letting two deplorable human beings out of a cell, he wrote, it was about that majesty of the law that the good guys spend their lifetimes upholding. He explained, "It will appear peculiar to many people that heinous criminals such as the defendants, having been found guilty on overwhelming evidence of the most despicable crimes of violence and treachery, should go unwhipped of justice. Yet our Constitution, statutes and morality require that we be ruled by law, not by vindictiveness or the advantages of the moment. If we are to be ruled by law, we must be limited by its protections. As Justice [Oliver Wendell] Holmes reminded us, it is 'A less evil that some criminals should escape than that the government should play an ignoble part.' Even during the great emergency of the Civil War, the courts rejected the theory that the rule of law could be twisted to meet the exigencies of the moment.'

"The government's case against these defendants stretches federal racketeering and conspiracy laws to the breaking point . . .

"The decision to enter a judgment of acquittal on the charge of racketeering conspiracy is required by the very essence of the rule of law." Weinstein did conclude that should he be reversed by the Court of Appeals the sentences he imposed of life-plus on both defendants should stand.

Steve Caracappa's first attorney, Ed Hayes, reportedly was "speechless" when reached at his office, but then he emphasized—happily—that the Feds had made a huge error by not permitting the case to be tried in state court, where there is no statute of limitations on murder. And then he added, "But this is a Justice Department that more than any in my lifetime has shown a mad-dog desire to control everything and to ignore the law. And they paid the price in this case."

Mike Vecchione read and reread Weinstein's decision, riding an emotional roller coaster between anger, satisfaction, and concern. "I guess my first thought was anger. I was furious that Feldman had not allowed us to at least go in to the grand jury and get an indictment on the Hydell or the Lino murders just in case something like this happened. We could have been waiting at the bottom of the courthouse steps to lock up Eppolito and Caracappa on state murder charges, where there is no statute of limitations.

"Admittedly, I felt some satisfaction because I'd been vindicated. My belief that the statute of limitations had expired had been borne out. I respected Judge Weinstein for this decision because I care deeply about justice. No matter how terrible someone is, you can't change the law to catch them; when you start doing that you no longer have a system of law that matters.

"On the other hand, I felt terrible because now Eppolito and Caracappa had the potential—although I couldn't imagine it would happen—of walking away from the worst crimes ever committed by cops." It also meant that Vecchione and Ponzi had to immediately begin working to put together a murder indictment against the cops. They had to be prepared to indict Eppolito and Caracappa if they were released.

Dades was also dealing with a great range of emotions. "I was confused," he remembers. "I'd never heard of anything like that before. I never heard of a judge going so far as to let families speak about how these guys affected their lives and then throwing out the case. If you were guessing he was going to do it, he would have thrown out the indictment or he would have heard some testimony and then thrown it out, but to let it go to a jury and actually allow the jury to deliberate on it and come up with a guilty verdict, then set a sentencing date and have the families come in and give impact statements, I didn't understand it."

Roz Mauskopf's spokesman issued a terse statement: "The jury in this case unanimously found Eppolito and Caracappa guilty of racketeering and murder based on overwhelming evidence. And based on the law that was given to them by the court, each of the 12 jurors specifically found that the defendants' heinous crimes were committed within the statute of limitations. We intend to pursue an appeal."

The federal prosecutor immediately asked the Court of Appeals to reinstate the verdict, claiming, basically, that the jury had heard the case, had weighed the arguments about the validity of the charge that concerned Weinstein, and had reached a decision. Guilty.

No one, absolutely no one, doubted the guilt of the two detectives. But the question that was being asked at the end was the same question Vecchione had asked at the beginning: Could the government make a federal case out of it?

Eppolito and Caracappa were denied bail, but at least they had a lifeline. A chance. For everyone involved, it had become a matter of waiting. And while the court of appeals wrestled with this complex decision, life moved forward. During this time, for Tommy

Dades, strained relationships ended. He and Ro tried to save their marriage, but too much had happened and eventually they divorced. He never again spoke with his father, although he continues to speak with his aunt. For a time, he was able to bandage the rift with Mark Feldman. "We would have dinner with Ponzi every few weeks. We'd talk about what happened; the only thing he would ever say was that what he did was best for the case. On a personal level I had always respected him, on a professional level I thought he was tremendous, but eventually that ended badly."

As he explains, "Mark was mad at me because he felt I got too much publicity and that hurt the case, but we got through that. Then, though, I started working on another cold case, a 1991 case regarding the murder of an innocent seventeen-year-old kid who was beaten to death. Two cooperators from another case came forward with the names of the people who did it. Feldman had three witnesses I needed to speak to. I asked him four or five times to speak to these people and ask them to talk to me. 'No problem,' he kept telling me, but it never got done.

"I was told by other people that he wasn't going to do it because I was working with Mike Vecchione. He and Mike just did not get along. So I told him, 'No matter what your feelings are toward Mike, this is an innocent kid that was killed and you should put your personal feelings aside and be more professional.'

"He responded by telling me that I was now a consultant to the DA's office and I shouldn't be involved. That a detective or an investigator should be calling him, not me. And that if he ever does put those witnesses on the phone an agent is going to have to be there as a witness. So I went nuts on him.

"This conversation took place right around the time Mark was leaving the U.S. Attorney's office to go into private industry. I told him, 'Mark, the best thing that can happen to you is to get out of this business, because what you're saying goes against every grain in my body.' And then I hung up on him.

"We spoke one more time, maybe a year later. We agreed that we had both lost our tempers. He wanted to forget about what happened, but the truth is I just never could respect him after that and we never spoke again."

As so often before in his life, Dades found contentment in the boxing gym. When he was working with teenagers in the Police Athletic League gym on Staten Island, literally showing them the ropes, he felt like he was where he belonged. He got a lot of satisfaction out of teaching those kids all the good lessons about life, about people, he'd learned over his two decades on the job. His reward came when one of those kids, a promising fighter named Terence Myers, showed him the essay he'd written for his college applications: "The people who inspire me are my mother, Patricia Myers, boxing trainer Tommy Dades and Floyd Mayweather Jr.," he wrote. "All of them went through a lot of ups and downs and a lot of problems in their lives, but they kept working hard and now they are successful . . . If it wasn't for my trainer, Tommy Dades, I probably would be in the streets doing nothing with my life."

A year passed and still the Court of Appeals failed to reach any kind of decision. There were all kinds of rumors about what was going on; several times it appeared that they had decided what to do, but the sound of their silence was overwhelming. During the waiting all the key members of the government's prosecution team left Mauskopf's office. Feldman and Henoch joined large firms, Mitra Hormozi was appointed Special Deputy Chief of Staff to New York State Attorney-General Andrew Cuomo, and President Bush appointed Roz Mauskopf to a federal judgeship.

Eventually undercover accountant Stephen Corso was sentenced to one year in prison. Corso had faced more than seven years, but Judge Janet Hall said, while pronouncing the reduced sentence, "I can't find the words to describe the value . . . of his cooperation." Corso, who made more than nine hundred tapes with Eppolito, refused an offer to enter the government's witness protection program when he finishes his sentence.

For his cooperation Burt Kaplan received a reduction in his twenty-seven-year sentence for marijuana trafficking and was released from prison. He also had to plead guilty to all the crimes to which he confessed as part of his plea agreement but will never have to return to prison for those crimes. He gave the prosecutors everything they needed. More than they imagined. For Burt Kaplan, his last payday is coming. After being released he seemed to have successfully disappeared, although it is doubtful he is in any danger. Almost all of the people against whom he testified are gone, dead or in prison.

Anthony Casso remains in his cell in Supermax, the maximum-security prison in Florence, Colorado, his ticket out having expired.

The waiting went on. Mike Vecchione prosecuted Clarence Norman in four trials on various corruption charges and earned convictions in three of those trials. Norman is in prison, serving his numerous sentences.

Vecchione's office also accepted guilty pleas from ten men involved in the macabre bones case, in which the body parts of more than a thousand corpses were taken and sold. And Vecchione and Tommy Dades worked together on one more high-profile cold case, but this one ended poorly.

After the Eppolito and Caracappa trials began, Vecchione received several letters from people asking him to pursue other cold cases. Among these letters was a folder full of documents sent by a private investigator who had been working on a case that she believed involved FBI misconduct. Former FBI agent Lin Devecchio was indicted for providing information to mobster Gregory Scarpa Sr.—who died of AIDS in 1994—in the late 1980s that led to four murders. Like Eppolito and Caracappa, rumors had been swirling around Devecchio for a long time, but prosecutors had not been able to make a case against him until Scarpa's former mistress came forward claiming to have intimate knowledge of Devecchio's cooperation with Scarpa. When the indictment was announced, many of Devecchio's former FBI colleagues rallied around him in support. Much of the prosecution's case centered around this former witness—but after the trial had begun a New York reporter produced audiotapes this woman had made ten years earlier for a book proposal. And in these tapes she had claimed Devecchio was not involved in two of the murders for which he was being prosecuted. As Vecchione explains, "We didn't find out about those tapes until she was in the middle of her testimony. At the time she made those tapes she was using drugs and was looking to protect herself and her son, but they were devastating to the prosecution. I was convinced we were on the right path and she was telling the truth, but those tapes damaged her credibility as a witness and we had no choice but to ask for a dismissal."

A second year passed without the Court of Appeals issuing a decision.

After leaving Hynes's office for the second time, Tommy Dades continued teaching boxing at the Police Athletic League gym on Staten Island—and his kids won two NYC Golden Gloves championships in 2008. Joe Ponzi continued supervising more than a hundred investigators, each of them working as many as twenty-five cases. And Mike Vecchione was finally ending the last of the funeral home ghouls prosecution when the Court of Appeals issued its verdict at last.

In October 2007 the Second Circuit Court of Appeals heard oral arguments from prosecutors and the defense attorneys. Representing the government, Mitra Hormozi contended that the conspiracy never ended because Eppolito and Caracappa continued to look for illicit ways to make money—and shared the secrets of their crimes. The three-judge panel then took almost another full year before finally reaching its seventy-page decision. "We reject the district court's view that . . . the enterprise that began in the 1980's and continued into the early 1990's could not be considered the same enterprise that engaged in the Las Vegas conduct . . ."

It was a long, carefully constructed decision, replete with numerous precedents that weaved a tight rope around the necks of the dirty cops. Guilty. Guilty of the worst crimes ever committed by New York City police officers. Guilty of murder and betrayal. Although defense lawyers promised an appeal to the Supreme Court, Louis Eppolito and Stephen Caracappa will spend the rest of their lives in prison. Ironically, there remains the possibility that eventually they will be assigned to Supermax—where, after all these years, they will finally get to meet Gaspipe.

As always, after the final verdict was announced, Tommy got on the phone with the mother. Betty Hydell had finally gotten justice. "How you feeling?" Tommy asked her.

There was no celebration in her, just quiet satisfaction. "I'm okay," she said. And finally they could begin talking about the future.

UPDATE

While the Mafia Cops case ended with the decision by the Second Circuit Court of Appeals, life went on for the major participants in the case—with one exception. In July 2009, 75-year-old Burt Kaplan, the one-eyed Jew whose fear that Louie Eppolito and Steve Caracappa were going to turn on him caused him to become a cooperating witness, died of prostate cancer. Kaplan had lived as a free man in an undisclosed location for three years after testifying against the cops. Legendary writer Jimmy Breslin provided Kaplan's epitaph when he said, "Who says he's dead? I made a study of the man and I wouldn't believe him if he told me today was Wednesday. He might have a reason to want me not to know it was Thursday . . . If he's dead it is a great loss to the romance of our times."

The decades-long friendship between Eppolito and Caracappa also ended forever. After spending several years locked up together twenty-three hours a day in a cell slightly larger than a walk-in closet in the Metropolitan Detention Center in Sunset Park, Brooklyn,

Eppolito was shipped to the high-security federal prison in Tucson, Arizona, near his family in Las Vegas, while Caracappa was assigned to Victorville Penitentiary, slightly more than an hour north of Los Angeles.

But ironically, the last answers in this case came from "Gaspipe" Casso, who finally decided to talk. One afternoon in May 2009, Vecchione received a phone call from *New York Times* reporter Ralph Blumenthal, who told him he was working on a story involving the theft of the French Connection heroin—and that Casso was willing to go on record about the theft and the ensuing murders. Vecchione tried to get in contact with John Lewis, Casso's old attorney, only to learn that the 64-year old Lewis, a non-smoker, had died of lung cancer. His new lawyer, Josh Draytel, confirmed to Vecchione that Casso was "anxious to talk to him," and arrangements were made for Vecchione, Joe Ponzi, and George Terra to visit the federal prison hospital in Butner, North Carolina, where Casso was being treated for prostate cancer. Ironically, this meeting was scheduled to take place just a few days before Eppolito and Caracappa were to finally be sentenced.

A brief note about this meeting appeared in the New York newspapers—and the next day U.S. Attorney Greg Andreas called to object. "You didn't ask us for permission."

Here we go again, Vecchione thought. "Of course I didn't," he replied, "why would I do that?"

It's common courtesy to let us know, Andreas complained, then asked, "What are you going down there to talk to him about?"

"Well that's really none of your business," Vecchione said. "We have open murders we want to talk to him about and I'm not going to share that information with you."

Andreas said that he was concerned about Casso giving them so-called Brady material about the Mafia cops case, meaning information that might be used to exculpate or clear Eppolito and Caracappa. In other words, Andreas was concerned they were going down there to screw up what was left of the case. Vecchione explained, "I have no intention to talk to him about that case. In fact, that was a specific requirement of mine when I agreed to do this with his attorney."

Andreas wasn't convinced. He was concerned Casso would make statements out loud and that the representatives of Hynes' office would legally be compelled to report it to the court—and that it could delay the sentencing. The conversation began to get a little tough, with Andreas complaining this visit hadn't been cleared with his office and Vecchione pointing out, "I don't work for you," and he didn't have to clear anything with the federal attorney's office.

Finally, Andreas told him that they were welcome to go, but it would be a complete waste of time. He had already notified the Bureau of Prisons not to allow them into Butner.

"Why didn't you start the conversation with that?" Vecchione snapped.

In the end they reached a compromise: If Vecchione agreed to postpone his trip until after the cops were sentenced, Andreas wouldn't interfere. To Andreas' credit, after the sentencing, he called the DA's office and lifted any objection he had.

Eventually, Vecchione, Terra, and Ponzi were waiting in the visitors' room at the prison hospital when

Casso walked in. It was the first time Vecchione had seen him and he noted that he was a lot smaller than he'd anticipated. When Terra introduced himself, Casso said, "I heard a you." When Joe Ponzi introduced himself, Gaspipe shook his hand and said, "Yeah, I know about you," then he turned to Vecchione. "You don't have to introduce yourself. I know exactly who you are. In fact, there's a bunch a guys in here that got your picture up on the wall that they use for a dartboard."

In the first ten minutes of the conversation Casso added, "And I read your book."

Vecchione smiled. Another critic waiting to be heard. "So how was it?" he asked.

"Pretty truthful," Casso said. "There's little things here and there, but it was pretty truthful."

With the cops sentenced there was no reason for Vecchione to avoid talking about his book. And one of his two biggest questions was answered when Casso told him that his late attorney D.B. Lewis had never contacted him to discuss Vecchione's offer. "The first time I found out you wanted to talk with me was when I read it in the book. That guy Lewis never told me that."

Casso said that Jimmy Hydell had not been picked up by the cops in a store by Dyker Park; instead they'd grabbed him coming out of a club owned by a Bonanno. He didn't know how the cops found out Hydell was there.

He also confirmed Tommy Dades' speculation that he'd found out the identities of the men who'd tried to kill him when Hydell's sister's boyfriend overheard a conversation and reported it to his father.

Finally, Vecchione asked the biggest question: Where was Jimmy Hydell's body? Believe it or not, Casso said, there was a big empty lot behind the Chinese restaurant he'd run into to avoid being killed. At that time the lot was basically being used to dump things—and one of those things was Hydell's body. It had been bulldozed into the earth.

Gaspipe provided a general location. When detectives drove over there to look at the lot, they found it was now a housing subdivision. It has been completely cemented over, covered with streets and houses, with no possible way of ever finding the spot where Hydell's body was buried.

During this meeting Casso provided potentially important information about three murders, one of them involving the French Connection theft.

It was a fascinating experience for the three men. It was clear Casso still loved being the star in the center ring. He told them the story in great detail of how the attempted assassination of John Gotti—which had been planned by Carmine Gigante and Casso—had gone so deadly wrong.

What became clear during this first meeting was that Casso's bitterness toward the federal government had grown. He claimed he'd given them good information about several cases, information that enabled them to solve those cases, and he never got credit for it, including the attempted assassination of Gotti.

Overall the three men spent about seven hours over two days with Casso. While the value of all the information he provided has yet to be tested, it provided Vecchione an odd kind of closure to the Mafia cops case.

No one knows for certain if Casso was telling the truth about the location of Hydell's body and no one ever will. That will remain the last mystery concerning New York's killer cops.

ACKNOWLEDGMENTS

Mike Vecchione would like to acknowledge the following people:

To my boss, District Attorney Charles "Joe" Hynes, without whose confidence in me this investigation could never have happened. To George Terra and the Detectives of the Special Investigation Unit of the Brooklyn DA's office for their great work and dedication to this case and countless others I have worked on with them. To the men and women of the Rackets Division in the Brooklyn DA's office, simply the best of the best. To my Uncle Louie, my mentor, role model, and the inspiration for me to become a lawyer, and Uncle Fred, the godfather, who always made me laugh and to whom I literally said my first words—keep fighting! I love you. And Aunt Jo, my second mom! I love you. To Jimmy Murphy, a great detective who brought me into the DA's office and whose stories inspired me. To Jerry Schmetterer, one of my newest and best friends, for his advice and for lending me an ear, and Morty Matz, for sharing with me the wealth of his experience and for all the lunchtime advice and support. To Ronnie, for being a wonderful mother to our sons. I couldn't have done law school without her. To Joe Petrosino, "grandpa," my great friend and my partner in the DA's office. To Anne Gutmann, a great lawyer and the best friend I could ever hope for, and The Cabal, for simply being my friends. To Brian Maher and Steve Bondor, for being there at the beginning in the homicide bureau—great detectives both. To Juliet P., for caring, you are truly "one of the great ones." And to Frances Mercurio, my great assistant, a true lady who does it all for me and who brightens every day I see her. To Chief Joe Ponzi, for his selfless contributions to this case, this book, and for his greatness as a detective. And to my friend Tommy D., for always being there for me and for his steady supply of "Dades specials." We kicked some ass!

Tommy Dades would like to acknowledge the following people:

To Jim Walden, Jimmy DiPietro, and Randy Mastro, thank you is an understatement. I'll never forget. God bless all of you and yes, Jimmy D., you are the best defense attorney I've ever faced!

To members of the groups D22 and D44 NY office DEA: Eric, Myron, Hunt, Brizz, Drew, Moran, Al, Cip, and all the rest of the boys. Thank you, a bunch of pros—no better. To Jimmy DeStefano and Gary "J" Pontecorvo, on both a personal and professional level; I'm proud to know you guys and thank you for letting me tag along. Thank you FBI–C38 NY office. Thank you Matt Tormey, C-31 FBI office NY, "What fun!" To Detective Nick Traffacenti and Detective John

Votto (Ret.). I learned from the best. To Sergeant Larry Ponzi (Ret.), the epitome of a squad boss. I love you. To Detective Robert Maladonich (Ret.). Thanks for your friendship and guidance both as a detective and as a boxer. To Jr. "Poisons" Jones, you will always be the champ in my eyes. To ADA Chris Blank of the Brooklyn DA's office—for all your hard work and for understanding me, thank you. To Detective Greg DeBor of the Brooklyn DA's office, for always being there; you're a great cop and friend. To "JC," friends for life. To "LM" the best of luck. To "GS," thank you for trusting me. To "SG," my partner on the same hit list—they missed! To Captain William Plackenmeyer (NYPD Ret.), words can't explain what I owe you, both personally and professionally. To Chief of Detectives William Allee, it was an honor to work for you and learn from you, the "cop's cop." All the best. To Supreme Court Judge Laura Ward, thanks for your friendship. To Chief of Rackets Michael Vecchione, the book says it all but we could have written a hundred more. God bless you. To Chief Joe Ponzi, what is it, five calls a day? I'm blessed with your friendship. To Detectives Mike Galletta and Jimmy Harkins, my partners for eleven and seven years. I miss you both— great partners, great detectives, and great friends. "We were surrounded by assassins"; you were right, Jimmy. To Chief Terra, "crazy as a fox." To Chief Anne Guttman, a sincere thank-you. To Chief Suzanne Corhan, thank you. To Sergeant Joe "Joe the Boss" Piraino, you drove me crazy, but I love you. To Inspector John Lynch (NYPD Ret.) who could have played a police inspector in any movie—a role you were born to be. God bless you. To Sergeant Pat Russo (Ret.), nobody has a bigger heart than you, you're a man's man, thank you, Patty! To Terence Meyers, thank you for letting me train you all those years and for bettering yourself. You're the poster boy for what the PAL is and for what its coaches do for the youth of our city. Keep punching and have a great life. To Detective Jimmy Sanseverino (Ret.), a gentleman, a great detective, and a good friend. To Nwachi Hartley, may you rest in peace. C-ya soon pal, I miss you. To Marty Ricco, I miss our talks; it seems like yesterday. I know you watch over me; I love ya, Rick. To my grandparents "Blackie" and Rosie, thank you for taking care of me. I would not be here if not for both of you. To Detective Joe Simone, Detective Patty Magiorie, and Angela Clemente. Three great friends; may God grant justice—never lose faith in Him. To New York Supreme Court Judge Leslie Crocker Snyder, thank you for showing integrity and that the system can be fair when in the hands of someone like you. To childhood friends Melfi and Pickett, to be your friends for thirty-five years is an accomplishment in itself—we're the last three standing. And to Jerry Capeci, I enjoy our friendship, you're a good man. To Sergeants Chris Straum and Jack Cucci, thank you for believing in me. You are two great bosses. To my godson, Frankie, I love you, God bless you. To Detective First Grade Frank Pergola, the epitome of a detective, lots of love and all the best.

David Fisher would like to acknowledge the following people:
　　I would like to thank our editor, Mauro DiPreta, for his confidence, his persistance, and his efforts to make this the best possible telling of the worst crimes in

NYPD history. I would also like to thank my friends Penny Farber and Jerry Stern for the use of their cyberspace, as well as Frank Biondo, Bart Reich, and Joe Maresca, my friends of a lifetime. I would like to thank our agents, Frank Weimann of the Literary Group and Peter Sawyer, for their efforts and their expertise. I also would like to thank Chief Joe Ponzi for his enthusiasm, his time, and his efforts to tell this story as accurately as possible. I would like to thank Patty Lanigan, George Terra, Josh Hanshaft, and those people I can't name who gave graciously of their time. I'd like to tell my sons, Jesse and Beau Stevens, how much I love them and appreciate their understanding of me. As always, I would like to thank Suzanne Copitzky and her staff at the Karmen Executive Center of Seattle, Washington, for their continued hard work and good humor. And I would like to add that working with Mike Vecchione and Tommy Dades, two of the most dedicated public servants I've ever met and two men I admire greatly, has been a great pleasure.

And last on the page, but first in my life, I would like to acknowledge my wife, Laura Stevens, who brightens my life with her endless support and enthusiasm. I am so lucky to have found her.